CANON REBEL
T6/EOS 1300D

THE EXPANDED GUIDE

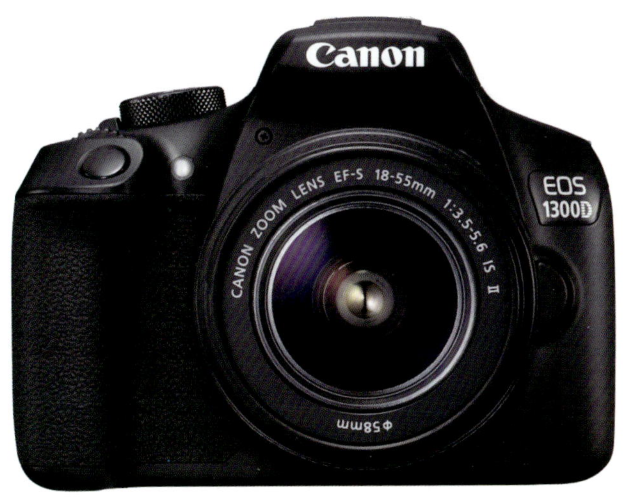

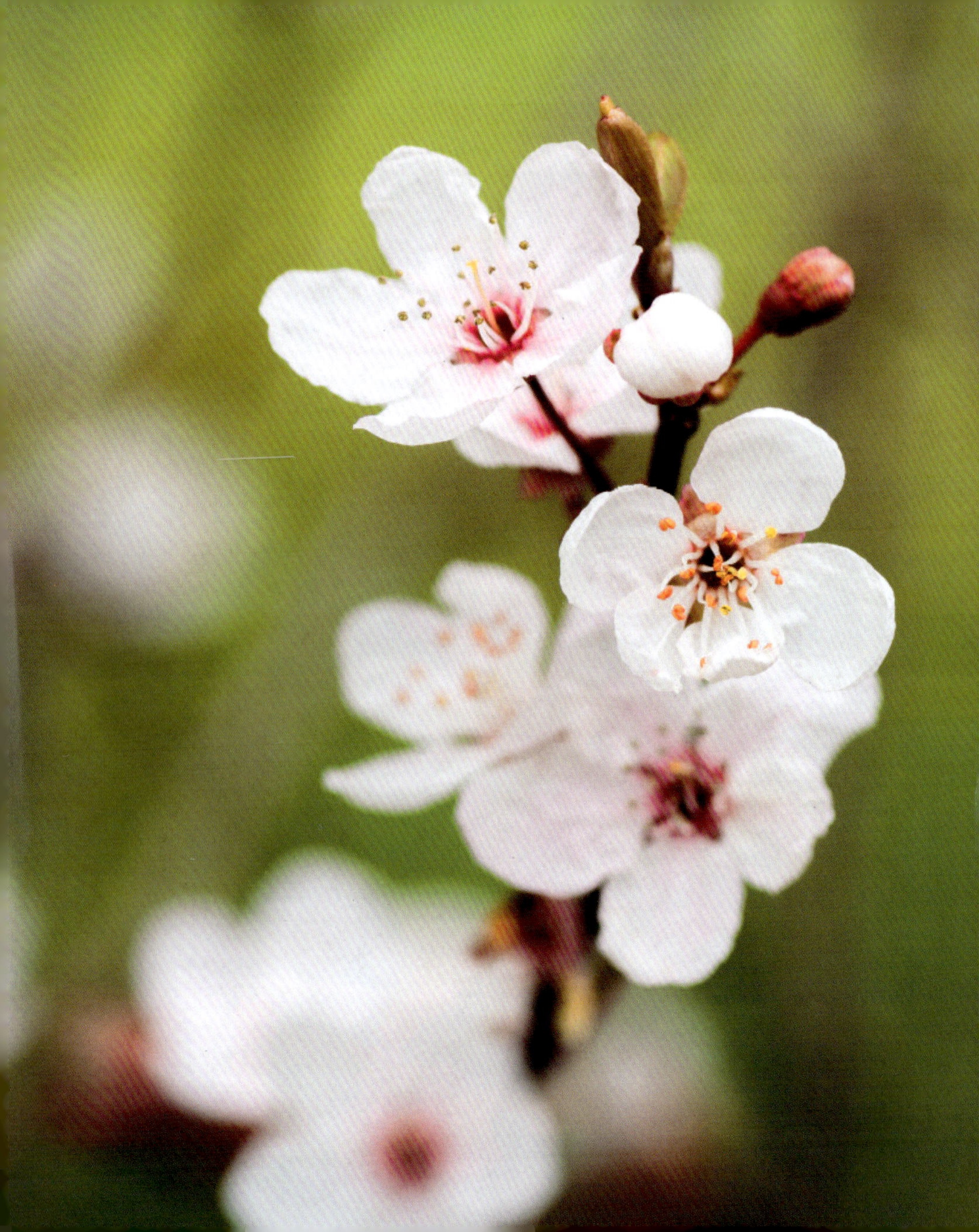

CANON REBEL
T6/EOS 1300D
THE EXPANDED GUIDE

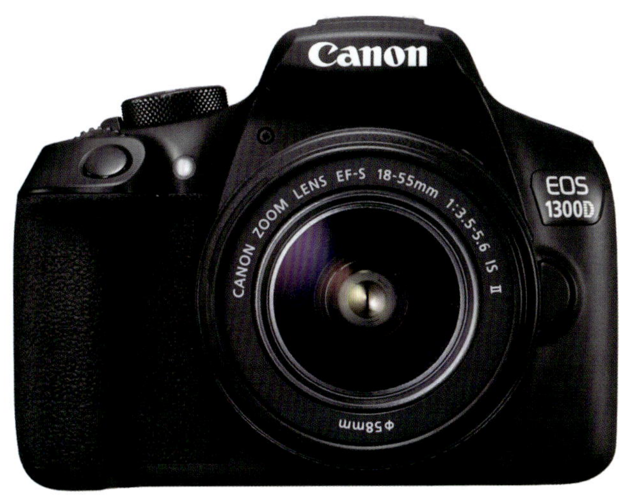

David Taylor

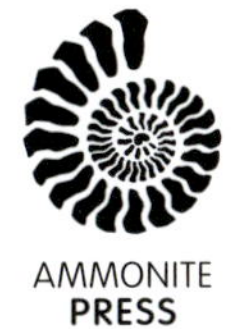

AMMONITE
PRESS

First published 2016 by
Ammonite Press
an imprint of AE Publications Ltd
166 High Street, Lewes, East Sussex, BN7 1XU, UK

ISBN 978-1-78145-282-0

British Library Cataloging in Publication Data: A catalog
record of this book is available from the British Library.

Publisher: Jason Hook
Art Director: Robin Shields
Editor: Chris Gatcum
Designer: Ginny Zeal

Typefaces: Giacomo
Color reproduction by GMC Reprographics
Printed in China

PAGE 2 «
Cherry blossom,
England.

CANON REBEL T6/EOS 1300D

» CONTENTS

1 OVERVIEW

The Rebel T6/EOS 1300D is Canon's latest entry-level digital SLR, but this doesn't mean that it's not well specified. In fact, many of its capabilities have filtered down from camera models higher up in Canon's EOS hierarchy.

The Rebel T6/EOS 1300D was announced on 10 March 2016, as the successor to 2014's Rebel T5/EOS 1200D. Many of the features of the older camera have been carried over to the Rebel T6/EOS 1300D, including an 18-megapixel digital sensor.

The headline changes are a switch to Canon's DIGIC 4+ processor, improved shooting speed, a higher-resolution LCD screen (increased from 460,000 pixels to 920,000 pixels), and the addition of built-in Wi-Fi. The latter is particulary useful for anyone who's interested in sharing their photographs on social media or wants to shoot remotely via Canon's Camera Connect app.

To aid smartphone connection, Canon has also implemented Near Field Communication (NFC) on the Rebel T6/EOS 1300D, which simplifies the task of making a Wi-Fi connection.

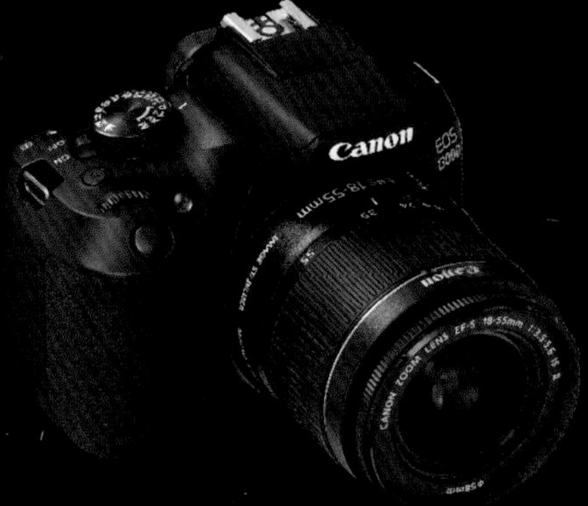

SIMPLICITY ⏫
The Rebel T6/EOS 1300D lacks some of the more esoteric features found on its expensive cousins, but there's something refreshing about using a simpler camera that has the essential features you need to make great photographs.
© Canon

LESS IS MORE ⏩
Keeping it simple applies to composition just as much as cameras. Excluding unnecessary distractions can make an image stronger.

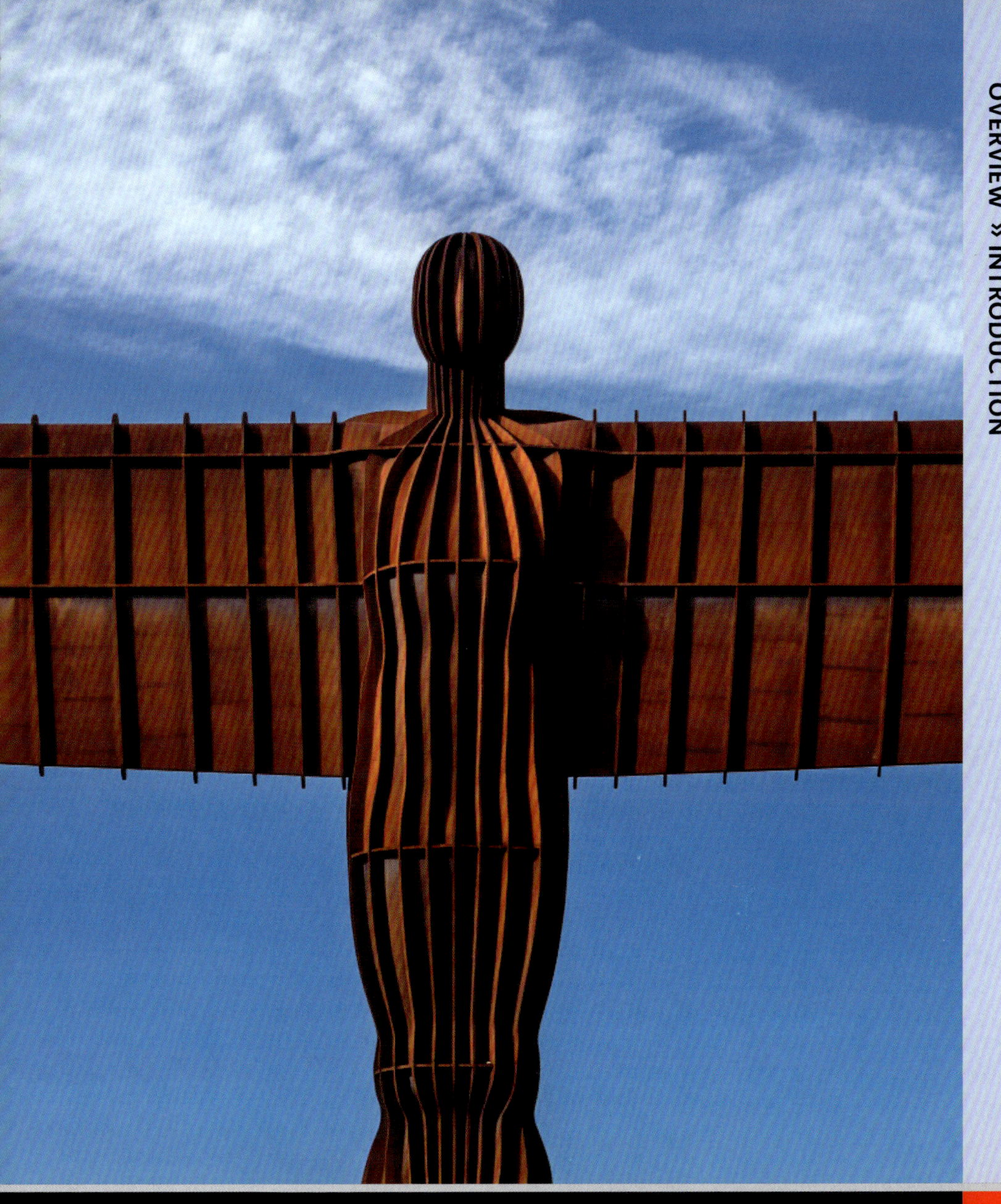

» MAIN FEATURES

Body

Dimensions (W x H x D): 5 x 4 x 3 in.
(129 x 101 x 77mm)
Weight: 17.1 oz (485g) with battery
Lens mount: Canon EF/EF-S
Operating environment: 32–104°F
(0–40°C) at 85% humidity maximum

Sensor and processor

Sensor: 22.3 x 14.9mm APS-C format
CMOS sensor
Aspect ratio: 3:2
Resolution: Approx. 17.9 megapixels
Image processor: DIGIC 4+
Automatic dust removal: No

Still images

JPEG resolution (pixels): 5184 x 3456 (L);
3456 x 2304 (M); 2592 x 1728 (S1);
1920 x 1280 (S2); 720 x 480 (S3)
JPEG Compression: Fine; Normal (not
available when S2 or S3 are selected)
Raw resolution (pixels): 5184 x 3456
Raw format: .CR2 (14-bit)
Raw + JPEG shooting: Yes

Movies

Movie format: .MOV
Image compression: H.264
Audio compression: Linear PCM
Movie resolution: Full HD (1920 x 1080
pixels); HD (1280 x 720 pixels);
SD (640 x 480)
Frame rates: 60; 50; 30; 25; 24
(available options determined by
resolution and local TV standard)

LCD monitor

Resolution: Approx. 920,000 million pixels
Size: 3.0 in. (7.5cm) diagonal
Live View: Yes
Touchscreen: No
Brightness levels: 7 user-selectable levels

Viewfinder

Type: Eye-level pentamirror
Coverage: Approx. 95%
Magnification: Approx. 0.8x
Eye point: 21mm
Diopter adjustment: $-2.5 - +0.5m^{-1}$

Focusing (viewfinder)

Focus modes: One-Shot; AI Servo AF;
AI Focus AF; Manual
Focus points: 9 AF points (automatic
or manual selection)
AF assist beam: Yes (using built-in flash)

Focusing (Live View)

Focus modes: FlexiZone-Single; ☺ Live
mode (contrast detection); Quick mode
(phase-difference detection)
Manual magnification: 5x; 10x

Exposure

Metering patterns: Evaluative;
Center-weighted; Partial
Exposure compensation: ±5 stops
(in ⅓- or ½-stop increments)
Automatic exposure bracketing: ±2 stops
(in ⅓- or ½-stop increments)
ISO: 100–6400 (expandable to H: 12,800)

Shutter

Shutter speeds: 1/4000–30 sec., plus Bulb
Drive modes: Single shot; Continuous
Max. frame rate: Approx. 3 fps
Max. burst depth: 1110 JPEG; 6 Raw;
4 Raw + JPEG
Self-timer: 2 sec.; 10 sec.; Continuous

Flash

Built-in flash: GN 30ft (9.2m) at ISO 100
Hotshoe: Yes (compatible with Canon
EX Speedlite flashes)
Sync speed: 1/200 sec.
Flash modes: Auto; Flash On; Flash Off;
Red-eye reduction; 1st/2nd curtain sync
Flash exposure compensation: ±2 stops
(in ⅓-stop increments)

Memory card

Type: SD; SDHC; SDXC
Eye-Fi compatible: Yes

Software (available to download)

Digital Photo Professional (DPP);
EOS Utility; Picture Style Editor; Lens
Registration Tool; EOS Web Service
Registration Tool

» FULL FEATURES & CAMERA LAYOUT

FRONT OF CAMERA

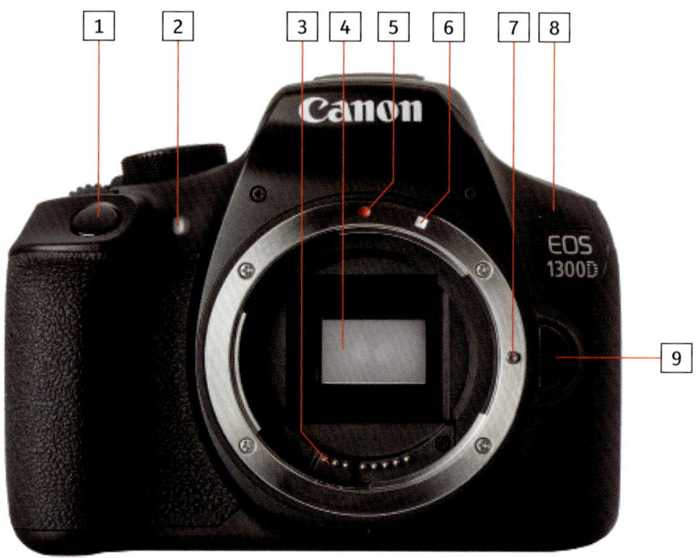

1	Shutter-release button
2	Red-eye reduction / Self-timer light
3	Lens electrical contacts
4	Reflex mirror
5	EF lens mount index
6	EF-S lens mount index
7	Lens locking pin
8	Microphone
9	Lens-release button

BACK OF CAMERA

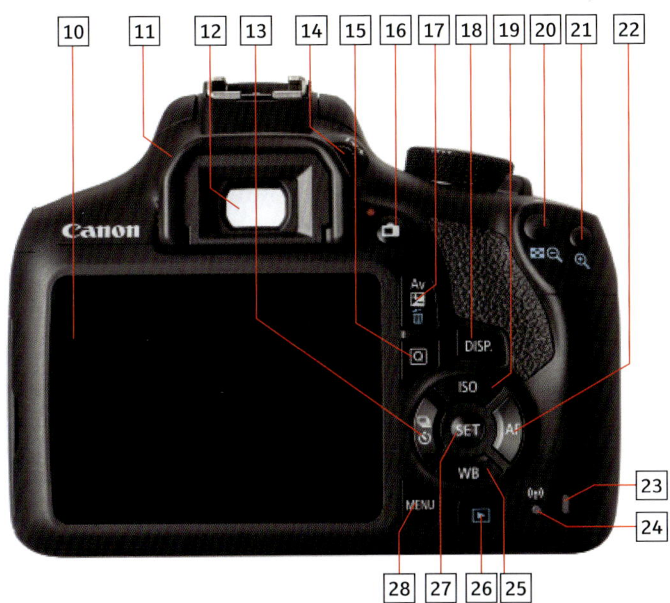

10	LCD monitor	20	AE lock / FE lock/ Index / Reduce button
11	Viewfinder eyecup	21	AF point selection / Magnify button
12	Viewfinder eyepiece	22	► / AF mode selection button
13	◄ / Drive mode selection button	23	Access lamp
14	Diopter adjustment knob	24	Wi-Fi status lamp
15	Quick control button	25	▼ / White balance selection button
16	Live View / Movie shooting button	26	Playback button
17	Aperture / Exposure compensation / Erase image button	27	(SET) button
18	Display button	28	MENU button
19	▲ / ISO selection button		

1 » FULL FEATURES & CAMERA LAYOUT

TOP OF CAMERA

LEFT SIDE

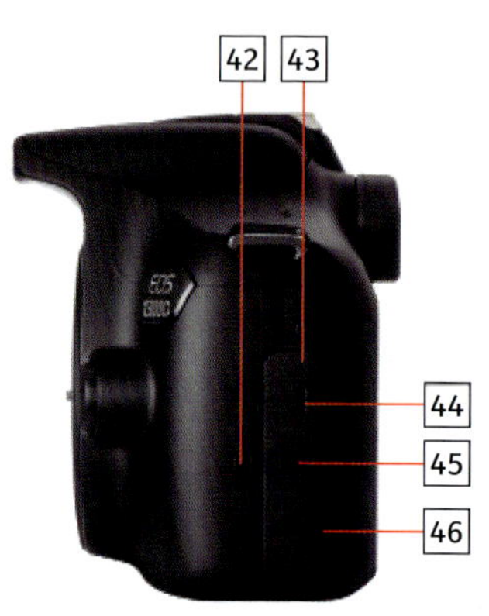

29	Left strap mount	37	ON/OFF switch
30	Focal plane indicator	38	Shutter-release button
31	Speaker	39	Main dial
32	Built-in flash	40	Flash button
33	External flash hotshoe	41	Right strap mount
34	External flash electronic contacts		
35	Mode dial index mark		
36	Mode dial		

42	NFC mark
43	Terminal cover
44	Remote control terminal
45	USB terminal
46	HDMI mini out terminal

RIGHT SIDE

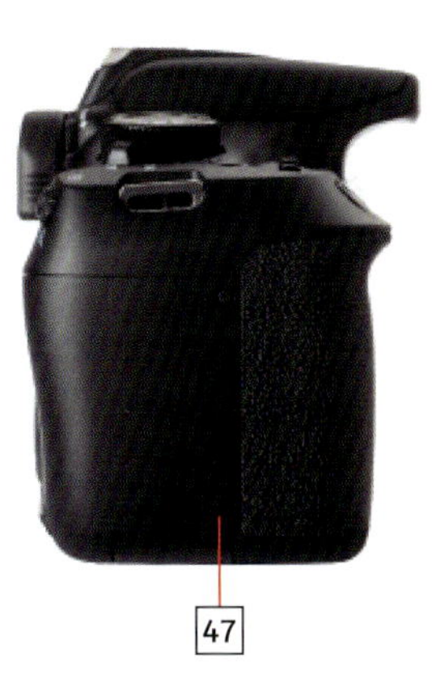

BOTTOM OF CAMERA

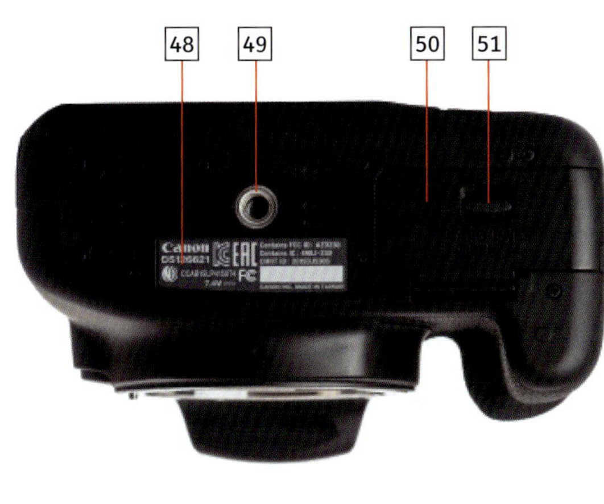

47 DC cord hole

48 Information panel
49 Tripod socket
50 Battery / Memory card cover
51 Battery / Memory card cover lock

1 » VIEWFINDER

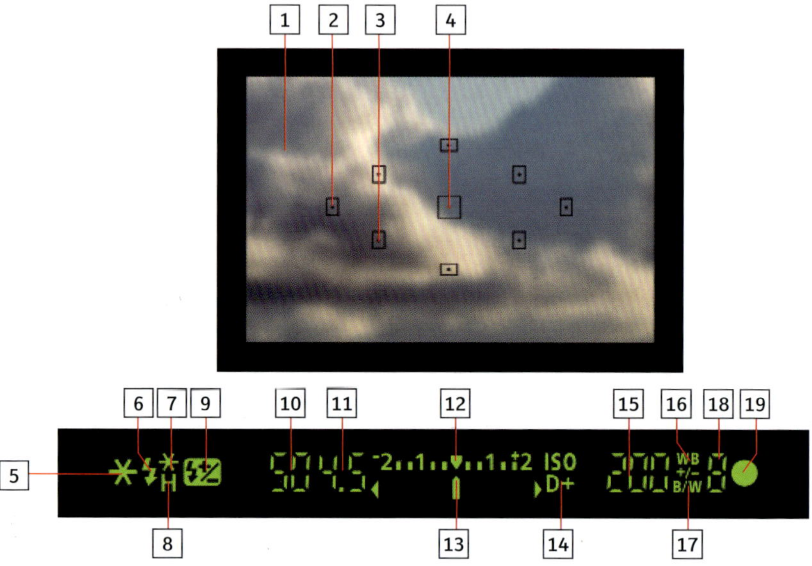

1 Focusing screen	**11** Aperture
2 AF point	**12** Standard exposure index
3 AF point activation indicator	**13** Exposure level indicator / Exposure compensation amount / AEB range / Red-eye reduction lamp-on indicator
4 Active AF point	**14** Highlight tone priority indicator
5 AE lock / AEB indicator	**15** ISO speed
6 Flash ready indicator	**16** White balance correction indicator
7 Flash FE lock / FEB indicator	**17** Monochrome shooting indicator
8 High-speed sync flash indicator	**18** Maximum burst indicator
9 Flash exposure compensation	**19** Focus confirmation indicator
10 Shutter speed / FE lock (FEL) / Busy (buSY) / Built-in flash recycling ($\frac{1}{2}$ buSY) / Card full warning (FuLL) / Card error warning / No card warning	

» QUICK CONTROL SETTINGS

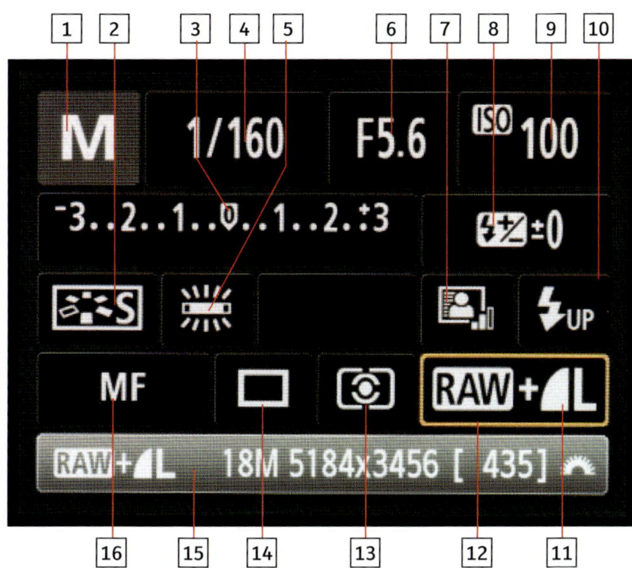

1	Shooting mode	13	Metering mode
2	Picture Style	14	Drive mode
3	Exposure level indicator / Exposure compensation / AEB	15	Information bar
		16	Focusing mode
4	Shutter speed		
5	White balance		
6	Aperture		
7	Auto Lighting Optimizer		
8	Flash exposure compensation		
9	ISO setting		
10	Raise built-in flash		
11	Image recording quality		
12	Q Option selection box		

» PLAYBACK SCREEN

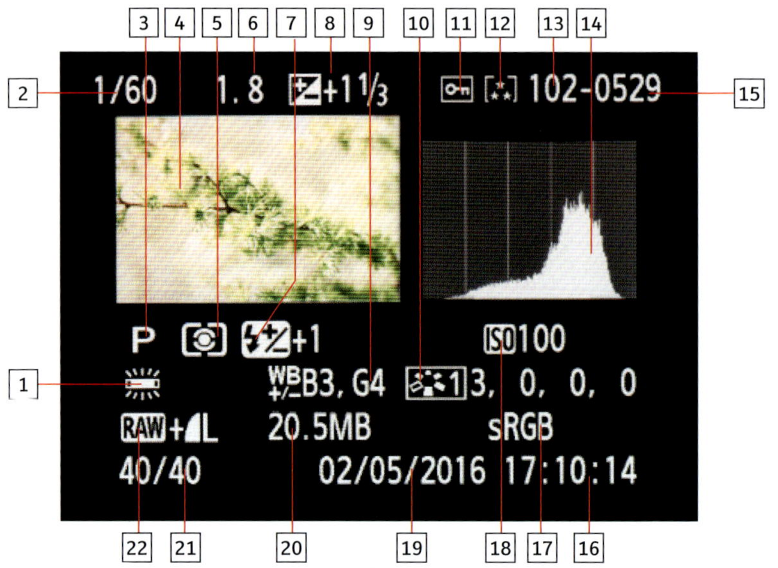

1	White balance setting	13	Current folder number
2	Shutter speed	14	Histogram (brightness)
3	Shooting mode	15	File number
4	Image thumbnail	16	Time of image capture
5	Metering mode	17	Color space
6	Aperture	18	ISO
7	Flash exposure compensation	19	Date of image capture
8	Exposure compensation	20	File size on memory card
9	White balance adjustment	21	Image number / Number of images on card
10	Picture style details	22	Image recording quality
11	Protection		
12	Rating		

» LIVE VIEW

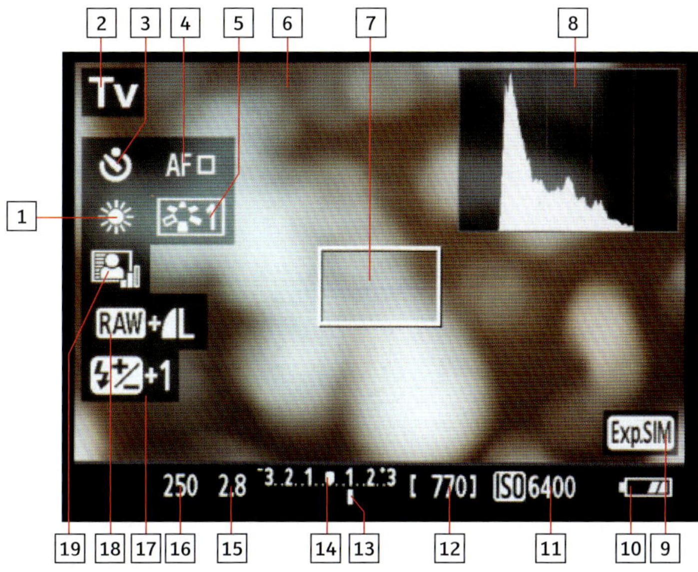

1	White balance setting	**11**	ISO
2	Shooting mode	**12**	Possible shots
3	Drive mode	**13**	Exposure level indicator / AEB range
4	AF mode	**14**	Standard exposure index
5	Picture Style	**15**	Aperture
6	Live View image	**16**	Shutter speed
7	Focus point	**17**	Flash exposure compensation
8	Histogram	**18**	Image recording quality
9	Exposure simulation	**19**	Auto Lighting Optimizer
10	Battery status		

2 FUNCTIONS

In a way, the Rebel T6/EOS 1300D is several cameras in one: in its automatic modes it can be used with point-and-shoot simplicity, or it can be controlled manually for more creative photography.

If you're familiar with Canon's design philosophy you'll find the Rebel T6/EOS 1300D an easy camera to pick up and use immediately, as many of the buttons and functions found on other Canon EOS cameras also make an appearance on this newcomer. These include the useful Quick Control button, Live View, and remote shooting via a Wi-Fi connection.

If the Rebel T6/EOS 1300D is your first EOS camera, this chapter will be particularly useful. In it you will find a guide to the camera's controls, how they work, and why they may occasionally need altering. Even if the camera feels daunting at first glance, with practice it is very easy to get to grips with.

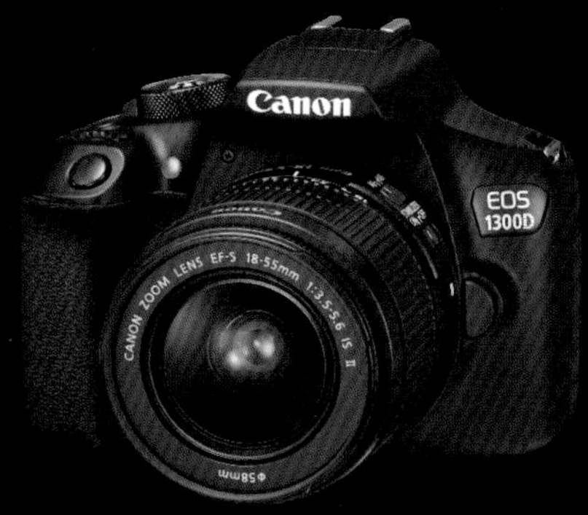

GETTING STARTED ⏫
Buy a Rebel T6/EOS 1300D with a kit lens and you'll have the basics to begin an exciting photographic journey.
© Canon

COMPLEX »
Despite its seeming complexity, there's a logic to how the Rebel T6/EOS 1300D operates, which is easy to pick up.

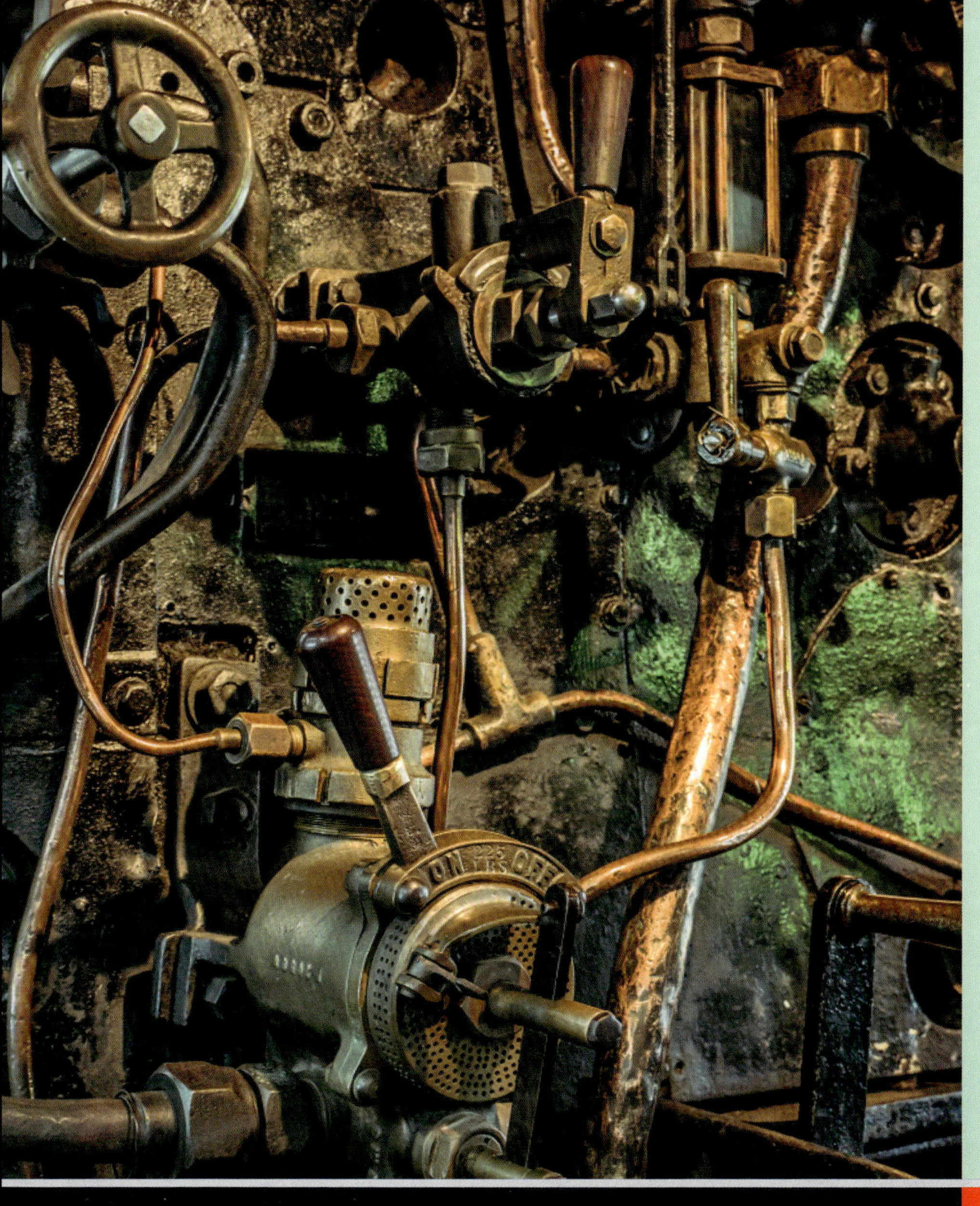

› Attaching the strap

The Rebel T6/EOS 1300D comes with a cloth strap that lets you wear it around your neck (or hold the camera with the strap wrapped around your wrist). Fitting the strap is an important first step as it will help to reduce the risk of you dropping the camera.

To attach the strap, pull one end of the strap out of the attached buckle and plastic loop and then feed it through either the right or left strap mount on the side of the camera. Feed this end back through the plastic loop and then under the length of strap still in the buckle. Pull the end of the strap so that is fitted snugly in the buckle. For safety, allow at least 2 inches (5cm) of strap to extend beyond the buckle.

Repeat the process on the opposite side of the camera.

› Using the viewfinder

Images can either be composed on the rear LCD screen in Live View, or through the optical viewfinder. The main advantage of using the viewfinder is power efficiency: you'll use significantly fewer batteries during a day's heavy shooting when using the viewfinder compared to the LCD.

The downside to the viewfinder is that it's not as easy to judge composition, as the viewfinder offers 95% coverage of the scene (Live View on the rear LCD gives you 100% coverage). This means that it's easy to miss important details around the edge of the frame. It's also more difficult to judge exposure decisions or the effects of functions such as WB correction, as these—and more—can be simulated on the LCD, but not through the viewfinder.

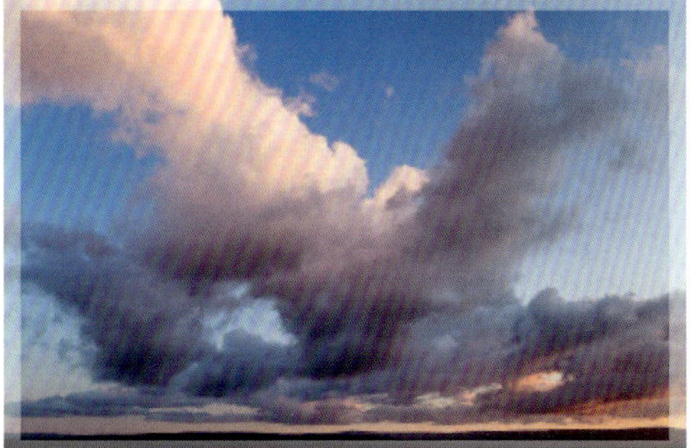

MISSING «

Looking through the viewfinder, the pale area around the edge of this image wouldn't be visible, but it would be recorded.

Note

The focus (or diopter) of the viewfinder can be adjusted to compensate for individual variations in eyesight. To adjust the diopter, look through the viewfinder and turn the diopter adjustment wheel until the text at the bottom of the viewfinder appears crisp. This will not affect the focus of the camera.

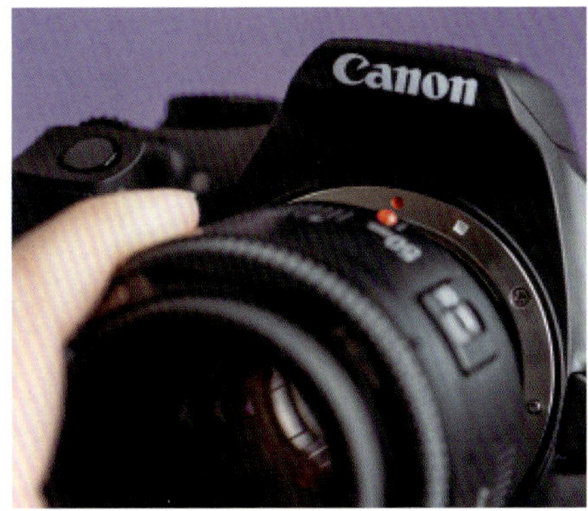

RED/WHITE ⨠

EF lenses fit on all types of EOS DSLRs and can be distinguished by the red mounting mark.

› Fitting and removing a lens

The beauty of a camera like the Rebel T6/ EOS 1300D is that you're able to change the lens to suit the types of images you want to shoot (while you may never need to do this if the kit lens is perfect for your needs, at least the potential is there).

To fit a lens, first switch off your Rebel T6/EOS 1300D. Next, hold the camera with the front facing toward you. Remove the body cap (or lens if one is already fitted) by pressing in the lens-release button fully and then turning the cap to the left until it comes free easily.

Remove the rear protection cap from your lens. If you're fitting an EF-S lens,

align the white index mark on the lens barrel with the corresponding white mark on the camera's lens mount; if you're fitting an EF lens, align the red index mark on the lens with the red index mark on the camera. In both cases, hold the solid part of the lens and gently push it into the lens mount until it will go no further. Turn the lens to the right until it clicks into place.

To remove a lens, reverse the procedure above. If you're not fitting another lens immediately, replace the body cap on the Rebel T6/EOS 1300D and fit the rear cap onto the lens you've just removed.

2

» POWERING YOUR CAMERA

Before you use your Rebel T6/EOS 1300D you must first install a charged battery. The camera is supplied with an LP-E10 battery, which is commonly used in Canon's smaller DSLRs. To charge the battery, first remove the terminal cover on the battery and then slide it in and then down into the supplied LC-E10 or LC-E10E charger (the word "Canon" should be in the same orientation on both the charger and battery).

Connect the LC-E10E charger to the AC power cord and insert the plug into a wall socket, or plug the LC-E10 charger directly into a wall socket after flipping out the power terminals. The "charge" lamp will glow orange as the battery charges; when charging is complete the "full" lamp will glow green.

Once the battery is charged, unplug the charger from the wall socket and remove the battery by pulling it up and out from the charger using the tab at the rear of the battery. The normal recharge time for a fully depleted battery is approximately 120 minutes.

› Inserting and removing the battery

To insert the battery, switch your Rebel T6/EOS 1300D off and turn it upside down. Push the memory card/battery cover release lever toward the front of the camera; the cover door should open easily.

With the battery contact terminals facing down and to the front of the camera, push the battery into the compartment with the side of the battery

Note
The Rebel T6/EOS 1300D's battery charger can be used overseas (100–240v AC 50/60hz) with a suitable plug adaptor and does not require a voltage transformer.

Approximate number of shots per battery charge

Composition method	Shooting style	Temperature	
		73°F (23°C)	32°F (0°C)
Viewfinder only	No flash	600 shots	500 shots
	Built-in flash (50% usage)	500 shots	410 shots
Live view only	No flash	190 shots	180 shots
	Built-in flash (50% usage)	180 shots	170 shots
Movie shooting	–	75 min.	70 min.

Notes

The battery charge indicator is shown at the bottom left of the rear LCD screen.

When shooting indoors, you can power your Rebel T6/EOS 1300D using mains electricity, via the optional CA-PS700 AC compact power adaptor.

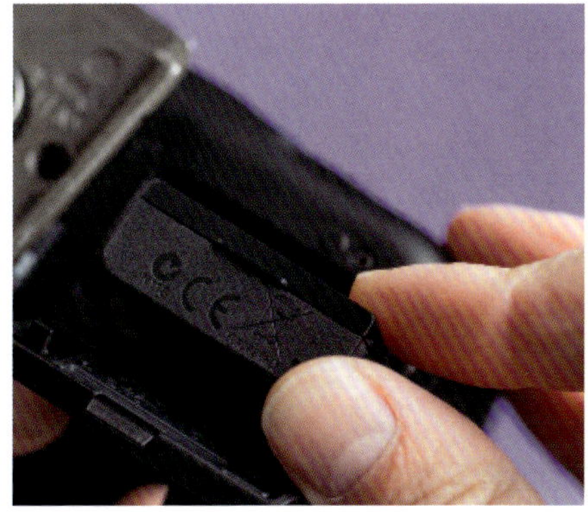

SHAPED ⌃

It is possible to insert the battery upside down, so always ensure that the end without the contacts faces outward.

pressing against the gray lock lever as you do so. Once the battery has clicked into place close the battery cover. To remove the battery, push the lock lever away from the battery and gently pull it out.

› Battery life

How quickly the battery depletes will depend on how you use your camera. Using the LCD and Live View is particularly power-draining, so you might want to try and keep your use of the screen to a minimum. Environmental conditions also affect the efficiency of a battery, with cold conditions causing the battery to deplete more quickly. When you're outside in winter, it's worth keeping a fully charged spare battery ready so your photography session doesn't come to a sudden stop.

Battery charge indicator

🔋	Battery adequately charged
🔋	Battery less than half charged
🔋	Battery almost depleted (flashes)
🔋	Battery depleted / requires recharging

2 » BASIC CAMERA FUNCTIONS

› Buttons and dials

The Rebel T6/EOS 1300D has plenty of external buttons (and a dial), and to get the most out of the camera it pays to be familiar with all of these controls. With practice this won't take long, and we'll be referring to the buttons and dial throughout the rest of the book by using a variety of shortcut symbols.

The main dial sits just behind the shutter-release button, while the cross keys are found at the right of the LCD (Left ◀ / Up ▲ / Down ▼ / Right ▶). These controls are used to select a variety of functions on the camera. If any of the cross keys can be used (such as when moving the focus point around the LCD) ✛ will be shown; it will then be up to you to decide which button is pressed. and the cross keys can usually be used interchangeably; any exceptions to this will be noted when necessary.

The cross keys are arranged around the Setting button, shown as ⓢⓔⓣ. Any other buttons on the camera will be referred to by their name or relevant symbol, while options that are visible on a menu screen will be shown in **bold** type.

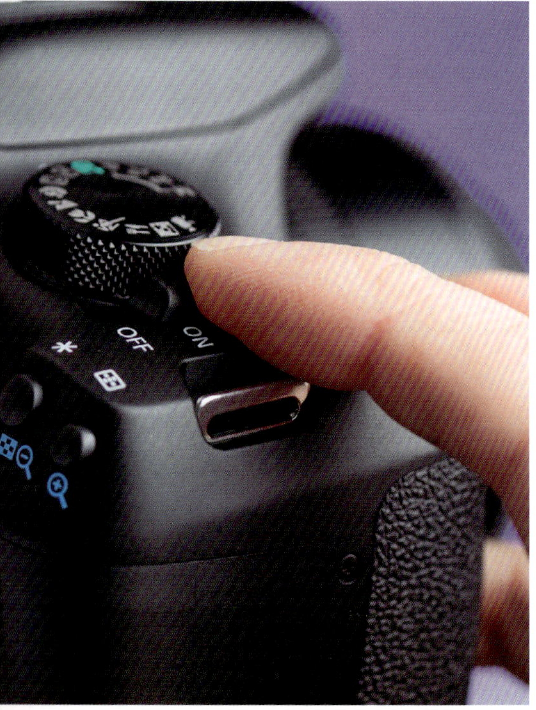

POWERING UP «

The power switch is to the right of the mode dial. Switched to OFF, the Rebel T6/EOS 1300D is entirely inactive. Switched to ON, the access lamp will briefly flicker and the LCD will light up.

› The menu system

The physical controls on the body of the Rebel T6/EOS 1300D let you quickly set a wide range of camera functions. However, you will need to delve into the camera's menu system to really configure it to your needs. Some of the more immediately useful menu options are referred to in this chapter—for details about other options see chapter 3.

The menu is divided into color-coded groups, each with its own icon: Shooting ◻, Movie (when the mode dial is set to), Playback ▶, Set-up , and My Menu ★. Each group is further subdivided into separate pages, with the page number indicated by one to four squares at the right of the group icon.

Notes

By default, the Rebel T6/EOS 1300D will automatically power down after 30 seconds if no controls are pressed. When the camera has powered down automatically lightly pressing down on the shutter button will re-activate it.

When using Live View it's a good idea to turn off the shooting information (even if it's just temporarily). The more cluttered the screen is with icons and text, the more likely it is that you'll miss an important detail in your shot.

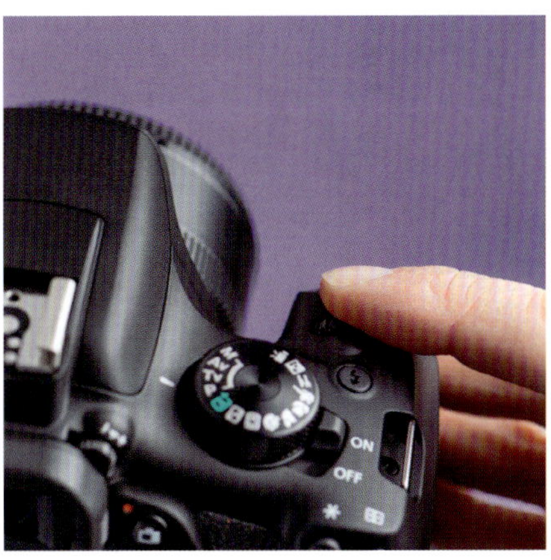

USING ⚙

In Aperture priority (**Av**) and Shutter priority (**Tv**) modes, ⚙ is used to set the aperture value and shutter speed respectively. In Program (**P**) mode, ⚙ can be used to "shift" the exposure values. In Manual exposure mode (**M**), turning ⚙ changes the shutter speed; to change the aperture value you need to hold down 🗑/Av at the same time as turning ⚙.

Changing menu options

1) Press MENU.

2) Press ◀ / ▶ or turn ⚙ to move left or right between the different menu pages. As you jump between the various menu pages that page's icon and number at the top of the LCD will be highlighted.

3) When you reach the required menu page press ▲ / ▼ to move up or down the options. Press (SET) when the function you wish to alter is highlighted.

4) Highlight one of the options for your chosen function by pressing either ▲ / ▼ for simple menu options, or ✛ when there is a series of options arrayed around the screen (the currently selected option is shown in blue). Press (SET) to make your choice. If you press MENU before making your choice you'll jump back up a level to the previous menu screen without making any alterations.

5) Press MENU, or lightly down on the shutter-release button, when viewing a main menu screen to return directly to shooting mode.

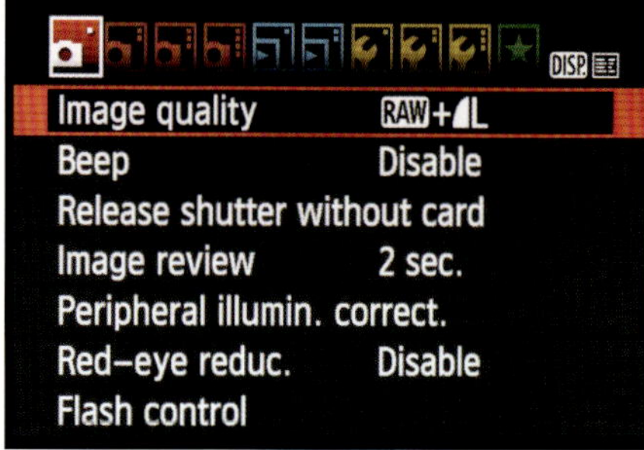

Notes

Some options will require you to confirm your choice before proceeding. This is done by selecting either **OK** to continue or **Cancel** to reject the choice. Highlight the required option and press (SET).

Fewer menu screens are shown when the mode dial is set to a Basic Zone mode. It's only when you select a Creative Zone mode that you have full access to the various menu screens.

› Quick Control menu

The Quick Control menu is displayed when you press the **Q** button and offers a useful shortcut to a variety of camera functions. The options shown vary depending on whether the mode dial is set to a Basic Zone or Creative Zone shooting mode, or whether you are viewing still images or movies in playback.

There are two ways to use the Quick Control menu. The first is to press ✛ to highlight the required option, followed by **SET** to view a detailed option screen. Alternatively, you can turn ⌒ to make the desired changes when the required option is highlighted on the main Quick Control menu screen.

Shooting function	Comments
Shutter speed	**Tv/M** modes only
Aperture	**Av/M** modes only
ISO	Not available in Basic Zone modes
Exposure compensation/ Bracketing	Not **M** or Basic Zone modes Not available in Basic Zone modes
Flash exposure compensation	Not available in Basic Zone modes
Picture Style	Not available in Basic Zone modes
White balance	Not available in Basic Zone modes
White balance shift	Not available in Basic Zone modes
Auto Lighting Optimizer	Not available in Basic Zone modes Disabled when Highlight tone priority is activated
Metering mode	Not available in Basic Zone modes
AF mode	Not available in Basic Zone modes MF only when lens is set to manual
Drive mode	Single shooting: selectable in all modes except ▨ and ▨ Continuous: selectable in all modes except ▨, ▨, ▨, ▨, and ▨ Self-timer: selectable in all modes
Image quality	Not available in Basic Zone modes
Ambience-based shots	▨, ▨, ▨, ▨, ▨, and ▨ only
Light/scene-based shots	▨, ▨, ▨, and ▨ only
Blurring/sharpening background	▨ only

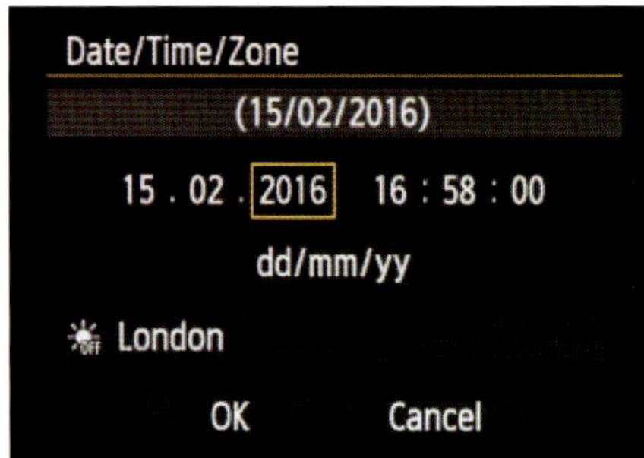

You'll be prompted to set the correct time and date on your Rebel T6/EOS 1300D the first time you switch it on. Setting the right time and date is important, as it can be a valuable method for sorting your images into order or finding a particular shot.

Setting the date and time

1) Turn your camera ON.

2) Press ◄ / ► to highlight the date or time value you want to alter; the highlighted value is surrounded by a yellow box. Press (SET) and the highlight box will change to ♦.

3) Press ▲ to increase the value shown, or ▼ to decrease it. Press (SET) to confirm your choice.

4) Set the way that the date is displayed: **dd/mm/yy**, **yy/mm/dd**, or **mm/dd/yy**.

5) Highlight ☼ to set whether daylight saving needs to be adjusted. Press ▲. When ☼ is displayed the time is advanced by one hour. Press (SET).

6) Highlight the time zone option. Press (SET) and then use ▲ / ▼ to find your current time zone. Press (SET) to select the time zone.

7) Select **OK** to continue (or **Cancel** to exit without saving).

> **Notes**
> If you want to alter your date and time settings again, press MENU and navigate to the ♈ tab. Highlight **Date/Time/Zone**, press (SET), and repeat steps 2 to 7 above.
>
> The date and time numerical values wrap around when they reach their highest or lowest limit; it's generally quicker to press ▼ to reach a high numerical value, particularly when setting the day or minute value.

› The shutter-release button

The Rebel T6/EOS 1300D's shutter-release button has two separate stages. When you press the shutter-release button down half way, the camera's AF system and exposure metering are activated (cancelling playback automatically). How and where the camera focuses is determined by the AF mode, which is described in more detail later in this chapter.

When the shutter-release button is pressed down fully, a photograph is taken (unless the AF system hasn't been able to acquire focus).

What happens next is now determined by the drive mode the camera is set to. Details about drive modes can also be found later in this chapter.

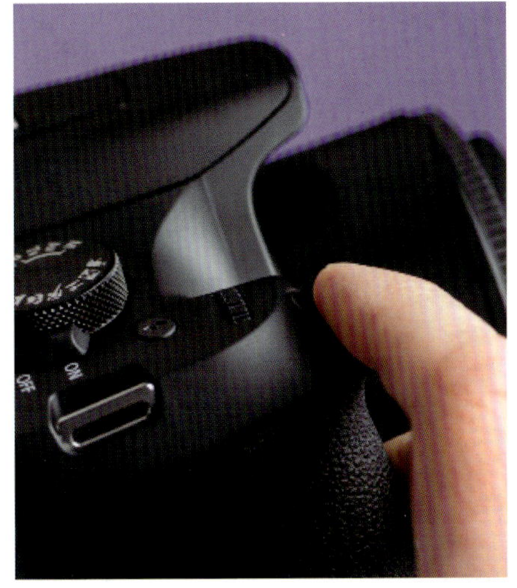

MANUALLY ⌃
You can press the shutter-release button down fully and take a shot when MF is selected, even if the image isn't in focus.

Note
The camera won't try to autofocus if manual focus (MF) has been selected, although the AF system can be used to confirm focus (see page 45 for details).

» MEMORY CARDS

› The SD standard

An SD memory card must be installed in the Rebel T6/EOS 1300D in order to store movies and still images. There are several types of SD memory card, with the latest variant being SDXC, which was introduced in 2009 and is currently available with a capacity of up to 512GB.

The biggest difference between SD cards (apart from their storage capacity) is the speed at which they can read or write data. When shooting still images this is often not an issue, unless you regularly shoot sports/action or are particularly impatient (the read/write speed also affects how long it takes to copy images from the memory card to your computer).

The speed of a memory card is usually shown in one of two ways: as a Class Rating (the higher the Class Rating, the faster the card) or as a figure followed by an "x" (referring to the speed of the card in comparison to the read/write speed of a standard CD-ROM drive). Canon recommends a Class 10 (or 66x) memory card or higher for shooting full HD video at 50/60.

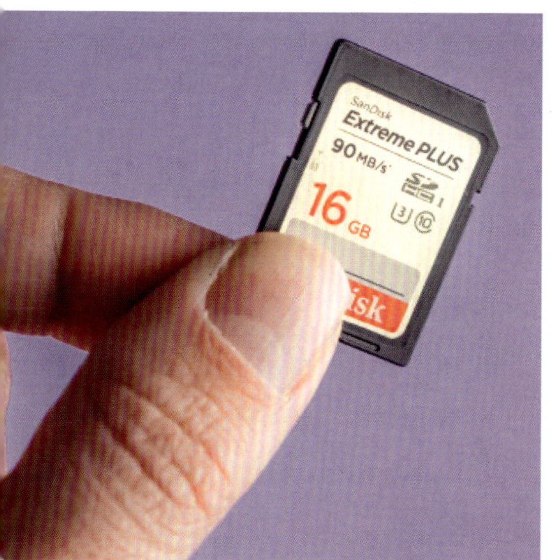

Speed	Read/write speed (Mb/s)	Class rating
13×	2.0	2
26×	4.0	4
40×	6.0	6
66×	10.0	10

UHS-1 «

UHS-1 cards are a new variant of SD memory cards, which potentially have faster read/write times than older types. UHS-1 cards can be used in the Rebel T6/EOS 1300D, but the camera is not fully compatible with the type. This means that the stated read/write time of the memory card will not be achievable.

Note

The Rebel T6/EOS 1300D can also use Eye-Fi memory cards. This is a type of memory card that features a built-in Wi-Fi transmitter, enabling you to copy files from your camera to a computer wirelessly.

Fitting and removing a memory card

1) Ensure that your Rebel T6/EOS 1300D is switched OFF, then open the battery cover door on the bottom of the camera.

2) If your memory card has a write protect tab, slide the tab to the "unlocked" position. If the card is locked, *Card's write protect switch is set to lock* will appear on the LCD and you'll not be able to take photos. Locking the card will ensure saved images will not be erased accidentally.

3) With the memory card contacts facing down and to the front of the camera, push the card into the slot until it locks with a click. Close the battery cover door.

4) To remove the memory card, push it down slightly until you hear a click. The card should now come free. Pull it out gently and close the battery cover door.

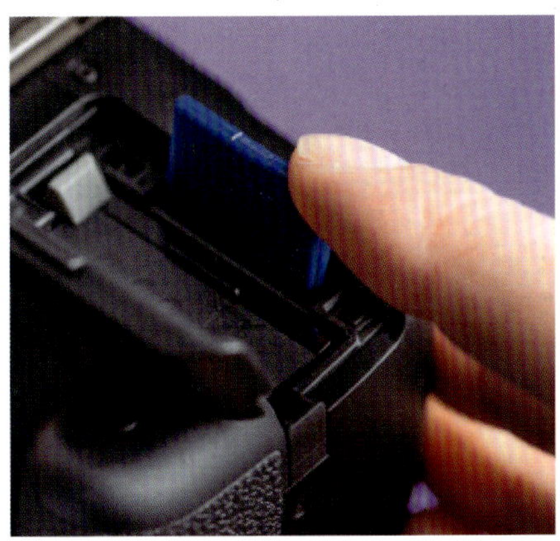

NO CARD ⌃

If there's no memory card in the camera it's still possible to shoot photos by setting **Release shutter without card** to **Enable**, via the ◻ menu. However, although you can fire the shutter, your photos will be not be saved.

Warning!

When the access lamp on the back of your Rebel T6/EOS 1300D is flashing, the camera is either reading, writing, or erasing image data on the SD card. Do not open the battery cover door, or remove the card or the battery when the lamp is flashing—doing so may cause data on the card to be corrupted and potentially damage your camera.

› Formatting a memory card

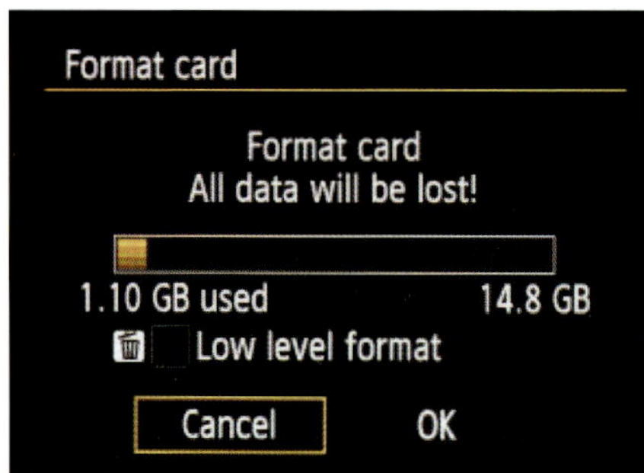

Most SD memory cards come pre-formatted, and although this means the memory card should be immediately ready for use, it's still good practice to format a card the first time you use it in your Rebel T6/EOS 1300D.

This is particularly true if you've used the card in another camera: files saved by another camera may not be visible to the Rebel T6/EOS 1300D, so you'll have less space on the card than you realize. However, before formatting the card, ensure you've copied any images stored on it somewhere else first!

1) Press MENU and press ◄ / ► to highlight the ♈ tab.

2) Select **Format card**.

3) Select **OK** to begin formatting the memory card (or select **Cancel** to return to the ♈ menu without formatting).

4) As the card formats *Busy...Please wait* will be displayed on screen. Once formatting is complete the camera returns to the ♈ menu.

5) Press down lightly on the shutter-release button to return to shooting mode.

» DRIVE MODE

Note

On the **Format card** screen is an option to **Low Level Format**. When you format a memory card, it is usually only the list of contents that is erased. This means that the original files are still on the card, it's just that the camera can't "see" them. As you shoot, these files are gradually overwritten and a new list of contents created.

The benefit here is that if you accidentally format a memory card, it's often possible to recover your files with file-recovery software—provided you don't use the card before you do so.

However, use **Low Level Format** and everything on the card is erased, not just the list of contents. This is a more secure way of clearing your card, but also a more permanent one. To use low-level formatting press 🗑/Av⊞ when you first enter the **Format card** screen at step 3. A ✔ will be displayed next to **Low Level Format** to show that you've chosen this option.

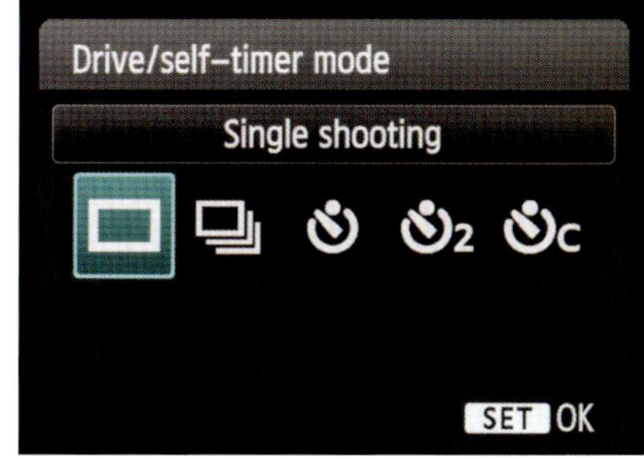

A camera's drive mode specifies when and how many still images are shot when the shutter-release button is pressed and held down. In terms of the numbers of images shot there are two choices: **Single** or **Continuous**. There are also three **Self-timer** modes that delay the firing of the shutter for a set period of time.

When you set the drive mode to **Single**, the Rebel T6/EOS 1300D will only fire the shutter once. If you want to shoot another image you'll need to take your finger off the shutter-release button briefly and then press down again. **Single** is suited to reasonably static subjects such as landscapes, portraits or still life.

If you are shooting moving subjects, the **Continuous** drive mode will likely be a better option. Set to **Continuous**, the Rebel T6/EOS 1300D will continue to shoot at a maximum shooting speed of 3 frames per second (fps) for as long as the shutter-release button is held down. The actual frame rate that is achieved will depend on the write speed of your memory card and the ambient lighting conditions.

Continuous shooting ends when you take your finger off the shutter-release button, but it will also stop if you run out of memory card space or the frame buffer fills. The frame buffer is the camera's built-in memory and is where images are temporarily stored until they've been written to the memory card. When shooting continuously, the frame buffer will gradually fill to the point where the camera can no longer continue shooting. When this happens the maximum burst indicator at the right of the viewfinder will show *0* and *buSY* will flash at the left. You won't be able to shoot any more images until the frame buffer is sufficiently clear and the queue of files has been written to the memory card.

To avoid the buffer filling up, it's a good idea to practice firing short bursts of frames. If not, you may find your camera

stopping at just the wrong moment, particularly when shooting Raw. When shooting JPEGs, the buffer will fill after 1110 shots (when using ◢**L**); Raw reduces this to just 6 shots; and Raw + JPEG to 4.

All of the drive modes are selectable when shooting using a Creative Zone mode, but in Basic Zone modes it is the mode that determines whether you shoot using Single or Continuous (Self-timer is available in all of the Basic Zone modes).

To adjust the drive mode, press ◄ and select the desired option from the drive mode screen. Alternatively, highlight the currently selected drive mode symbol on the Q screen and alter the setting as required.

Drive mode	Action	Symbol
Single	One shot fired with each press of the shutter-release button	☐
Continuous	Shutter fires continuously until memory card/frame buffer fills	⊒
10-sec. Self-timer	Shutter fires after 10-second delay	↻
2-sec. Self-timer	Shutter fires after 2-second delay	↻2
Self-timer continuous	Shutter fires 2–10 shots after a 10-second delay	↻c

» SPEED

If you shoot a moving subject using a fast shutter speed, the subject's movement will be frozen. This often fails to convey a sense of speed, making the final shot feel strangely static. Blur—created by using a longer shutter speed—is often more pleasing.

However, too much blur can make the subject unidentifiable. For this shot I panned the camera to follow the vehicle as it passed, shooting roughly half way through the panning motion. This caused the background to blur, but left the vehicle reasonably sharp.

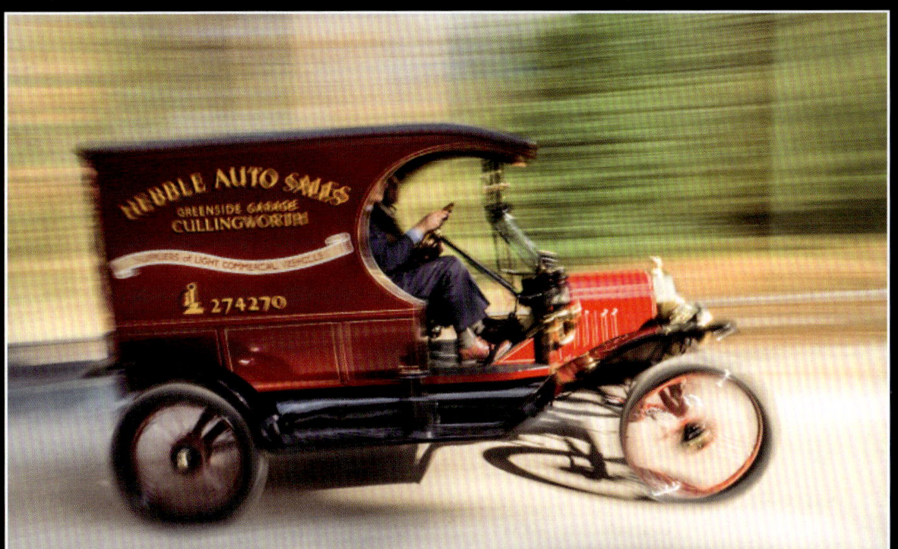

Settings
> Focal length: 24mm
> Aperture: f/22
> Shutter speed: 1/5 sec.
> ISO: 100

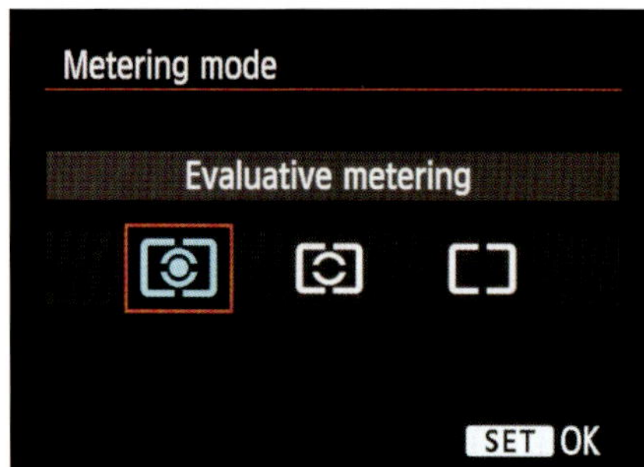

› Metering modes

To select one of the three metering modes on your Rebel T6/EOS 1300D press [Q] and highlight ◉ (the default metering mode). Turn ⬚ until the required metering option is displayed.

Evaluative ◉

Evaluative metering uses 63 separate metering zones arrayed across the image space to calculate the exposure. Each zone is assessed separately, and the overall exposure is calculated by combining the results from the zones, biasing the exposure to where the focus point is.

This system is generally accurate, but not infallible. Evaluative metering can cause underexposure if the camera focuses on a lighter-than-average subject, while focusing on a darker-than-average subject can cause overexposure.

> **Note**
> In the Basic Zone modes, the metering is set to ◉ and can't be altered.

There are two steps required to produce a correctly exposed image. The first step is to measure the amount of light either falling onto or reflected by the scene in front of the camera. The second step is setting the required shutter speed, aperture, and ISO values so that just the right amount of light reaches the digital sensor inside the camera. If too little light reaches the sensor the image will be dark and underexposed; too much light and the image will be burnt-out and overexposed.

The Rebel T6/EOS 1300D has a built-in exposure meter that is used for the first step. There are three different metering modes available, each with advantages and disadvantages that are discussed below. The required shutter speed, aperture, and ISO values are set automatically in the Basic Zone modes or can be controlled by you in the Creative Zone modes.

Center-weighted average ⬚

As with ◉, all 63 metering zones are used when ⬚ is selected. However, the exposure is biased very heavily to the central zones, with the zones at the edge of the frame affecting the exposure less. This makes ⬚ ideal for central subjects, particularly those that are backlit.

Partial ⬚

Partial metering restricts the metering area to a small circle at the center of the image. This is useful when you only want to meter a particular area of a scene (typically this would be something with an average reflectivity to avoid under- or overexposure). Used with AE lock, you can even set the exposure using something outside your intended composition before recomposing to take the shot.

› Exposure compensation

When you select any of the Creative Zone shooting modes (with the exception of **M**) you can override the exposure settings suggested by the camera using exposure compensation. This can be done in increments of ⅓ or ½ stops, up to ±5 stops. Applying negative exposure compensation will darken the image (either by making the aperture smaller or by setting a faster shutter speed),

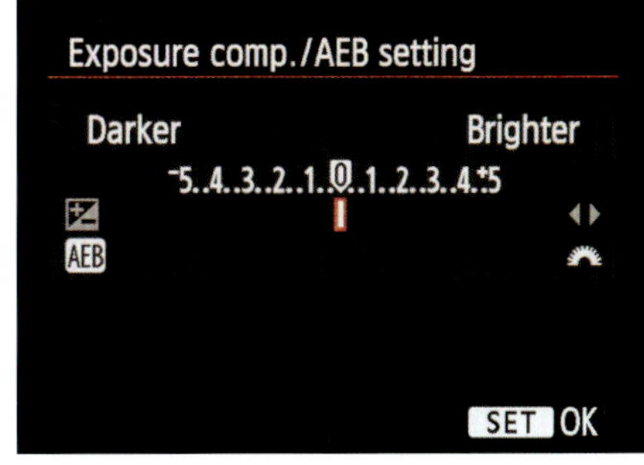

while positive exposure compensation will lighten the image (by opening the aperture or setting a slower shutter speed). Exposure compensation allows you to correct any exposure errors the camera may make, or adjust the exposure for creative effect.

The simplest way to set exposure compensation is to hold down Av⊞ and turn ⬙ at the same time. The degree of alteration can be seen on the standard exposure index in the viewfinder or on the LCD.

The downside to this method (when using the viewfinder) is that the standard exposure index only shows exposure compensation up to ±2 stops. If you dial in a value greater than this, the levels of under- and overexposure are shown with less accuracy, with ◀ and ▶ shown respectively at the side of the standard exposure index.

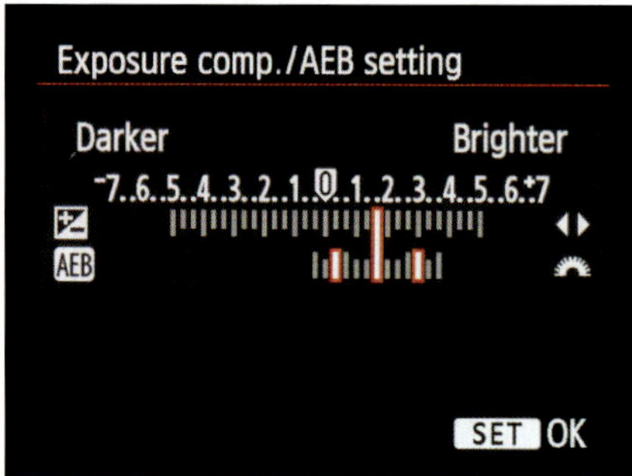

increased; turn to the left and the difference is decreased. As with exposure compensation, press SET to confirm the new setting.

A more accurate way of setting exposure compensation is via the **Q** screen, or by selecting **Expo. comp./ AEB** from the menu. Press ◄ / ► to apply exposure compensation as required, followed by SET to confirm the setting.

› Auto exposure bracketing

Bracketing is a term used to describe the technique of shooting two or more images at different settings. Bracketing is usually applied to exposure, but the Rebel T6/EOS 1300D also lets you bracket white balance.

Canon refers to exposure bracketing as "auto exposure bracketing" (AEB). When applying AEB, the first shot is "correct," the second shot is darker, and the third shot is lighter. The bracketing sequence can be set to ±2 stops in ⅓-stop increments.

AEB is set on the **Expo. comp./ AEB** screen by turning . Turn to the right and the difference in the exposure of the bracketed sequence is

Notes
Reset exposure compensation to 0 when you're finished, otherwise it will be applied to all your subsequent exposures.

AEB can be used in conjunction with exposure compensation.

To deactivate AEB, turn to the left until only the standard exposure index is shown.

If you apply AEB in addition to exposure compensation, the bracketing values will be centered on the compensated exposure.

» SHADOWS

It is often necessary to apply negative compensation when a scene is dominated by deep, dark shadows. This image required exposure compensation of -2 stops to ensure that the shadows remained dark and the highlight around the edge of the pot didn't burn out to pure white.

Settings
> Focal length: 50mm
> Aperture: f/2.8
> Shutter speed: 1/50 sec.
> ISO: 100

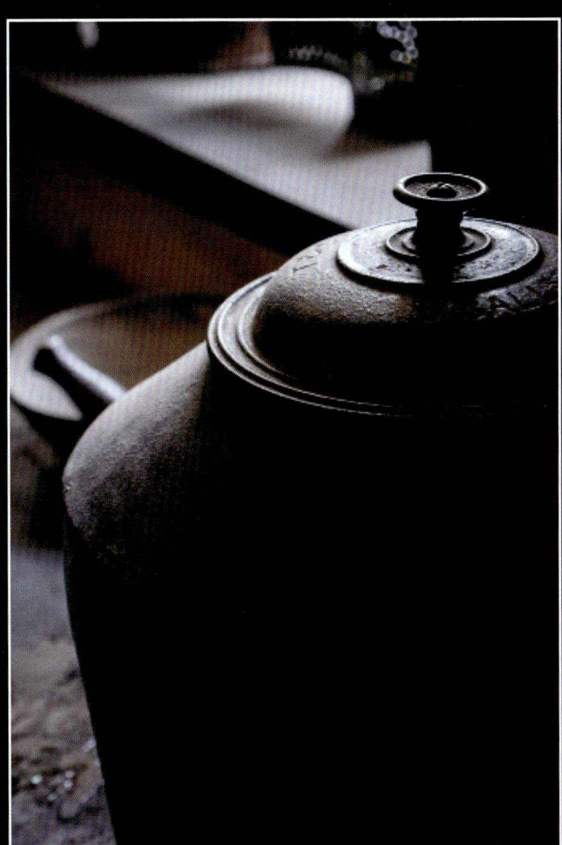

› ✳ AE lock

AE lock is a useful function that temporarily locks the shutter speed, aperture, and Auto ISO (if set) until you take a shot or until it is automatically cancelled after the period of time set using **Metering timer** (see page 110). Holding the shutter-release button down half way also locks exposure, but the difference is that the shutter release button will lock focus as well (AE lock only locks the exposure).

Activating AE lock

1) Press the shutter-release button down half way to activate the exposure meter in the camera.

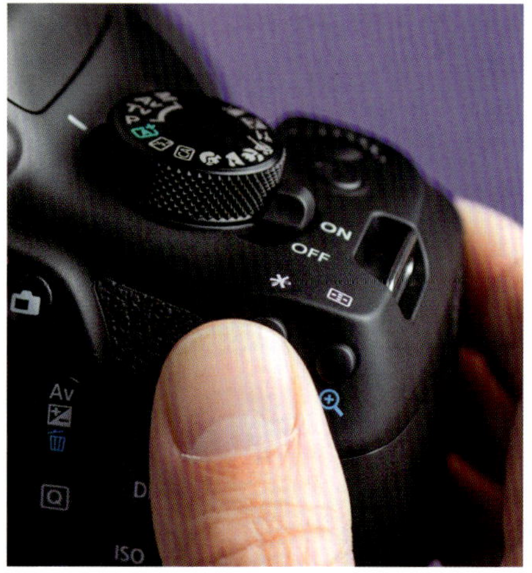

2) Press ✳. ✳ will light in the viewfinder to show that AE lock has been activated (or on the LCD if you're using Live View).

3) Recompose (if necessary) and press the shutter-release button down fully to take the shot.

4) AE lock is cancelled after you've taken the shot. If you want to keep the exposure locked, hold down ✳ as you shoot.

Metering mode	AF point selection method	
	Automatic	**Manual**
◉	Exposure is determined and locked at the AF point that achieved focus. (AE lock is applied to the central AF point if the lens is set to MF.)	Exposure is determined and locked at the selected AF point. (AE lock is applied to the central AF point if the lens is set to MF.)
◎ / ▭ / ◦	Exposure is determined and locked by the central AF point.	

» ISO

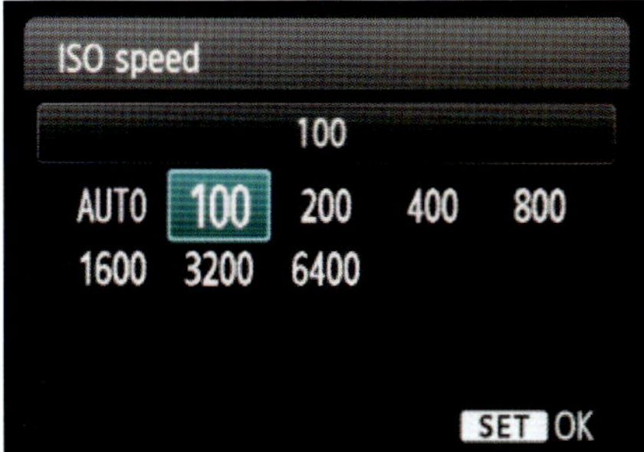

ISO determines exactly how much light is needed by the camera's sensor to make an acceptably exposed image (the other two exposure controls—aperture and shutter speed—determine how much light physically reaches the sensor).

The default ISO range on the Rebel T6/EOS 1300D is ISO 100–6400. As you increase the ISO, the sensor will need progressively less light to make a usable image (it may help to think of using higher ISO values as turning up the volume on the sensor). Unfortunately there's a price to pay for increasing the ISO: image noise. Image noise is seen as reduction in fine detail and an increase in "grittiness" in the image. The higher the ISO value you use, the "grittier" the image becomes.

On the Rebel T6/EOS 1300D the optimal ISO setting for the digital sensor is ISO 100. This is the setting that will give you the very best image quality. However, the ability to alter the ISO is one of the most useful aspects of a digital camera. If you're handholding your camera in low light, for example, you may not be able to keep the camera steady because the shutter speed is too slow. Increasing the ISO will let you use a faster shutter speed and in this instance an increase in image noise would be preferable to losing shots because of camera shake.

Noise is most visible on screen when an image is viewed at 100% magnification. However, when you reduce the resolution of an image, noise becomes less visible. Using a higher ISO setting is therefore less of an issue if you know that the image will be reduced in size later.

Notes
Increasing the ISO also reduces the dynamic range that the camera can capture. When shooting a scene with bright highlights and dark shadows you'll have a greater chance of capturing the full tonal range by using a lower ISO.

Noise can be removed in-camera by setting **C.Fn II-5 High ISO speed noise reduct'n** to **1: Low** or **2: Strong** (see page 135) or it can be removed during postproduction.

ISO 100
This image was shot at ISO 100. The cropped details on the page opposite were shot at a variety of different ISO settings, showing the difference in noise levels as ISO increases.

You don't just have to set a particular ISO value, though. The Rebel T6/EOS 1300D also offers you the choice of ISO AUTO. This sets the ISO automatically, according to the ambient light levels. ISO AUTO is particularly useful when you're shooting with the camera handheld and will be moving between scenes with varying levels of ambient light (such as outdoors and indoors).

There are several ways to set the ISO. The simplest method is to press the ▲ / ISO button and then set the required value on the LCD screen. ISO can also be set via the Q screen.

Notes
Don't use ISO AUTO if you're using ND filters (see page 190), as the camera will simply increase the ISO to try and counter the effect of the filter.

You can expand the ISO range and use H, which is equivalent to ISO 12,800. This is set via **C.Fn I-2 ISO expansion** on the menu. However, this option is not recommended for everyday shooting, as image quality is extremely low at this setting.

CANON REBEL T6/EOS 1300D

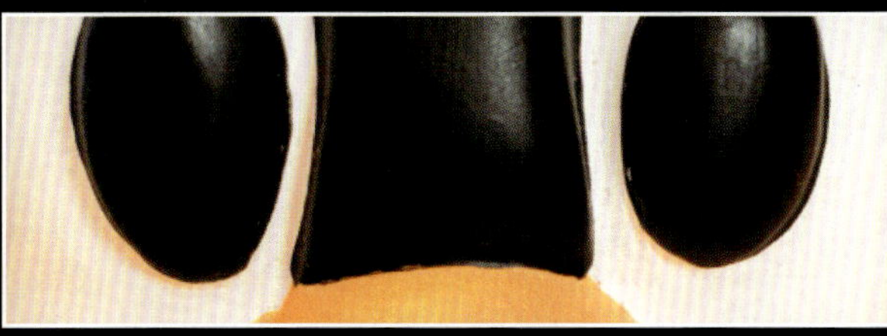

ISO 100

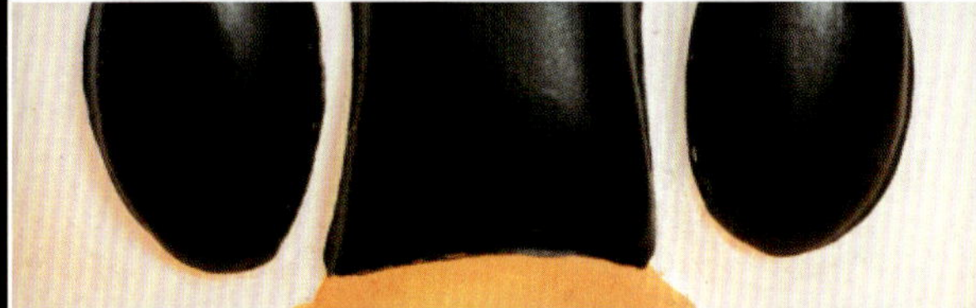

ISO 1600

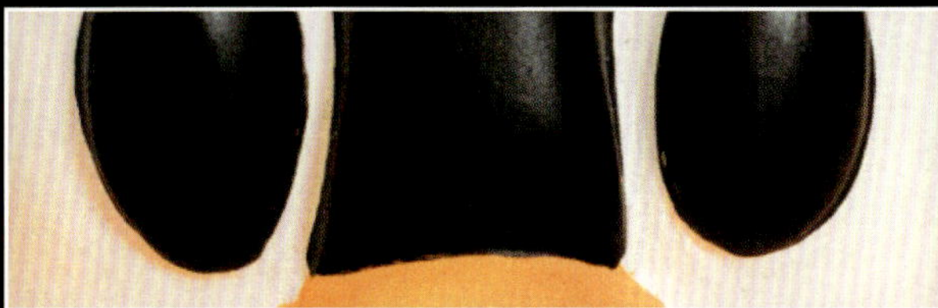

ISO 6400

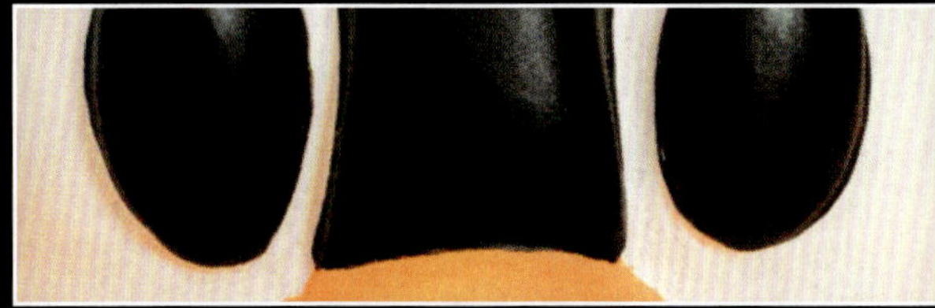

ISO (H) 12,800

A lens is necessary to focus light onto a camera's digital sensor to form a sharp image, but where the image is sharp will depend on the focus distance. This can be anywhere between a lens' minimum focusing distance through to infinity (the maximum focusing distance, typically shown as ∞).

Focus can be achieved automatically using the camera's autofocus (AF) system, which moves the lens elements into place to focus the lens by driving motors within the lens barrel. When you look through the viewfinder, you will see nine rectangles arranged in a flattened diamond shape: these are AF points and show the relative position of the AF sensors built in to the camera. When AF is activated, one or more of the AF points will determine the camera-to-subject distance and focus the lens accordingly.

You can also focus manually (MF) by physically turning a lens' focus ring. Although AF is convenient, there may be times when you need to switch to MF for reasons other than personal preference. AF can struggle when light levels are low, for example, either because of the ambient lighting conditions or because light-sapping filters are fitted to the lens. AF can also fail when there is insufficient contrast in a scene. In these situations the lens may start to "hunt" and be unable to

Note
The Rebel T6/EOS 1300D actually has two AF systems: one for when the viewfinder is used (phase detection), and another that is activated when the camera is switched to Live View (contrast detection). Although you don't need to understand how they work, it's important to understand that the two systems have different advantages and disadvantages. Phase detection is far faster, but slightly less accurate than contrast detection (although accuracy is still excellent). Therefore the viewfinder AF is better suited to fast action, such as sports, whereas Live View AF is best left to still life, portraiture, and landscape subjects.

achieve focus lock. When this happens the green ● focus confirmation indicator in the viewfinder (and on the LCD in Live View) will blink. To solve this you may need to move the AF focus point or switch the lens to MF.

› Using viewfinder MF

1) Set the focus switch on the lens to MF.

2) Look through the viewfinder and rotate the focus ring. Turn the focus ring to the right to focus on subjects close to the camera, or to the left to focus on subjects further away.

3) Hold down the shutter-release button half way as you focus and the ● focus confirmation indicator will light when your subject is in focus (if your subject is behind one of the nine focus points in the viewfinder).

SWITCHED
Some lenses (typically USM and STM lenses) let you turn the focus ring even when the AF/MF switch is set to AF. Don't try and force a focus ring though, particularly if there's slight resistance.

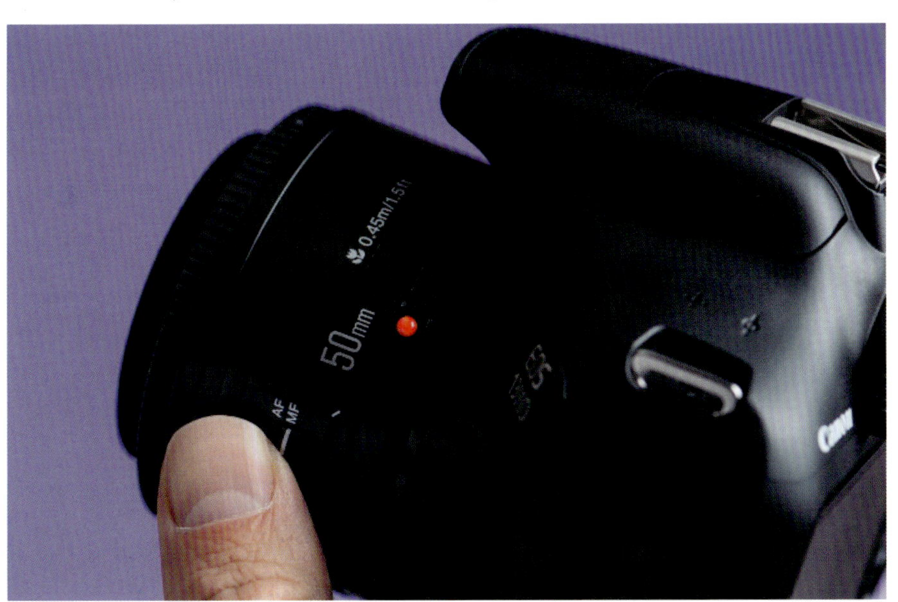

› Using viewfinder AF

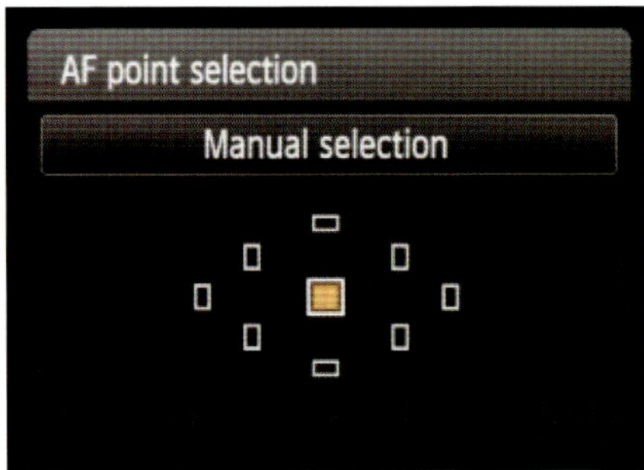

AF can be usefully split into two steps, with a decision needing to be made at each step. The first step is deciding where in the scene to focus; the second is whether the camera stops focusing once focus has been achieved or whether it's updated continuously until the shutter is fired. The "where to focus" step is solved by selecting which one or more of the nine AF points is used to set focus. The second step is set by the selection of the required AF mode.

› AF point selection

By default, your Rebel T6/EOS 1300D is set to **Automatic selection** of the AF points. This means that your camera automatically chooses which of the nine focus points should be used to set the focus distance. Typically the Rebel T6/EOS 1300D focuses on the closest point in the scene to the camera (if more than one AF point has

been selected, the AF system has found and focused on several areas of the scene that are exactly the same distance from the camera).

Automatic selection generally does a reasonable job at deciding where to focus, but as with other automatic camera functions it's not foolproof. It can sometimes fail when you're shooting an off-center subject, for example, particularly if there's something else in the scene that's closer to the camera.

The easiest way to solve this problem is to switch to **Manual selection** of the AF points. This lets you specify exactly which AF point should be used to determine focus.

Notes
Although there are nine AF points, they aren't all equal in their capabilities. The most sensitive AF point is the one at the center, and in low light the central AF point will be able to focus more accurately then the other eight. If your dimly-lit subject isn't central, aim the camera at the subject, focus, and recompose—keeping your finger held half way down on the shutter-release button.

Manual selection of the AF points is only possible in the Creative Zone modes.

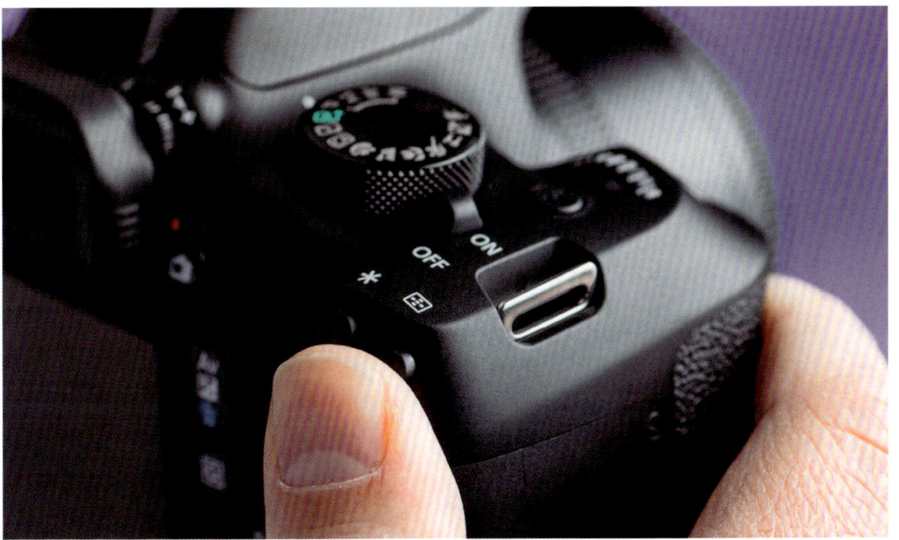

Switching AF point selection mode

1) In shooting mode press ⊕/▦, followed by (SET) to toggle **Automatic selection** and **Manual selection**.

2) Look through the viewfinder. Press ✛ to select the desired focus point, the center of which will light red. ⛯ can also be used to move quickly around the nine focus points.

3) Once all the focus points have been highlighted in turn, point selection will return to **Automatic selection** (all the AF points on the LCD will have an orange center or will light red in the viewfinder).

4) Once you've selected the desired AF point, press down half way on the shutter-release button to return to shooting mode. When you next focus, only the selected focus point will be used.

> **Note**
> Press (SET) at step 2 to jump back to the central AF point.

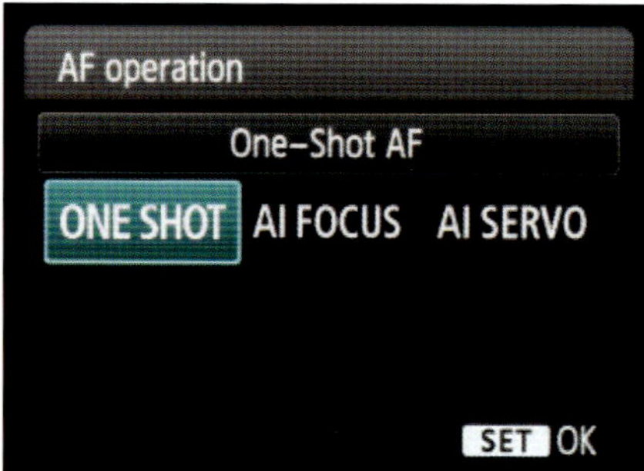

The Rebel T6/EOS 1300D has three subtly different AF modes. Which you choose will depend on whether you're shooting a still subject; whether the subject is moving; or whether your subject has the potential to move before you take the shot. To choose the required AF mode set the lens to AF and either press the ▶/AF button or change the AF mode using the 🇶 screen.

One-Shot AF

With **One-Shot AF** selected, focus is locked when you press the shutter-release button down half way (and focus is confirmed by the ● focus confirmation indicator lighting green).

This means **One-Shot AF** is only suitable for static subjects (if the subject moves before you take the shot you'll need to release the shutter-release button and refocus). It is worth noting that if you are using Evaluative metering, the exposure will also be locked when you press the shutter-release button half way down.

AI Servo AF

AI Servo AF tracks moving subjects, adjusting focus (and exposure) until you press the shutter-release button down fully to take the shot. **AI Servo AF** is a predictive AF system that calculates how your subject is moving and uses that information to keep focus updated. It is not perfect, though: it can fail if your subject is moving too fast, or if your subject moves outside the diamond shape made by the nine AF points (and therefore outside the range of the AF system).

With **AI Servo AF** selected, the camera chooses the appropriate AF point to begin focusing with when **Automatic selection** is used. If the subject moves out from under that AF point, focusing switches automatically to one of the other eight AF points.

When AF point selection is set to **Manual selection**, focus will still update using the selected AF point, but tracking

> **Note**
> The AF mode is selected automatically when the camera is set to a Basic Zone mode.

will stop once the subject moves out from under that AF point. ● does not light in **AI Servo AF** and no sound is made when focus is acquired.

AI Focus AF

AI Focus AF is essentially a hybrid of **One-Shot AF** and **AI Servo AF** modes. Focusing initially behaves exactly like **One-Shot AF**, but will effectively switch to **AI Servo AF** if the camera detects your subject has started to move (as long as you keep the shutter-release button pressed down half way). When the focusing has switched to **AI Servo AF**-type behavior, the beeper will continuously sound very softly as focus is tracked.

FLIGHTY ⌄

AI Focus AF may seem an ideal combination of One-Shot AF and AI Servo AF, but it isn't quite as snappy to begin tracking your subject as AI Servo AF. If you know for certain that your subject will move, use AI Servo AF instead.

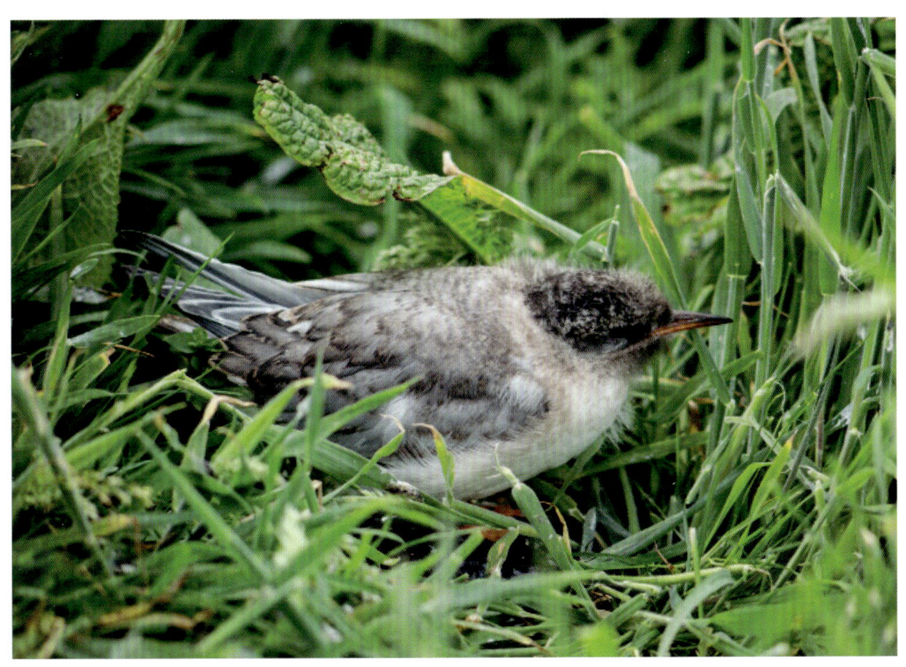

» LIVE VIEW

Live View sends a live feed from the camera's sensor to the rear LCD screen, where you can compose your shots. The advantage of using Live View over the viewfinder is that the effects of functions such as white balance can be seen before you take the shot (see the grid below for a list of these functions).

When **Exp. SIM** is shown in white on the LCD you can also see a reasonable simulation of the final exposure. **Exp. SIM** will blink if the image on the LCD is displayed at a different brightness to the final exposure or, if the final exposure cannot be simulated (when you're using flash, for example), **Exp. SIM** will be grayed out.

Press **Q** to display the Quick Control options available when using Live View. Icons for these options are overlaid at the left edge of the Live View image. You can also choose how much, or how little, shooting information is shown on screen by pressing **DISP.** repeatedly. One particularly useful piece of information is the live histogram showing the tonal range of the image (see page 220 for more about using a histogram).

Function	Comments
Exposure	Not when using flash
Peripheral illumination correction	Selected lenses only
Aspect ratio	Black borders are used to define image shape
Highlight tone priority	Not available when Auto Lighting Optimizer is enabled
Depth of field preview	When C.Fn IV-9 is set to 4
White balance/WB correction	–
Lighting/scene-based shots	Certain Basic Zone modes only
Ambience-based shots	Certain Basic Zone modes only
Auto Lighting Optimizer	Not available when Highlight tone priority is enabled
Picture Style	–

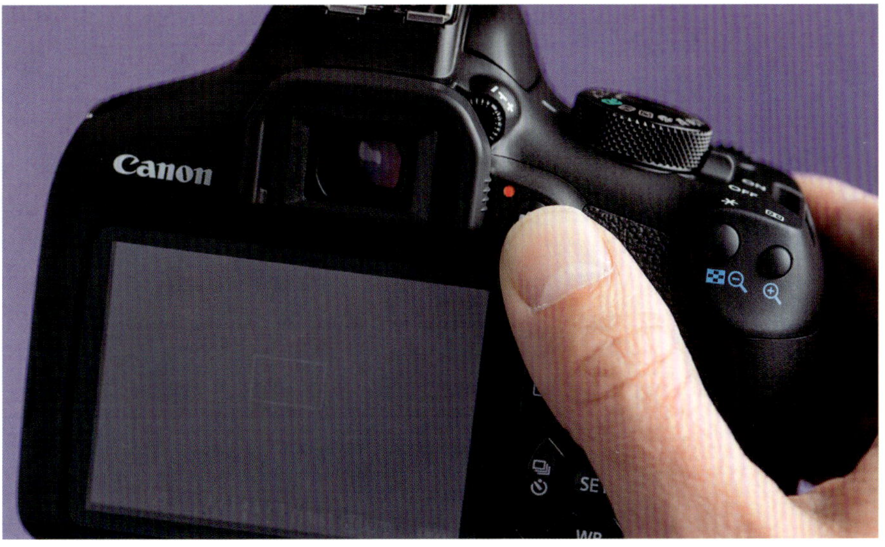

Using Live View

1) Press ◻. The mirror inside the camera will rise and, after a short delay, the Live View image will be displayed on the LCD.

2) The AF point mode is set to FlexiZone **AF** ◻ by default. To move the white focus point rectangle around the LCD press ✛. To re-center the AF point press (SET).

3) Press the shutter-release button half way down to focus and then down fully—once focus has been achieved—to take the shot.

Notes

You can magnify the Live View image by 5x or 10x: press ⊕ to magnify the Live View image 5x, again to magnify 10x, and a third time to restore the display to normal. Magnifying the Live View image is particularly useful for checking critical focus in the scene, such as when shooting macro subjects. Use ✛ to pan around the magnified image.

AF is set to One-Shot AF in Live View mode; AI Servo AF and AI Focus AF are not available.

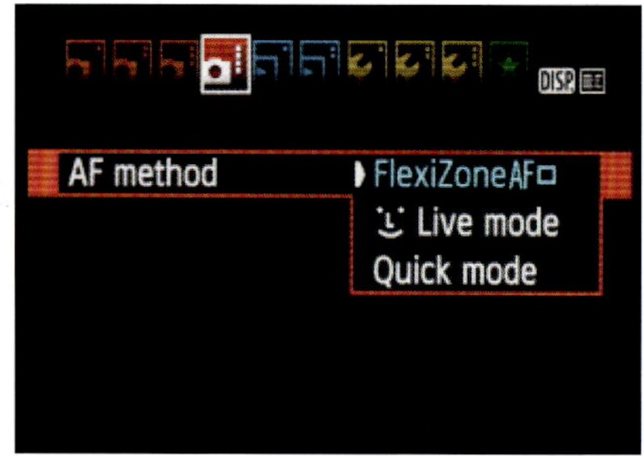

When you switch to Live View you have the choice of three AF modes: FlexiZone **AF □**, **AF :** Live mode, and Quick mode. Each has it strengths and weaknesses and should be used for very specific purposes.

FlexiZone **AF □**

This simple, but effective, AF mode features only one AF point. Although this sounds like a limitation, it's made up for by the fact that you can move the AF point (using ✛) all around the LCD. FlexiZone **AF □** is ideal when shooting static subjects that are close to the edge of the image space. Press (SET) to reset the AF point to the center of the LCD.

AF : Live mode

This AF mode is specifically designed to detect and focus on faces within the image space. A white ⌐ ⌐ AF point is drawn around an automatically-detected face as confirmation. If there are multiple faces in the shot, ⌐ ⌐ will be displayed instead; by pressing ◀ / ▶ you can move the AF point to the desired face.

Press the shutter-release button down half way to focus, and once focus has been achieved the target box will turn green as confirmation (or orange if AF can't be confirmed). Press the shutter-release button down fully to take your shot.

If a face isn't detected, the **AF □** point will be displayed instead and focus will be set at the center of the frame.

Quick mode

Quick mode is a hybrid AF system that uses the Rebel T6/EOS 1300D's standard viewfinder AF sensors to achieve focus. This means that Live View is temporarily turned off when you press half way down on the shutter-release button. Once focus has been achieved, the Live View image returns and the focus point that achieved focus will turn green. Press the shutter-release button down fully to take the shot. If focus cannot be achieved the focus point will turn orange and blink.

> **Note**
> Live View AF can be changed via **Q** or on the **◻:** menu.

» WHITE BALANCE

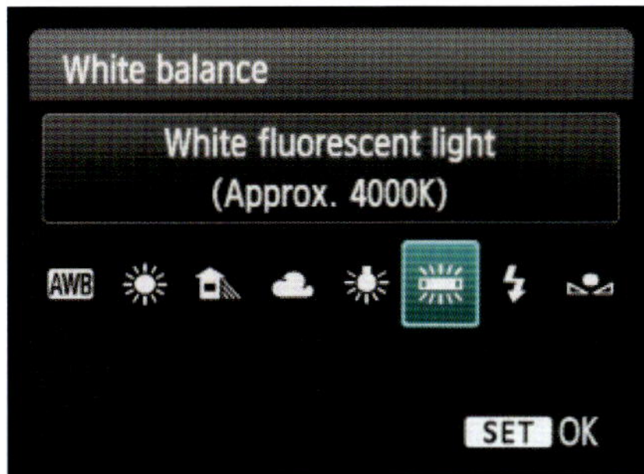

Most light sources have a color bias. This is often either a red bias (resulting in the light being "warm") or a blue bias (or "cool" light). This variation in the red/blue color bias of light has been quantified and is known as the color temperature of light, measured using the Kelvin Scale (K).

White balance (WB) is a camera function that compensates for this color bias (without adjustment your images would look unnaturally warm or cool depending on the light source illuminating

your subject). White balance is so called because the camera adjusts images so that any whites are neutral and don't display a color tint.

Your Rebel T6/EOS 1300D lets you set the WB either by using preset options built into the camera, by letting the camera automatically adjust WB, or by specifying a Kelvin value. The preset you choose is the one that most closely matches the light source illuminating your subject. For greater accuracy you can also create a custom white balance.

Setting white balance
1) Press the ▼/ WB button.

2) Highlight the desired white balance preset and press (SET).

Notes
The WB preset can also be set via the Ⓠ screen.

Some light sources have either a magenta or green bias. This can be compensated for using **WB Shift/ Bkt.** (see page 100).

WB settings

AWB White balance is set automatically

☀ Tungsten (3200K): incandescent lighting

☀ White fluorescent lighting (4000K)

⚡ Flash (5500K)

☀ Daylight (5500K): sunny conditions

☁ Cloudy (6000K): overcast light

⌂ Shade (7000K): open shade

Custom white balance

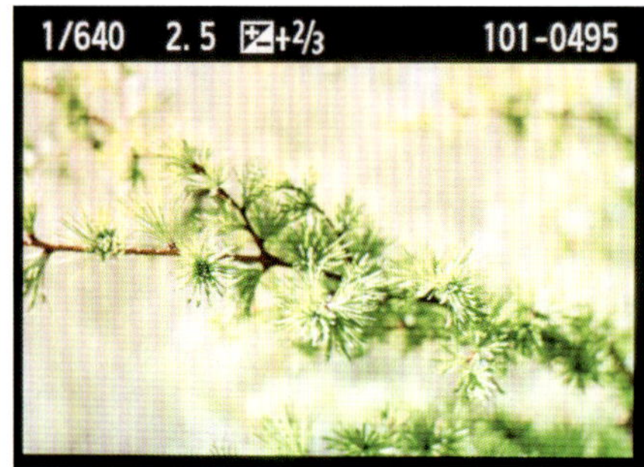

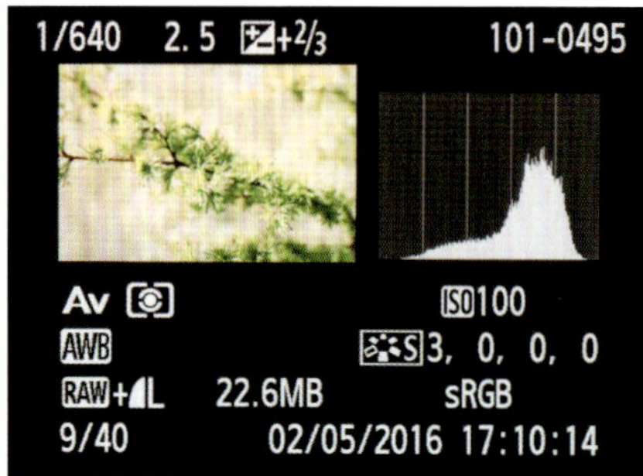

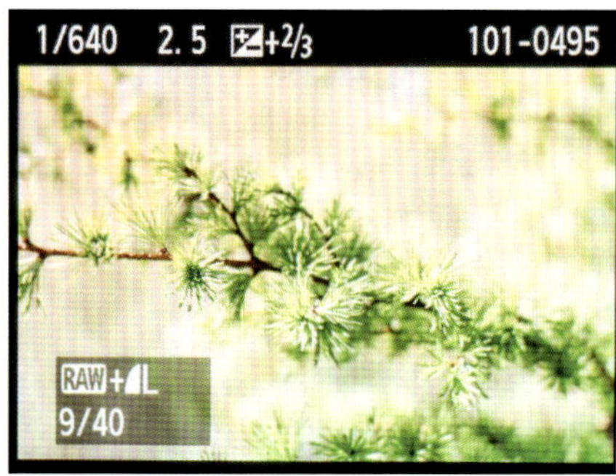

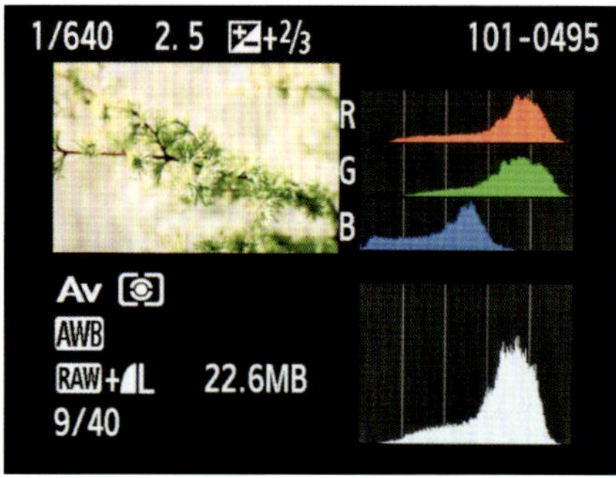

Immediately after you've shot an image, it will be displayed on the Rebel T6/EOS 1300D's rear LCD screen for two seconds. If you want to view images shot previously, you first need to press ▶. The first image shown is the last image viewed previously (if you've just shot an image it will be that one). Both still images and movies can be viewed on the LCD; movies are identified by a 🎬 **SET** or 🎬 **SET** icon at the top left corner of the LCD screen.

When there's more than one image on the memory card you can skip backward or forward through them by pressing ◀ / ▶ respectively. Turning ⚙ skips through your images using the jump method selected on **Image jump w/⚙** on the ▶ menu (see page 119).

Pressing **DISP.** toggles between playback display showing four different levels of image information (above).

› Playback Q

If you press Q during playback you can set the following functions: ⊶ Protect images, ⟳ Rotate, ★ Rating, ◒ Creative filters, ⊡ Resize (JPEG only), or ⌐1 Jump method. Options in gray are not available when viewing movies.

To select a Q option press ▲ / ▼ to highlight the desired control and then ◀ / ▶ to choose the required option (the only exceptions to this are ◒ and ⊡).

Notes

One useful feature of detailed shooting information playback is that overexposed areas of an image (where the pixels in the image are completely white) will blink white/black as a warning.

You can change the duration of automatic playback or even turn it off entirely by adjusting the settings of **Image review** on the ◻ menu (see page 96).

› Magnifying images

Still images can be magnified up to 10x their normal size on playback, which can be used to check critical focus of a particular area of an image. This is especially useful when you are using longer focal length lenses at maximum aperture—depth of field will be minimized, so correct focus is more important. A good example of when this is useful is when shooting portraits. In this instance it's important to ensure that your subject's eyes are in focus. Magnifying the image immediately after shooting will either confirm this or quickly show that you need to reshoot.

Magnify images

1) Navigate to the image you want to view.

2) To zoom into an image press ⊕. Use ✛ to move around the zoomed display. A white box within a small gray box, at the bottom right corner of the LCD, will show your position in the image.

3) To zoom back out press ▦/⊖.

› Image index

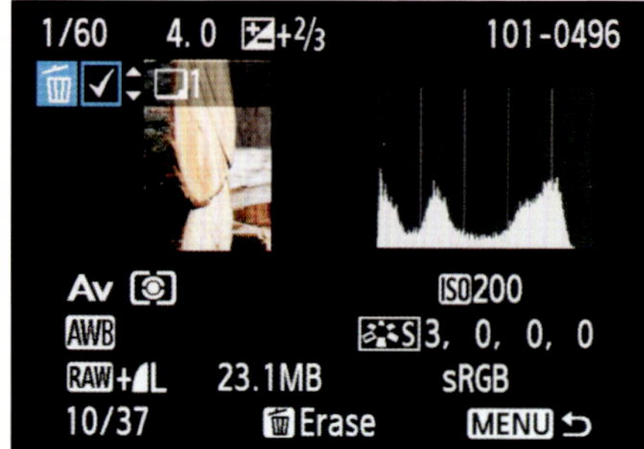

As well as single images, you can call up either four or nine image thumbnails on screen at any one time using image index. Image index is a very effective way to speed up the task of scanning through your images.

1) In non-magnified playback press ▓/🔍 once to view an index of four images and again to view nine.

2) The current image will be highlighted with an orange box. Use ✛ to select another image on the screen or turn 🖘 to move up and down the pages of images on the memory card (assuming there are more than nine on the memory card).

3) When the image you wish to view is highlighted, press (SET) to revert to single-image display (or press ⊕ twice).

› Erasing images

You can erase an image immediately after shooting by pressing 🗑/Av🔲 and selecting **Erase** (or **Cancel** if you change your mind). The same method of erasure can be used when reviewing pictures shot previously, unless the image is protected. To erase multiple images at the same time you need to use the Rebel T6/EOS 1300D's menu system.

Selecting a range of images for deletion

1) Press MENU, navigate to ▶, and select **Erase images**.

2) Choose **Select and erase images**.

3) Press ◀ / ▶ to skip through the images on the memory card. To view three images on screen at once press ▓/🔍; to restore single-image view press ⊕.

4) When the image you want to delete is displayed, press ▲ / ▼ to toggle the erase marker. A ✔ will be displayed in a box in the top left corner of the LCD to show that the image has been marked for deletion. The number of images marked for deletion is shown at the right of the ✔ icon. Repeat steps 3–4 to mark more images for deletion as required.

5) When you're ready, press 🗑/Av⊞ to erase all the marked images. Select **OK** to erase the selected images, or choose **Cancel** to return to step 3.

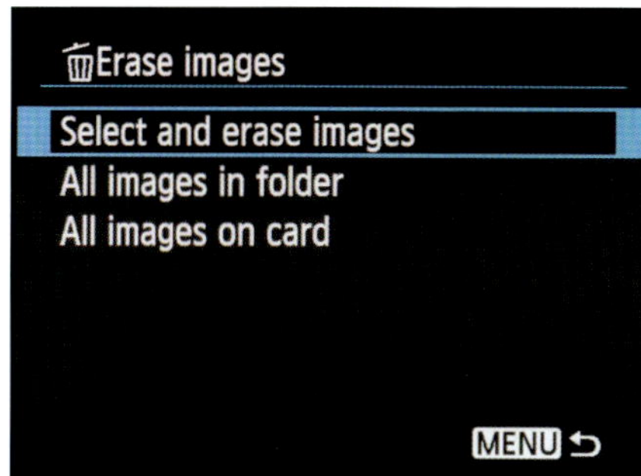

Other deletion options

1) Press MENU, navigate to ▶, and select **Erase images**.

2) Select **All images in folder**. Press ▲ / ▼ to choose the folder you wish to erase images from and press (SET). Select **OK** to continue (or **Cancel** to return to the **Select folder** screen).

3) To erase all the images on the memory card (except those that are protected) select **All images on card** at step 1. Select **OK** to continue, or **Cancel** to return to the main **Erase images** menu.

› Protecting images

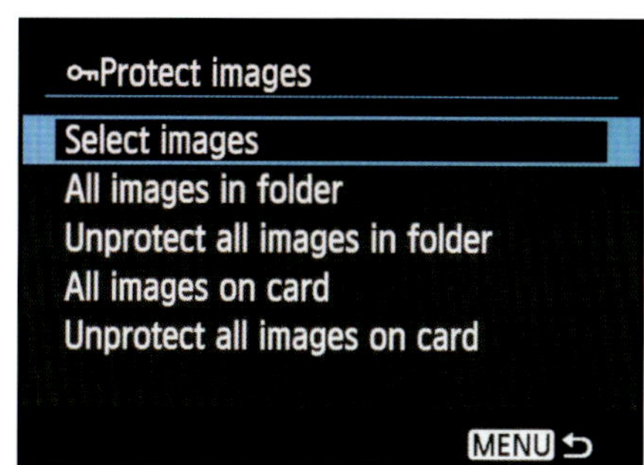

It's frustrating and annoying to accidentally delete an image. To stop this happening you can protect images either individually or as a group. Once an image has been protected, the only way to erase it is to "unset" protection or to format the memory card (formatting removes both protected and unprotected images alike).

Selecting a range of images for protection

1) Press MENU, navigate to ▶, and select **Protect images**.

2) Choose **Select images**.

3) Press ◄ / ► to skip through the images on the memory card. To view three images on screen at once press ▦/⊖. To restore single-image view press ⊕.

4) When the image you want to protect is displayed, press (SET) to toggle the protection marker **O─π**. This marker will be displayed at the top of the LCD to indicate that the image has been protected. Repeat steps 3–4 to protect other images as required.

5) When you're ready, press MENU to return to the main **Protect images** menu.

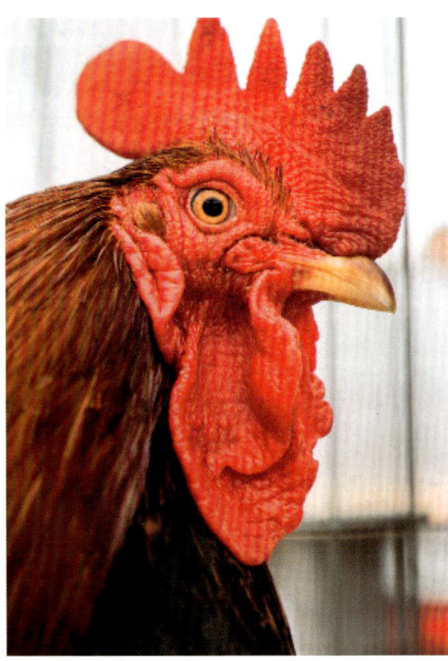

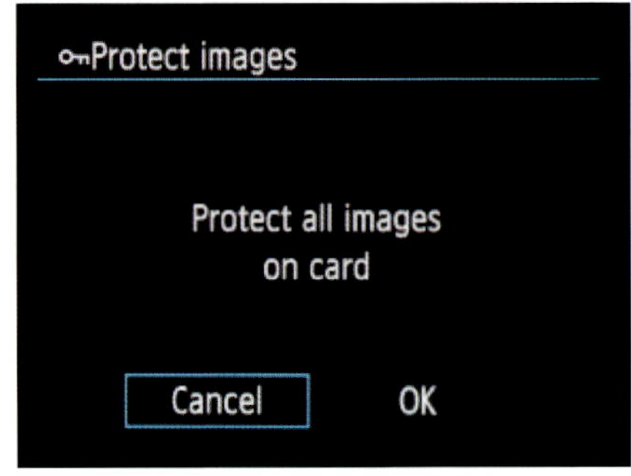

Other protection options

1) Press MENU, navigate to ▶ , and select **Protect images**.

2) Select **All images in folder**. Press ▲ / ▼ to highlight the folder you want to protect, and press (SET). Select **OK** to continue, or **Cancel** to return to the **Select folder** screen.

3) To protect all the images on a memory card select **All images on card**. Select **OK** to continue, or **Cancel** to return to the main **Protect images** menu.

4) Repeat steps 2–3 to remove protection, this time selecting either **Unprotect all images in folder** or **Unprotect all images on card**.

OUT FOR THE DAY «
The easiest way to avoid deleting images accidentally is not to delete as you shoot.

» MODE DIAL

The mode dial is used to select the required shooting mode. There are 14 settings to choose from in total: 13 still image modes and ▶🎥 for shooting video.

These modes are grouped into two types: Basic Zone and Creative Zone. The various Basic Zone modes are highly automated and are designed to help you successfully make images in specific shooting situations. The Creative Zone modes are far less automated. This makes them harder to use successfully, but arguably more satisfying.

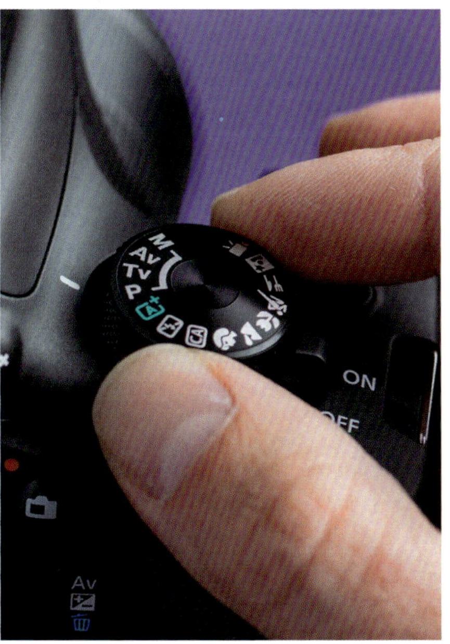

Creative Zone	
Program	**P**
Shutter priority	**Tv**
Aperture priority	**Av**
Manual	**M**
Movie	▶🎥

Basic Zone	
Scene Intelligent Auto	A⁺
Flash Off	🚫⚡
Creative Auto	CA
Portrait	👤
Landscape	🏔
Close-up	🌷
Sports	🏃
Food	🍴
Night Portrait	🌃

SELECTING «

To select the desired mode, turn the dial until its icon is aligned with the white mark at the left of the dial.

» BASIC ZONE MODES

The Basic Zone exposure modes are designed to let you get satisfying results without worrying too much about exposure and other camera settings. That doesn't mean that all control is taken out of your hands, though. For a start, you can select a limited number of drive mode options for all the Basic Zone modes. You can also change **Ambience-based shots** when shooting using CA, 🧑, 🏔, 🌷, 🏃, and 📷, as well as **Light/scene based shots** when shooting 🧑, 🏔, 🌷, and 🏃. 🍴 also offers a **Color tone** adjustment, while CA Creative Auto provides you with control over the depth of field by setting **Background blur**.

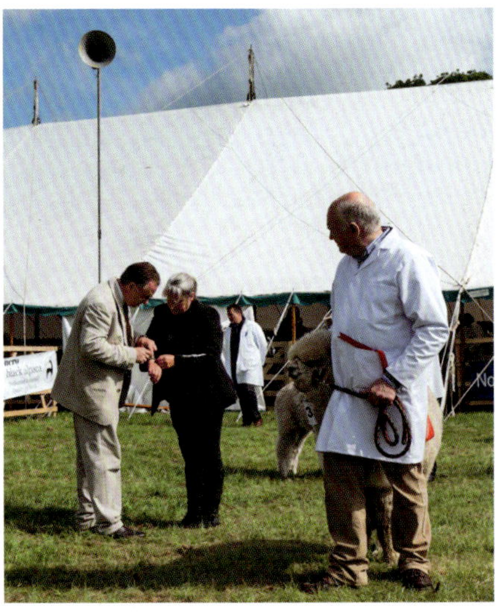

› Scene Intelligent Auto A⁺

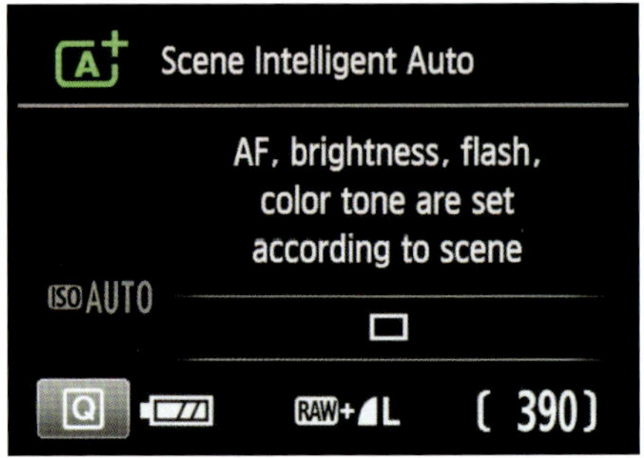

A⁺ is very much the Rebel T6/EOS 1300D's "point-and-shoot" mode. Virtually all the shooting functions are set automatically and cannot be altered. The only function you can change is the drive mode (via the Q screen).

This leaves you free to compose your images without worrying about technical details, although the downside is that you have no creative control over your shots. However, if you just want to shoot and have a better than average chance of success—such as at social or sporting events—A⁺ is ideal.

Q options: Drive mode

EVENTS «
Scene Intelligent Auto means you'll be ready to shoot, without worrying too much about exposure technicalities.

› Flash Off

is essentially the same as , but the flash will never fire, no matter how little light there is. Even an external flash will refuse to fire.

At first glance, this may seem like an unnecessary restriction, but there are many occasions when flash is unwelcome (a wedding—particularly during the service itself—is one such occasion). ensures that the flash won't even fire accidentally, while still retaining all the other useful automatic functions of .

To compensate for the lack of flash, increases the ISO automatically to try and maintain a shutter speed fast enough to avoid camera shake. If you have a lens with image stabilization, this will help, and using a wide-angle lens will further reduce the risk of camera shake compared to a telephoto lens. If camera shake is likely, the shutter speed display in the viewfinder will blink to warn you.

Q options: Drive mode

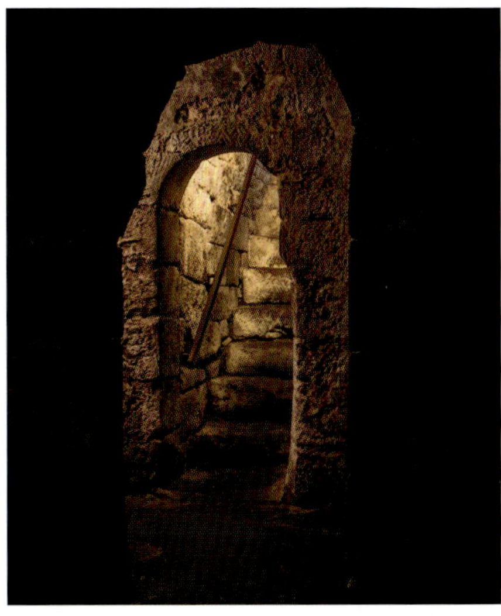

ATMOSPHERE »

There are times when flash will detract from a shot, even though the ambient light levels would suggest that flash would be useful. This shot was taken without flash and relied on a long shutter speed to make the correct exposure. The camera needed to be mounted onto a tripod to avoid camera shake.

Ambience-based shots options

Setting	Options	Notes
Standard	None	The standard image setting for the chosen shooting mode.
Vivid	Low; Standard; Strong	Increases the intensity (saturation) of the colors in an image.
Soft	Low; Standard; Strong	Reduces contrast to produce a softer effect.
Warm	Low; Standard; Strong	Adds red to an image to make it appear warmer.
Intense	Low; Standard; Strong	Contrast is increased to add drama to an image.
Cool	Low; Standard; Strong	Adds blue to an image to make it appear colder.
Brighter	Low; Medium; High	Creates a "high-key" effect; lightens shadows, but can lead to burnt-out highlights in high-contrast lighting.
Darker	Low; Medium; High	Creates a "low-key" effect; darkens highlights, but can lead to dense, black shadows in high-contrast lighting.
Monochrome	Blue; B/W; Sepia	Turns your shots to black and white (or tones them with an optional Blue or Sepia color).

Light/scene-based shots options

Setting	Result	Notes
Default	Image stays relatively true to the light source.	The default setting; good for general-purpose photography.
Daylight	Colors are correctly balanced for shooting during the middle of the day under sunlight.	Images will appear too warm when shooting indoors under artificial lighting.
Shade	Colors are rendered true when shooting in open shade.	Shade light is very blue; this option adds red to the image to correct for this tendency.
Cloudy	Colors are rendered true when shooting under cloudy conditions.	As with shade, overcast light has a tendency to blueness, but not as dramatically.
Tungsten light	Corrects color when shooting under household lighting.	Tungsten lighting is biased toward red; this option adds blue to compensate. Not available when shooting using ▲.
Fluorescent light	Corrects color when shooting under white fluorescent lighting.	White fluorescent is warmer than daylight, but not as warm as tungsten lighting, so less blue is added to compensate. Not available when shooting using ▲.
Sunset	Keeps the warmth of sunlight at sunrise and sunset.	Direct sunlight at either end of the day is very warm in color.

› Creative Auto [CA]

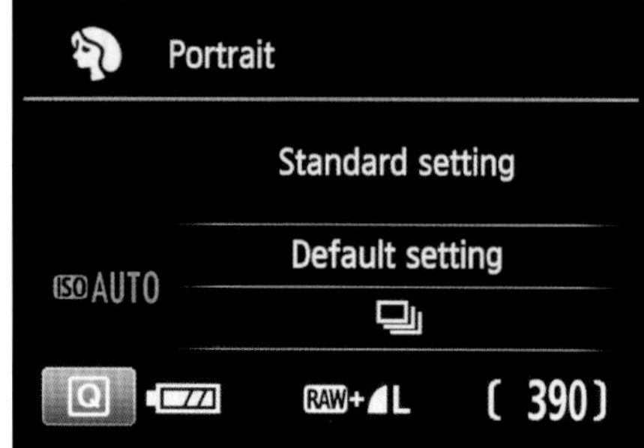

Creative Auto offers four shooting options, which are altered via the **Q** screen.

Ambience-based shots lets you set the visual style of your shots by choosing from a range of different presets, such as **Monochrome**, which can then be further refined in intensity once selected.

Background blur sets the depth of field of your images. When set to ▣, depth of field is minimized, making the background softer; ▣ maximizes depth of field, making the image sharper overall.

The **Drive/self-timer** mode can be changed, using the same range of options as described earlier in this chapter.

Finally, you can control the flash by setting **Flash firing** to **Auto flash, Flash on**, or **Flash off**.

Q options: Ambience-based shots; Background blur; Drive mode; Flash

› Portrait ♪

♪ mode is designed to help you create pleasing shots of people's faces. To achieve this, the Rebel T6/EOS 1300D biases the aperture setting so that depth of field is minimized. This means that backgrounds will be relatively soft and less distracting (the effect is more pronounced with telephoto lenses than wide-angle lenses).

Note that when depth of field is minimized, focusing needs to be very accurate, so you should ensure that your subject's face is within the AF focusing area when using the viewfinder.

Q options: Ambience-based shots; Light/scene-based shots; Drive mode

› Landscape ▨

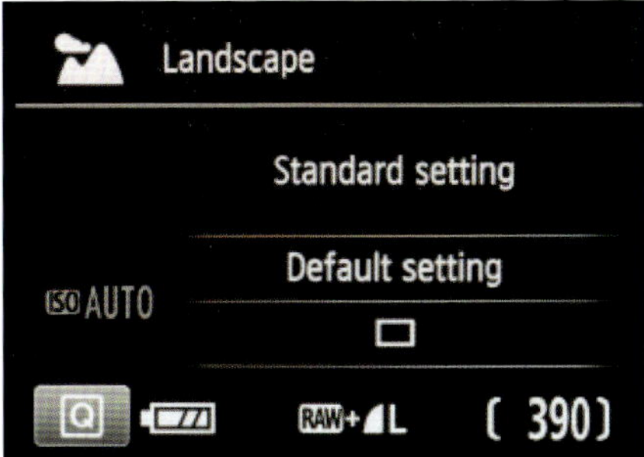

▨ is the mode to use in a natural (or even urban) landscape environment. ▨ influences the resulting images in a number of ways. The most obvious trait is that greens and blues are more highly saturated than they are in any of the other Basic Zone modes. More subtly, sharpness and contrast are also increased.

▨ also prioritizes depth of field over shutter speed, to give front-to-back sharpness. This is a common requirement in landscape imagery. Depth of field is covered in more detail on page 74.

[Q] options: Ambience-based shots; Light/scene-based shots; Drive mode

UPWARD
Tilting your camera upward is an easy way to convey the sense that a tall landscape subject, such as a tree, towered over you.

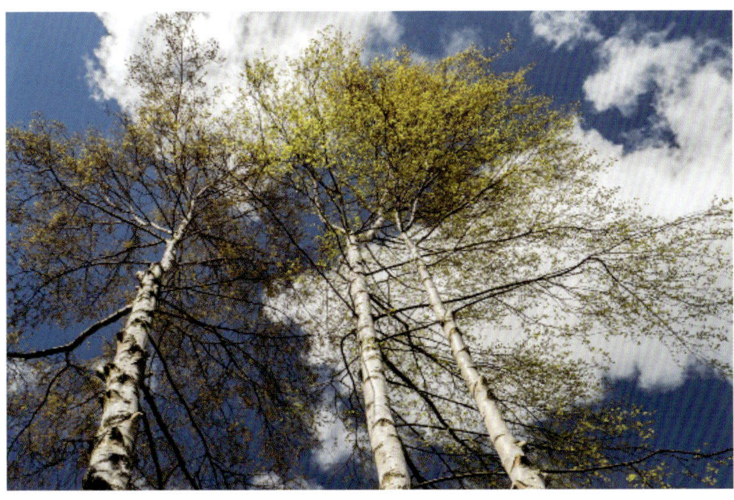

› Close-up 🌷

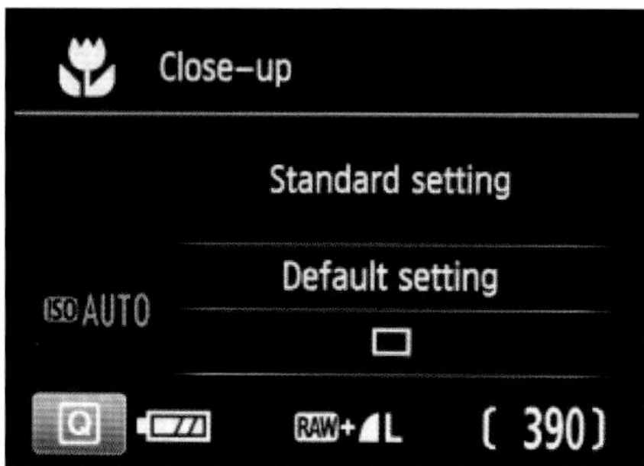

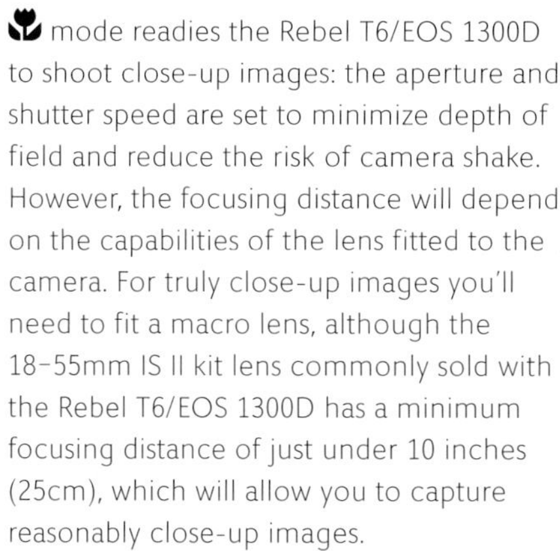

🌷 mode readies the Rebel T6/EOS 1300D to shoot close-up images: the aperture and shutter speed are set to minimize depth of field and reduce the risk of camera shake. However, the focusing distance will depend on the capabilities of the lens fitted to the camera. For truly close-up images you'll need to fit a macro lens, although the 18–55mm IS II kit lens commonly sold with the Rebel T6/EOS 1300D has a minimum focusing distance of just under 10 inches (25cm), which will allow you to capture reasonably close-up images.

Q options: Ambience-based shots; Light/scene-based shots; Drive mode

› Sports 🏃

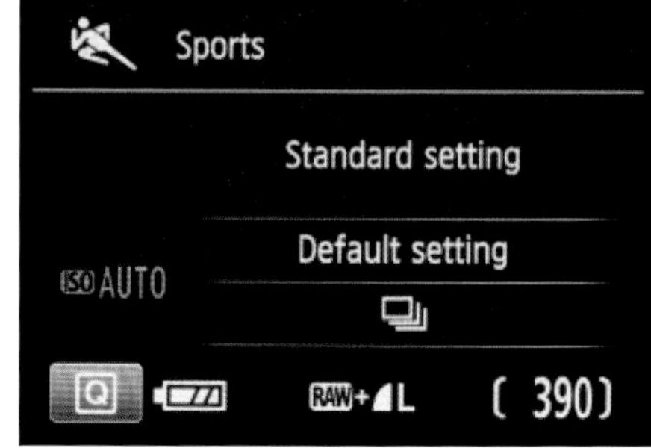

🏃 mode sets your camera up to capture fast action. This is done by maximizing shutter speed and using a larger aperture and/or increasing the ISO value up to a maximum of ISO 6400. This means that depth of field may be an issue (focusing needs to be accurate) and that your action images may look "noisy" if you shoot in a dimly-lit sports hall.

However, capturing fast action successfully isn't just about using a fast shutter speed, shooting wildly, and hoping you get at least one good frame. The most successful sports photographers understand their subject, which means they're able to anticipate when the peak of action will occur and be ready to shoot at that point.

Q options: Ambience-based shots; Light/scene-based shots; Drive mode

› Night Portrait

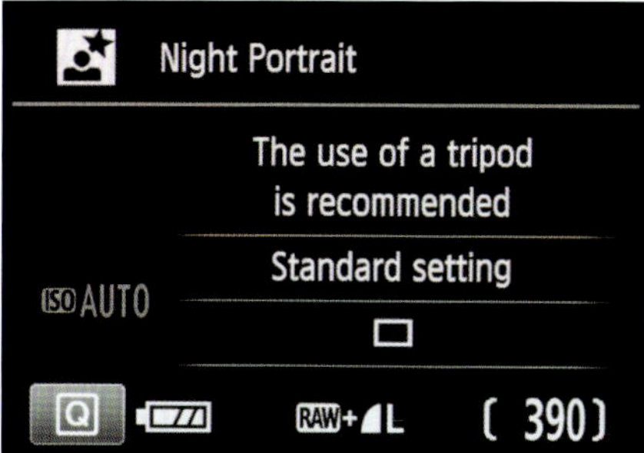

highly recommended. If you are shooting a human subject with a shutter speed below 1/4 sec., ask them to keep as still as possible during the exposure. If they move during the exposure they will be recorded as a ghostly double image; the first (sharp) image lit by flash, the second (more blurred) lit by the ambient light.

Q options: Ambience-based shots; Drive mode

is an automated slow sync flash mode. This is a technique that combines the use of flash with a slow shutter speed that's long enough to expose the non-flash-lit areas of a scene. It's particularly useful when there's low—but enough—ambient light; pre-sunrise or post-sunset outdoor scenes are a good time to use this.

In low-light conditions, the shutter speed can be lengthy, so mounting your camera on a tripod (or other support) is

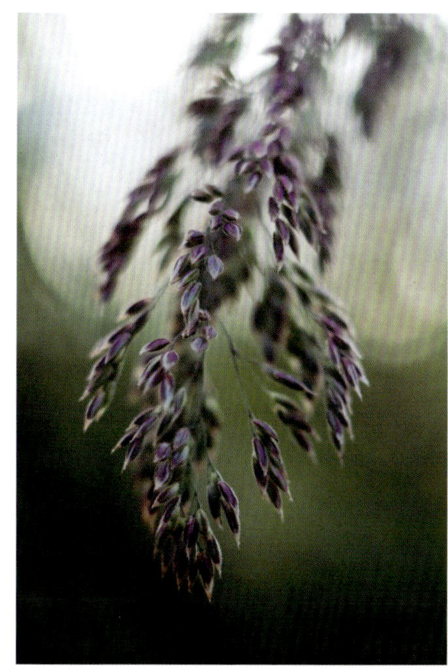

CLOSE-UP »
You don't necessarily need a dedicated macro lens to shoot really close-up imagery. This shot was created using an 85mm lens combined with a set of extension tubes.

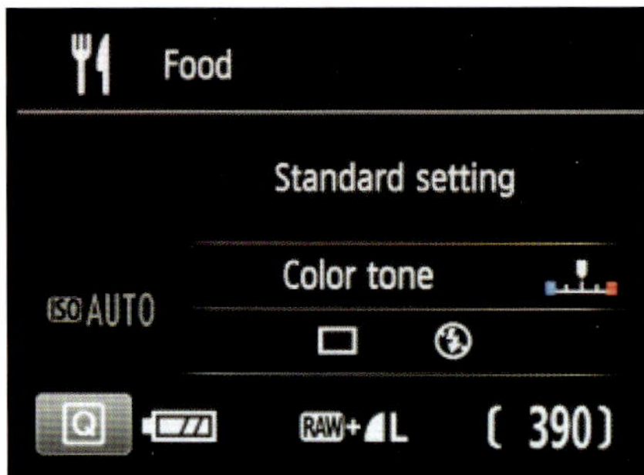

Note
Don't use 🍴 when shooting subjects other than food.

🍴 mode is specifically designed to help you achieve mouth-watering images of tasty food. Food is an essential part of everyone's lives, so it's a popular subject—there are even professional photographers who specialize in food photography, for use in advertising, magazines, books, and shop displays.

A key part of good food photography is lighting. The most flattering way to light food is from behind (with the light aimed toward the camera). Supplementary lighting or reflectors can be used close to the camera to bounce light back into the shadows to reduce contrast if necessary.

A unique **Q** option in 🍴 is **Color tone**, which lets you add more blue to an image (making it cooler) or more red (to make it warmer).

Q options: Ambience-based shots; Color tone; Drive mode; Flash

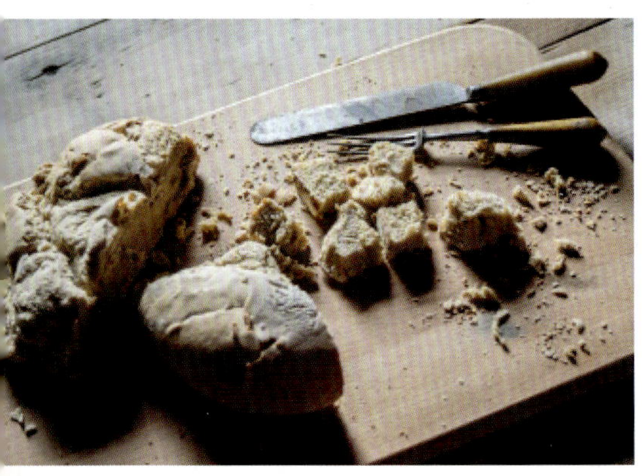

EXTRAS «
Props, such as cutlery, will add interest to a food photograph.

» CREATIVE ZONE MODES

If you want to take full control of your Rebel T6/EOS 1300D, you'll need to use one of the camera's Creative Zone modes. These modes require you to understand some of the basic concepts of photography and how they apply to various shooting situations.

Settings available in the Creative Zone modes

Focus settings
One-Shot AF; AI Servo AF; AI Focus AF; AF point selection; AF-assist beam; MF; Live View only; ☺ Live mode; FlexiZone–Single; Quick mode

Image settings
JPEG (Fine/Normal; Compression levels: L; M; S1; S2; S3); Raw + JPEG; Raw Other: Aspect ratio; Peripheral illumination correction

Exposure settings
Metering: Evaluative; Center-weighted average; Partial Settings: Program shift (**P** only); Exposure compensation (not **M**); AEB; AE lock (in **M** with ISO AUTO you can set a fixed ISO); Bulb (**M** only); Long exposure noise reduction

Tone settings
White balance (AWB; Preset; Custom; Correction/Bracketing); Auto Lighting Optimizer; Highlight tone priority; Color space (sRGB; Adobe RGB); Picture Style

Drive mode
Single; Continuous; Self-timer (2; 10 seconds; ☉c)

ISO settings
ISO AUTO; Manual selection (100–6400); Maximum for Auto; High ISO speed noise reduction

Built-in flash settings
Manual firing; Flash on; Flash off; Red-eye reduction; FE lock; Flash exposure compensation

External flash settings
Function settings; Custom function settings

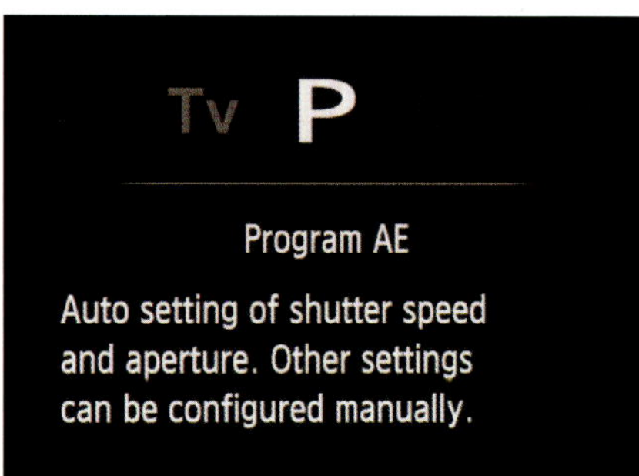

Note
Underexposure is likely if *30"* blinks in the viewfinder or on the LCD. This will occur when the aperture required isn't available (a larger aperture is required than is possible on the lens fitted to the camera). To avoid underexposure you'll need to either increase the ISO or add extra illumination to the scene.

If *4000* blinks in the viewfinder or on the LCD this indicates overexposure (again because the required aperture isn't available— this time because the aperture needs to be smaller than the smallest possible on the fitted lens). In this case you'll need to decrease the ISO or reduce the amount of light reaching the sensor.

P is a more sophisticated version of [A+]. Just like [A+], the Rebel T6/EOS 1300D will automatically set the shutter speed and aperture. This means that you can essentially point-and-shoot. However, unlike [A+] you aren't locked out of making decisions about exposure—you can alter the ISO setting, for example, and apply exposure compensation.

While **P** sets both the shutter speed and aperture, you don't have to settle for the selected combination of values. Program Shift lets you freely adjust (or shift) the shutter speed/aperture combination. To set Program Shift, turn once you've pressed the shutter-release button down half way to activate the camera's exposure meter. Once you've taken the shot, Program Shift is cancelled.

Although **P** is an automatic mode, it's better to think of it as a useful half way point between [A+] and the semi-automatic modes **Tv** and **Av** described on the following pages.

Using **P** mode

1) Turn the mode dial to **P**.

2) If you're using the viewfinder, press the shutter-release button down half way to focus.

3) Once focus has been achieved, the active focus point(s) will flash red, the camera will beep, and the focus confirmation light ● will be displayed (One-Shot AF/viewfinder) or the focus box will turn green and the camera will beep (Live View).

4) Press down fully on the shutter-release button to take the shot. The captured photograph will be displayed on the LCD for 2 seconds, unless the review time has been adjusted.

FLEXIBILITY ⌄
The real appeal of **P** is that you can worry less about the exposure, but still have the option to make adjustments in tricky lighting situations.

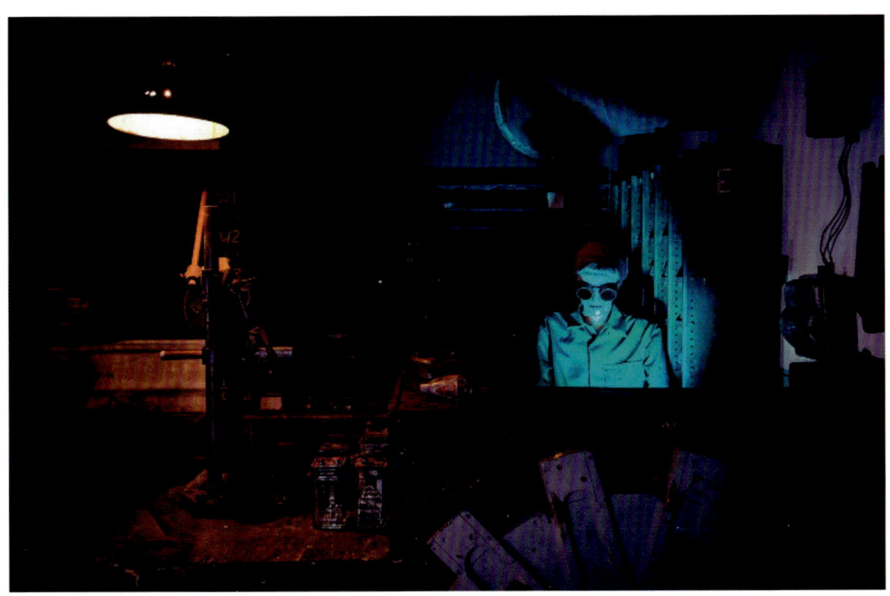

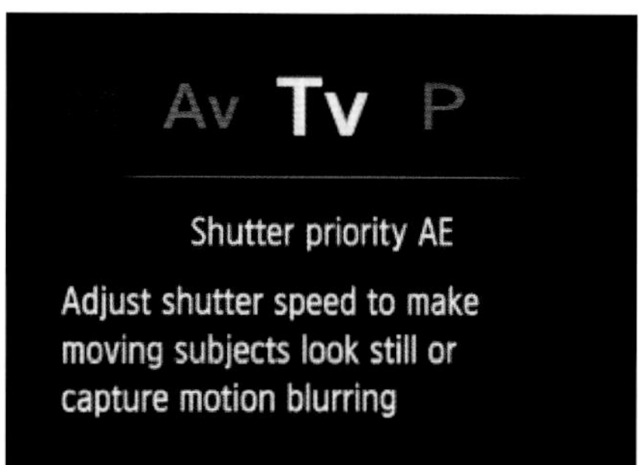

Tv and **Av** are both semi-automatic exposure modes, where you set one aspect of the exposure and your Rebel T6/EOS 1300D automatically sets the other. **Tv** lets you set the required shutter speed, with the camera choosing a suitable aperture.

Shutter speed is important for two reasons. First, if you are handholding the camera and use a shutter speed that is too slow, your images may be marred by camera shake. Second, the shutter speed is important if there's movement in the scene you're shooting: depending on the shutter speed you use, you can either "freeze" movement or you can deliberately blur it.

Freezing movement means using a fast shutter speed: the faster the movement, the faster the shutter speed will need to be. You also have to take into account the distance between you and your moving subject. The closer the subject is to the camera, the faster the shutter speed will need to be. A subject moving across the image frame will also need a faster shutter speed than one moving toward or away from the camera.

Blurring movement means using a long shutter speed, although the further the subject is from the camera, the longer the shutter speed will need to be in order to blur it.

ND filters are useful to further extend shutter speed. With a suitably dense ND filter it is often possible to extend shutter speed from fractions of a second to whole seconds (see page 190).

> **Note**
> A good rule when handholding a camera is to match the shutter speed to the focal length of the lens. So, when using a 50mm lens you'd use a shutter speed of 1/50 sec. or higher; a 200mm lens would require a shutter speed of 1/200 sec. or higher, and so on. (A shutter speed that is twice as fast as the focal length is better still.)

Using **Tv** mode

1) Turn the mode dial to **Tv**.

2) Turn to the right to set a faster shutter speed or to the left to set a slower shutter speed. As you change the shutter speed, the Rebel T6/EOS 1300D will adjust the aperture to try and maintain the same level of exposure overall.

Note

There's usually a greater range of available shutter speed settings than aperture settings. This means it's quite possible to select a shutter speed that would result in under- or overexposure because the required aperture isn't available on the lens. If the maximum aperture figure blinks in the viewfinder or in Live View, your image will be underexposed. When this happens you'll need to use a longer shutter speed (or increase the ISO). If the minimum aperture figure blinks, the image will be overexposed, and you'll need to use a faster shutter speed (or decrease the ISO).

SUPPORT »

In low light it's important to support the camera somehow. To take this shot of a model train I pressed the camera gently against the glass of the display case. This gave enough support to keep the camera steady.

3) Press lightly down on the shutter-release button to focus. Once focus has been achieved, the active focus point(s) will flash red, the camera will beep, and the focus confirmation light ● will be displayed (One-Shot AF/viewfinder) or the focus box will turn green and the camera beeps (Live View).

4) When the lens is focused, press down fully on the shutter-release button to take the shot. The captured photograph will be displayed on the LCD for 2 seconds unless the review time has been adjusted.

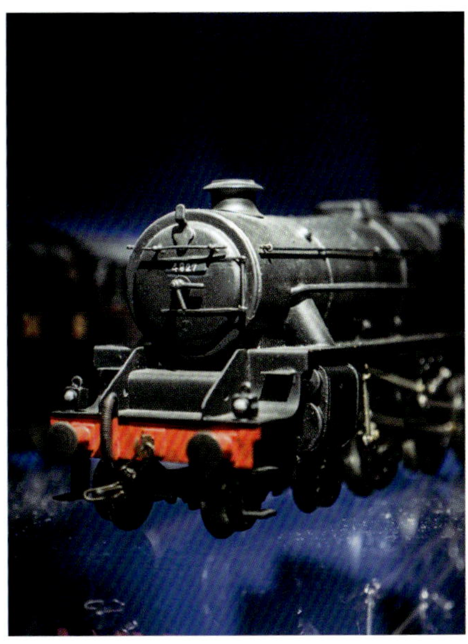

› Aperture priority (**Av**)

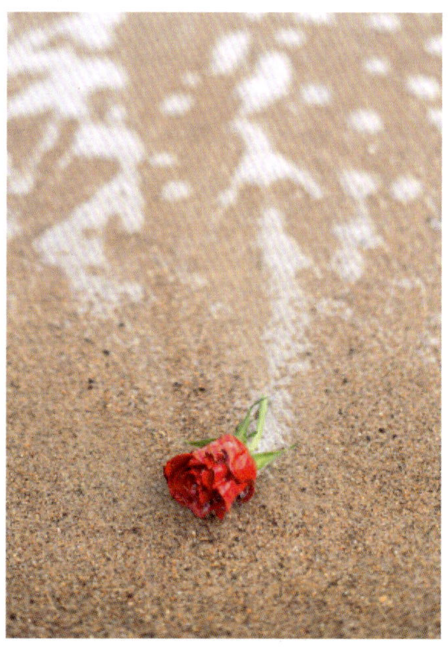

Inside every EOS lens is a variable iris known as the aperture, which can be varied in size to control the amount of light that enters the camera.

When the aperture is set at its widest setting (slightly counter-intuitively this is its lowest numerical value—f/2.8 or f/3.5, for example) the greatest amount of light is let into the camera. This allows you to use a faster shutter speed or a lower ISO setting.

Conversely, when a lens is used at its minimum aperture setting (f/16 or f/22, for example), the least amount of light is allowed into the camera. This will require the use of a longer shutter speed or higher ISO setting.

The aperture also has an effect on the degree of acceptable sharpness in an image. The smaller the aperture, the more of a scene will appear to be "in focus"— the extent of this zone of sharpness is known as "depth of field."

Depth of field is influenced by three factors. The first is the aperture setting; the smaller the aperture, the great the depth of field.

The second factor is the lens' focal length; depth of field is always greater at any given aperture when using a shorter (wider angle) focal length lens.

The third factor is the camera-to-subject distance; the closer you focus (and the shorter the camera-to-subject distance) the less depth of field you'll be able to achieve.

Using **Av** mode

1) Turn the mode dial to **Av**.

2) Turn ⚙ to the right to set a smaller aperture (reducing depth of field) or to the left to set a larger aperture (increasing depth of field). As you change the aperture, the camera changes the shutter speed automatically to maintain the same level of exposure overall.

3) Press down lightly on the shutter-release button to focus. Once focus has been achieved, the active focus point(s) will flash red, the camera will beep and the focus confirmation light ● will be displayed (One-shot AF/viewfinder) or the focus box turns green and the camera beeps (Live View).

4) When the Rebel T6/EOS 1300D has focused, press down fully on the shutter-release button to take the shot. The photograph will be displayed on the LCD for 2 seconds, unless the default review time has been adjusted.

SOFT «

To minimize depth of field you need to get in close to your subject and set the largest aperture possible on the lens. Minimizing depth of field is a great way to focus attention on your subject.

Notes

If the shutter speed indicator in the viewfinder or on the LCD blinks *30"*, your image will be underexposed. You'll need to use a larger aperture (or increase the ISO). If the shutter speed shows *4000* and the figure blinks, the image will be overexposed. You'll need to use a smaller aperture (or decrease the ISO). As there's usually a smaller range of available aperture settings than shutter speed settings you're less likely to encounter this problem than when using **Av**. Typically this will only occur when shooting in very low light, very bright light, or when light-sapping filters have been fitted to a lens.

When you look through the viewfinder or are viewing a Live View image, you are seeing the scene at maximum aperture (and so at minimum depth of field). The Rebel T6/EOS 1300D doesn't have a dedicated depth of field preview button, but you can assign this task to the (SET) button (see page 138). Once assigned, holding down (SET) will close the aperture to the selected value.

Manual exposure

Set shutter speed and aperture manually for greater freedom of expression in shots

When you set your Rebel T6/EOS 1300D to **M**, you're in full control of your exposures—you have to set both aperture and shutter speed, with no camera automation to help. If the resulting image is incorrectly exposed then there's no-one to blame but yourself.

However, this shouldn't put you off using **M**—it may not be suited to everyday shooting, but in certain situations it's ideal. For example, **M** is the exposure mode of choice if you need to maintain the same exposure over a series of shots. This is necessary when shooting a sequence of images that will be stitched together to produce a panorama. It's also useful if you're shooting a series of images over a longer period of time to produce a time-lapse movie.

You also need to select **M** to shoot **BULB** exposures. **BULB** is used to shoot images that require an exposure of more than 30 seconds. When the Rebel T6/EOS 1300D is set to **BULB**, the camera will continue to expose for as long as the shutter-release button is held down (typically by using a remote switch to lock the shutter open).

BULB is only really necessary when shooting in very low light, such as in dimly lit interiors or at night when shooting cityscapes or star trails. If long exposure noise reduction is switched on, exposure times will double, making **BULB** exposures lengthy affairs. For this reason it's a good idea to start with a freshly charged battery and keep a spare or two handy if you intend to shoot more than a few images.

> **Note**
> You should always use a fixed ISO when using **M** mode.

Using **M** mode

1) Turn the mode dial to **M**.

2) Turn [main dial] to adjust the shutter speed, or hold down [trash/Av±] and turn [main dial] to set the aperture.

3) When you're happy with the exposure, press lightly down on the shutter-release button to focus, and then press down fully to take the shot.

4) The captured photograph will be displayed on the LCD screen for 2 seconds, unless the review time has been adjusted.

Note

In **M** mode, the correct exposure is set when the exposure level mark is centered in the exposure level indicator in the viewfinder or LCD. In the viewfinder, when the set exposure exceeds the "correct" exposure by ±2 stops, ◀ will be shown at the left of the exposure level indicator to warn of potential underexposure, or ▶ at the right to warn of potential overexposure. On the LCD, when the set exposure exceeds the "correct" exposure by ±3 stops, the exposure level indicator will blink.

Using **BULB** mode

1) Turn the mode dial to **M**.

2) Turn [main dial] beyond 30" to **BULB**. Hold down [trash/Av±] and turn [main dial] to set the required aperture.

3) Press lightly down on the shutter-release button to focus.

4) Once focus has locked, press down fully on the shutter-release button to take the shot. Keep the shutter-release button pressed down until the required exposure is achieved. The accumulated length of the exposure—in minutes and seconds—will be shown on the LCD during the exposure.

5) The captured photograph will be displayed on the LCD for 2 seconds, unless the review time has been adjusted.

A successful portrait conveys something of the character of the subject and where your subject looks is particularly important in achieving this goal. If a subject looks directly at the camera, there's an air of confidence projected out of the photo. There's a more ambiguous emotion conveyed when the subject looks away from the camera.

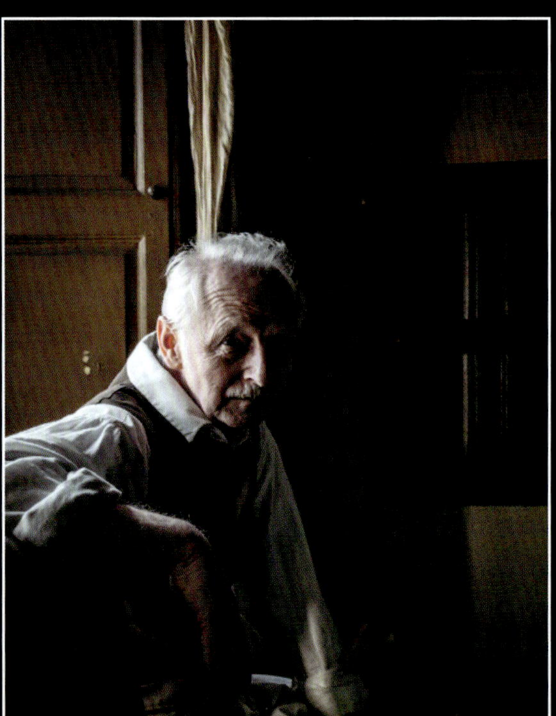

Settings

> Focal length: 28mm
> Aperture: f/2.8
> Shutter speed: 1/60 sec.
> ISO: 400

» MAKING MOVIES

At first glance, shooting a movie is superficially like shooting a still image.

The two main differences are that you need to think about how the scene you're shooting will change over time and how sound should be recorded. Another difference is that you can't compose movies through the viewfinder; movies are always shot in Live View.

Notes
The longest movie clip size you can shoot is 4GB. If a clip exceeds that length during recording a new clip is started automatically.

The camera will switch off Live View after a set period if no controls are pressed. Press 📷 to resume Live View.

Warning!

Do not touch the microphone on the front of the camera during movie recording, as this will create extraneous noise.

› Memory cards

Creating a movie means capturing a continuous stream of digital data. Fortunately, the Rebel T6/EOS 1300D compresses this data—if it didn't, the memory card would be quickly filled.

The compression process works by comparing individual frames within the movie. If there is little or no difference between two or more successive frames, the camera doesn't save the data for every frame over and over again; only the changes are recorded. Therefore, the more static a scene is, the more easily the resulting movie data can be compressed.

However, more kinetic scenes result in movies that are less easily compressed, which means that the movie footage will take up more room on a memory card. Shooting movies with a high-capacity card with a fast read/write speed is therefore highly recommended; Canon suggests using at least a Class 10 memory card when shooting movies.

› H.264

The Rebel T6/EOS 1300D's movies are recorded in .MOV format using the H.264 video-encoding standard, which is used in a wide variety of applications from Blu-Ray players to YouTube. MOV is also supported by movie-editing software such as Adobe Premiere Elements.

› Shooting a movie

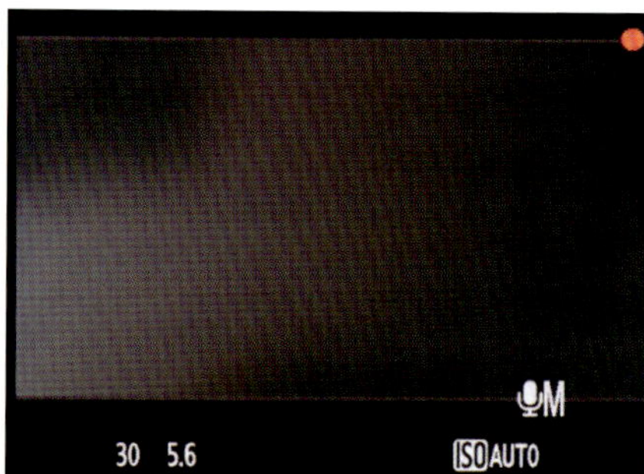

Shooting movies is similar to shooting still images, in as much as you have to compose your shot and then set the exposure (if it is not set automatically) before shooting. However, the similarities end there and a slightly different procedure must then be followed:

Starting recording

1) Turn the mode dial to movie.

2) Press the shutter-release button half way to focus. Once the Rebel T6/EOS 1300D starts recording a movie it will no longer focus automatically—if focus adjustments need to be made during shooting, switch the lens to MF.

3) Press ●/◻. A red ● mark will be displayed at the top right of the LCD to show that recording has started. The duration of the movie is shown at the left of the LCD, along with the resolution and frame rate.

4) Press ●/◻ to stop recording.

› Quick Control

The movie Q screen is controlled in the same way as the Q screen in Live View when shooting still images. Press Q to alter any or all of the following before movie recording: **AF method, White balance, Picture Style, Auto Lighting Optimizer, Movie recording size,** or **Video snapshot.**

› Exposure control

Just like still images, movie exposures rely on balancing the shutter speed, aperture, and ISO. The first step in deciding how these are set is to go to **Movie exposure** on the '🎥' menu, where you will find two options: **Auto** and **Manual**.

If you select **Auto**, the Rebel T6/EOS 1300D automatically sets the exposure, selecting the required shutter speed, aperture, and ISO (between ISO 100–6400) according to the ambient lighting conditions. You do have some control over exposure, though: you can lock and unlock exposure by pressing 🔲 and ✳ respectively and you can set exposure compensation by holding down Av⊡ and turning ⚙. However, it's not a good idea to do either once recording begins, as the noise of using the controls may be picked up by the camera's microphone.

If you select **Manual**, you have far more control over the exposure, as you can set ISO, shutter speed, and aperture. ISO is set by pressing ⚡, followed by either ◀ / ▶, or by turning ⚙ to highlight the required ISO, followed by ⑤ℇ⑤.

The shutter speed is set by turning ⚙. The available range is 1/4000–1/60 sec. when using a frame rate of ⎵50/⎵60, or 1/4000–1/30 sec. when using ⎵24/⎵25/⎵30.

The aperture is set by holding down Av⊡ and turning ⚙.

› LCD information

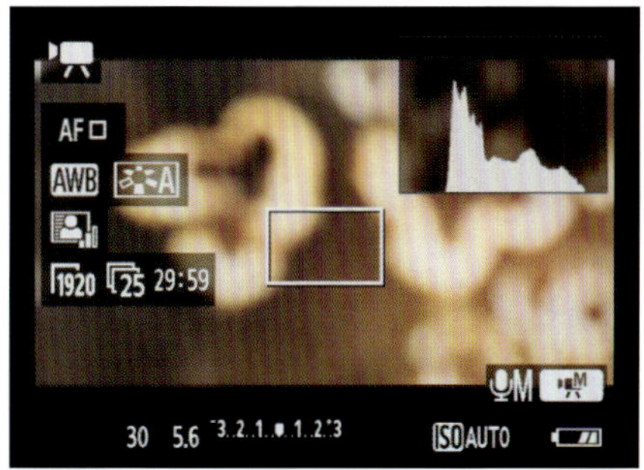

Just like using Live View in other shooting modes, pressing **DISP.** toggles between screens with different levels of shooting information; it is a good idea to use the least cluttered option when initially composing your shot.

Note that the image displayed on the rear LCD screen (both before and during recording) adjusts as you change the following functions: **Auto Lighting Optimizer**, **Picture Style**, **White balance**, **Peripheral illumination correction**, and **Exposure compensation**.

» MOVIE SHOOTING TIPS

› Color

You can apply a Picture Style to movies, just like a still image (see page 101–103). If you want to use your movie straight out of the camera then choose a Picture Style that is most pleasing, but if you intend to alter the look of your movie in postproduction (known as "grading"), it is a good idea to set a style that has both low contrast and low color saturation.

› Shutter speed

A movie is shot at a certain frame rate (⊏50, ⊏60, ⊏24, ⊏25, or ⊏30, depending on the video resolution and video system). Each frame of the movie is exposed for a set period of time, and logically you might think that the shutter speed should match the frame rate (so, when shooting at ⊏50 a shutter speed of 1/50 sec. would be used).

Strangely, this isn't the case. The general rule when shooting at a particular frame rate is to use a shutter speed that's *twice* as fast (so, when shooting at ⊏50 the ideal shutter speed is actually 1/100 sec.).

If you use a shutter speed that's three or four times faster, the resulting footage will appear too sharp and staccato. This is effective for short action sequences, but isn't comfortable to watch for long periods.

However, using a shutter speed that's double the frame rate will result in a slight amount of blurring between frames, which results in smoother footage that's more comfortable to watch.

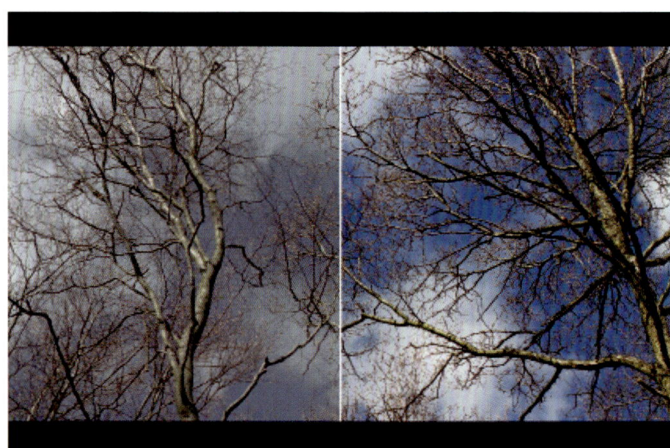

GRADING «
It's better to add color saturation and contrast to flat footage (left) than to remove unwanted color saturation and contrast (right).

» MOVIE PLAYBACK AND EDITING

You can view your movies and make simple trimming edits using your Rebel T6/EOS 1300D.

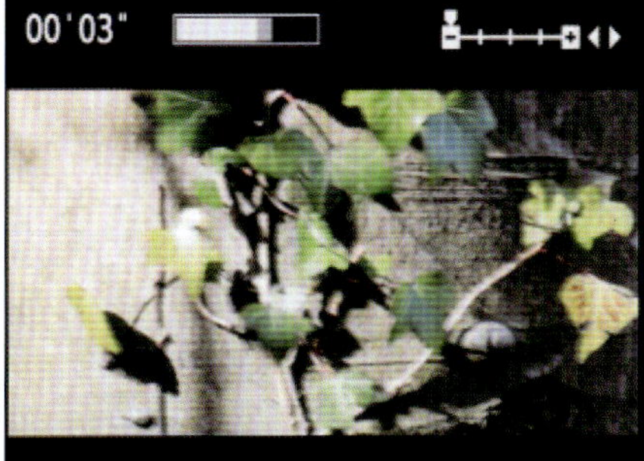

Playing back a movie

1) Press ▶. Navigate to the movie you wish to view by pressing ◄ / ►. Movie files are distinguished from still images by a 🎞 **SET** icon (for standard movies) or 🎞 **SET** (for video snapshots—see page 114) at the top left corner of the LCD.

ORIENTATION　　　　　　　　　　　»

Typically you'd shoot movies with the camera held horizontally. This is particularly important if your movies will ultimately be watched on a TV, but there's nothing to stop you from shooting vertically if you plan to show your movies purely on social media.

2) When you've navigated to the movie you want to view, press ⬟ to display the playback panel.

3) The play symbol, ▶, is highlighted by default when you first view the playback panel. Press ⬟ to play the movie and again to pause and return to the playback panel.

4) When the movie finishes you'll be returned to the first frame of the movie.

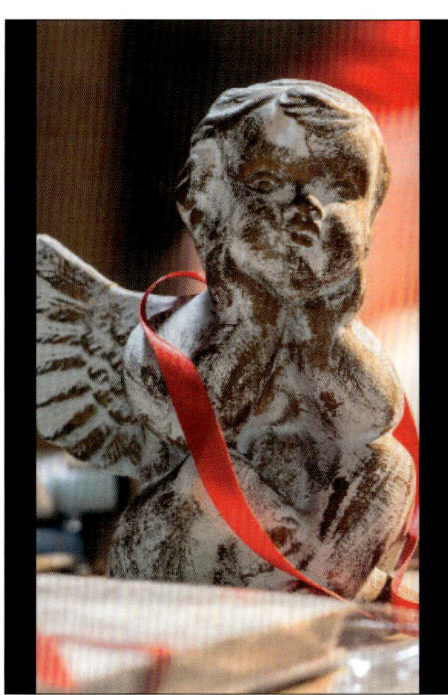

› Other playback options

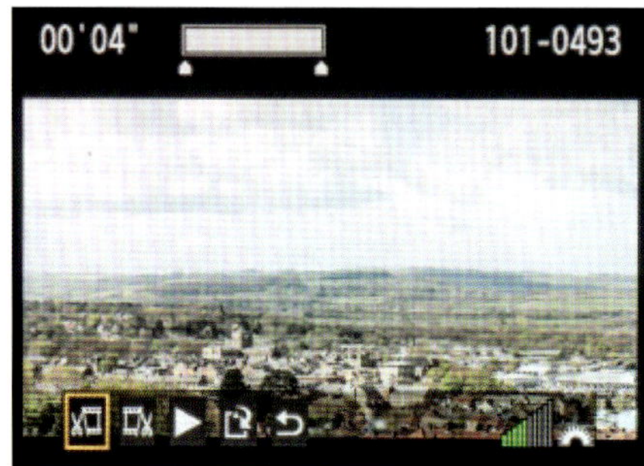

As well as ▶, there are other options on the playback control panel. See the grid below for an explanation of these options.

1) Follow steps 1 to 2 in *Playing back a movie* on the previous page.

2) Press ◀ / ▶ to highlight the desired option on the playback control panel and press (SET).

› Editing movies

Your Rebel T6/EOS 1300D has a mini movie-editing suite built into it. Although it's not as sophisticated as postproduction editing software, it does allow you to trim movies in-camera. Unfortunately, it doesn't allow particularly precise trimming: movies are edited in 1-second increments and you can only trim either the start or the end of the movie (not slice out sections from the middle). However, it's better than nothing.

Movie playback panel

▶ Movie playback

I▶ Slow motion: press ◀/▶ to decrease/increase speed

◄◄ Jump back to the first frame of the movie

◄II Move back one frame by pressing (SET) (hold down (SET) to skip backward quickly)

II▶ Move forward one frame by pressing (SET) (hold down (SET) to skip forward quickly)

▶▶I Jump forward to the last frame of the movie

✂ Edit movie

♫ Plays movie accompanied by music copied to the memory card using EOS Utility software

Editing movies

1) Follow steps 1 to 2 in *Playing back a movie* on page 83.

2) Select ✂ from the movie playback control panel.

3) To cut the start of the movie select ✂, or choose ✂ to cut the end. Press ◀ / ▶ to move the orange trimming point backward or forward through the movie (hold down ◀ / ▶ to move the trimming point more quickly). The white section of the time bar at the top of the LCD shows how much of the movie will be left once it's been edited. Press (SET) when you're happy with the positioning of the trimming point(s).

4) Select ▶ to view the trimmed movie.

5) Select ⬆ to save the movie to the memory card if you're happy with the edited version. Choose **New File** if you want to create a new movie file with the edit applied, **Overwrite** if you want to save over the original movie, or **Cancel** to return to the editing screen.

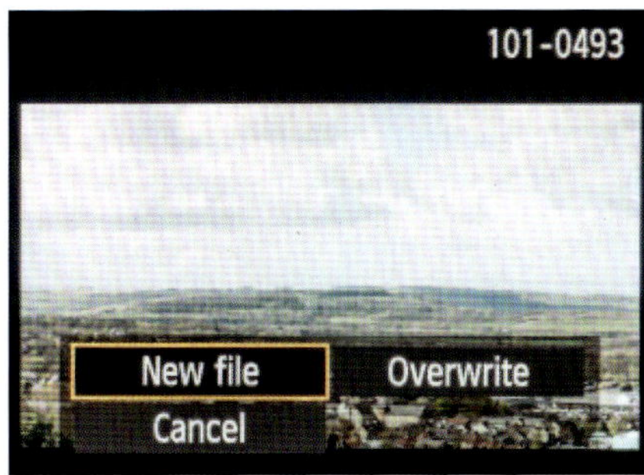

Notes
If there's not enough room on the memory card to save a new movie, **New File** will not be selectable.

6) At any point in the editing process, pressing MENU will take you back to the movie playback control panel. If you've set the trimming points, select **OK** to exit without saving your changes, or **Cancel** to return to the editing screen.

MENUS

The various buttons and dials on the body of the Rebel T6/EOS 1300D enable you to quickly change various aspects of the way the camera behaves. However, if you really want to configure your camera you'll need to delve into its menu system.

Every photographer has a unique way of working, which means that your factory fresh camera may not be set up quite right for your needs. Thankfully, the Rebel T6/EOS 1300D has a comprehensive menu system that lets you configure your camera in a wide variety of ways. Once you've set your camera, you should find there's less need to access the menu (particularly if you get into the habit of using Q instead), but it still pays to familiarize yourself with the menu system. There may be occasions when you're presented with a unique photographic challenge, and a working knowledge of the menu system will prove invaluable in helping you rise to—and overcome—that challenge.

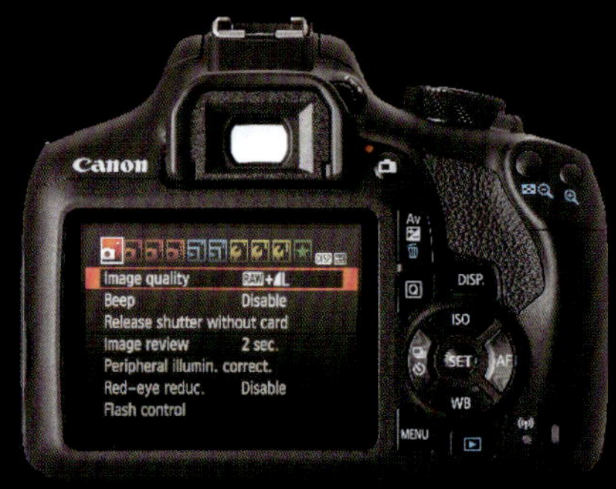

MENU ⌃
The Rebel T6/EOS 1300D's menu system is logical and easy to navigate.
© Canon

DRESSY »
You often don't know what photographic challenges await you on a day out. This high-contrast scene needed a few camera functions (such as Highlight tone priority) to be changed, in order that it could be captured successfully.

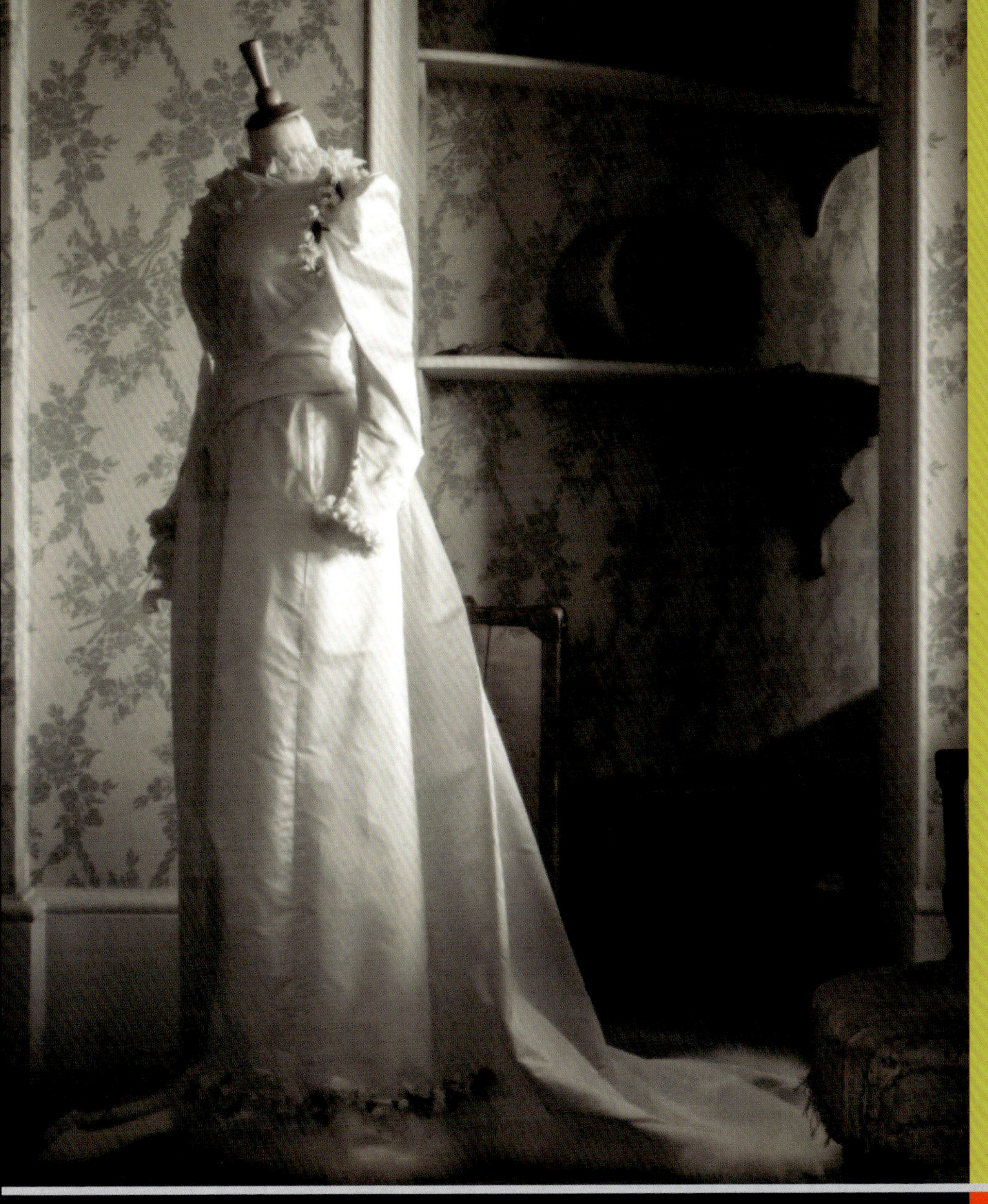

Menu settings shown in gray are not available in the Basic Zone modes.

Shooting 1 ◻ (Red)	Options
Image quality	JPEG: ◢L Large Fine; ◢L Large Normal; ◢M Medium Fine; ◢M Medium Normal; ◢S1 Small 1 Fine; ◢S1 Small 1 Normal; S2 Small 2; S3 Small 3
Raw	Raw **RAW**; Raw + JPEG ◢L
Beep	Enable; Disable
Release shutter without card	Enable; Disable
Image review	Off; 2 sec.; 4 sec.; 8 sec.; Hold
Peripheral illumination correction	Enable; Disable
Red-eye reduction	Enable; Disable
Flash Control	Flash firing (Enable; Disable); Built-in flash func. setting (Flash mode; Shutter sync.; Flash exp. comp; E-TTL II meter.); External flash func. setting (Speedlite dependent); External flash C.Fn setting (Speedlite dependent); Clear ext. flash C.Fn set.

Shooting 2 ◻ (Red)	Options
Expo. comp./AEB	Exposure compensation (±5 stops in ⅓- or ½-stop increments); AEB (±2-stops)
Auto Lighting Optimizer	Disable; Low; Standard; High
Metering mode	▣ Evaluative; ◉ Partial; ▢ Center-weighted average
Custom white balance	Manual setting of white balance
WB Shift/BKT	White balance correction; White balance bracketing
Color space	sRGB; Adobe RGB

| Picture Style | 🎨A Auto; 🎨S Standard; 🎨P Portrait; 🎨L Landscape; 🎨N Neutral; 🎨F Faithful; 🎨M Monochrome; User Def. 1-3 |

Shooting 3 📷 (Red)	**Options**
Dust Delete Data	Image capture for automatic dust removal in Digital Photo Professional
ISO AUTO	Max.: 400; Max.: 800; Max.: 1600; Max.: 3200; Max.: 6400

Shooting 4 📷* (Red)	**Options**
Live View Shooting	Enable; Disable
AF method	FlexiZone-Single; 😊 Live mode; Quick mode
Grid display	Off; Grid 1 ⌗; Grid 2 ⧉
Aspect ratio	3:2; 4:3; 16:9; 1:1
Metering timer	4 sec.; 8 sec.; 16 sec.; 30 sec.; 1 min.; 10 min.; 30 min.

Movie 1 🎥 (Red)	**Options**
Movie exposure	Auto; Manual
AF method	FlexiZone-Single; 😊 Live mode; Quick mode
AF with shutter-release button during 🎥	Enable; Disable
🎥 Shutter/AE lock button	AF/AE lock; AE lock/AF; AF/AF lock, no AE lock; AE/AF, no AE lock
🎥 Highlight tone priority	Enable; Disable

Movie 2 🎥 (Red)	**Options**
Movie rec. size	1920 x 1080 (30/30/24); 1280 x 720 (60/50); 640 x 480 (30/25)

* In Basic Zone modes Shooting 4 📷 is renamed Shooting 2 📷

Sound Recording	Sound recording (Auto; Manual; Disable); Recording level; Wind filter (Enable; Disable)
Metering timer	4 sec.; 8 sec., 16 sec.; 30 sec.; 1 min.; 10 min.; 30 min.
Grid display	Off; Grid 1 ╫; Grid 2 ▦
Video snapshot	Disable; 2 sec. movie; 4 sec. movie; 8 sec. movie
Video system	For NTSC; For PAL

Movie 3 🎥 (Red)	**Options**
Exposure compensation	⅓-stop increments; ±5 stops
Auto Lighting Optimizer	Disable; Low; Standard; High
Custom White Balance	Manual setting of white balance
Picture Style	ⓐ Auto; ⓢ Standard; ⓟ Portrait; ⓛ Landscape; ⓝ Neutral; ⓕ Faithful; ⓜ Monochrome; User Def. 1–3

Playback 1 ▶ (Blue)	**Options**
Protect images	Select images; All images in folder; Unprotect all images in folder; All images on card; Unprotect all images on card
Rotate	Rotate images by 90–270° clockwise
Erase images	Select and erase images; All images in folder; All images on card
Print order	Selection of images for printing
Photobook Set-up	Select images; All images in folder; Clear all in folder; All images on card; Clear all on card
Creative Filters	Grainy B/W; Soft focus; Fisheye effect; Toy camera effect; Miniature effect
Resize	Reduce the resolution of compatible images

Playback 2 ▶ (Blue)	**Options**
Histogram display	Brightness; RGB

Image jump w/ ⛭	Jump by 1; 10; 100 images; Display by Date; Folder; Movies; Stills; Rating
Slide show	Select images for automatic slide show
Rating	Rate images (Off; 1–5 ★)
Set Up 1 ☝ (Yellow)	**Options**
Auto power off	30 sec.; 1 min.; 2 min.; 4 min.; 8 min.; 15 min.; Disable
Auto rotate	On ◻🖳; On 🖳; Off
Format card	Format memory card
File numbering	Continuous; Auto reset; Manual reset
Select folder	Create and select folders
Screen color	1 black; 2 light gray; 3 brown; 4 green
Eye-Fi settings	Settings for Eye-Fi card use (only visible when an Eye-Fi card is used)
Set Up 2 ☝ (Yellow)	**Options**
LCD brightness	Seven levels of brightness
LCD off/on button	Shutter-release button; Shutter/DISP; Remains on
Date/Time/Zone	Sets current date/time/time zone; daylight saving time; time zone
Language	English; German; French; Dutch; Danish; Portuguese; Finnish; Italian; Ukrainian; Norwegian; Swedish; Spanish; Greek; Russian; Polish; Czech; Hungarian; Romanian; Turkish; Arabic; Thai; Simplified Chinese; Chinese (traditional); Korean; Japanese
Clean manually	Lifts reflex mirror to allow manual cleaning of the sensor
Feature guide	Enable; Disable
GPS device settings	Settings available when GPS unit GP-E2 is fitted

Set Up 3 �'(Yellow)	Options
Wi-Fi/NFC	Disable; Enable; Allow NFC connections
Wi-Fi function	Connect to smartphone; Upload to Web service
Certification logo display	Displays the logos of the camera's certifications
Custom functions (C. Fn)	C.Fn I: Exposure (Exposure level increments; ISO expansion; Flash sync in **Av** mode) C.Fn: II Image (Long exposure noise reduction; High ISO speed noise reduction; Highlight tone priority) C.Fn III: Autofocus/Drive (AF-assist beam firing) C.Fn IV: Operation/Others (Shutter/AE lock button; Assign (SET) button; Flash button function; LCD display when power ON)
Copyright information	Display copyright info.; Enter author's name; Enter copyright details; Delete copyright information
Clear settings	Clear all camera settings; Clear all Custom Func. (C.Fn)
Firmware Ver.	Currently installed camera firmware version number; Install new camera firmware

My Menu ★ (Green)	Options
My Menu Settings	Choose your most commonly used menu options for easy accessibility

» SHOOTING 1 📷

› Image quality

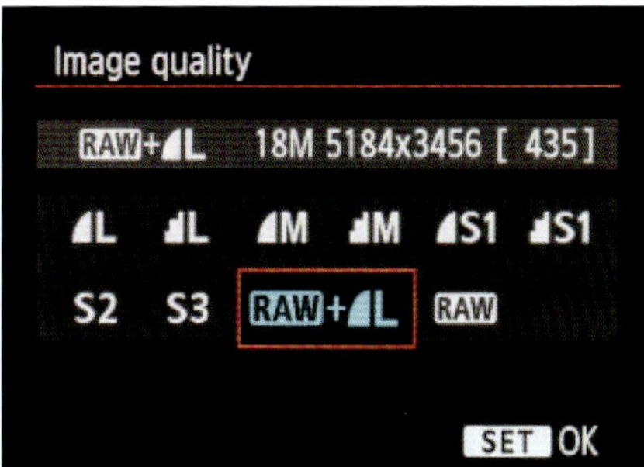

The Rebel T6/EOS 1300D can shoot Raw, JPEG, or Raw+JPEG, but there's no right or wrong answer to which option to choose. If you shoot JPEG you'll have a finished image ready for immediate use (such as uploading to social media sites or printing directly from the memory card). The key thing here is that the look of the image—how the white balance is set or which Picture Control is applied—is essentially fixed at the time of shooting. Slight adjustments can be made to the image in postproduction, but these adjustments cannot be pushed too far without an unacceptable loss of image quality.

Raw gives you far more scope for postproduction alteration, as images are (usually) processed using software on your computer, rather than in-camera. The downside to this freedom is that Raw files are far less useful immediately, and you have to set time aside to work on your Raw files after shooting—they need to be imported into Raw conversion software, adjusted, and then exported as a more useful file type, such as JPEG or TIFF.

A useful rule of thumb when deciding which format to use is to think about how you'll be shooting on a particular day. If you're at a social event and intend to shoot hundreds or even thousands of shots then JPEG would be a good choice. However, if you're going to shoot more sparingly and want to have finer control over your images then Raw is a better option. If you have a large enough memory card then shooting Raw+JPEG gives you the best of both options.

JPEGs can be shot at two different quality settings and five different resolutions. The lower quality and lower resolution options will all save space on your memory card, allowing you to shoot

> **Note**
> Image quality can also be set via 🅀 when the mode dial is set to a Creative Zone mode.

Quality (pixels)	Resolution	Possible no. of shots[1]	Printable size: cm[2]	Printable size: in.[3]
JPEG ⬛L	5184 x 3456	2280	52 x 35	20.7 x 13.8
⬛L		4480		
⬛M	3456 x 2304	4300	35 x 23.2	13.8 x 9.2
⬛M		8400		
⬛S1	2592 x 1728	6700	26.1 x 17.4	10.3 x 6.9
⬛S1		12720		
S2	1920 x 1280	11140	19.3 x 13	7.7 x 5.1
S3	720 x 480	43120	7.2 x 4.8	2.9 x 1.9
Raw ⬛L	5184 x 3456	580	52 x 35	20.7 x 13.8
Raw+JPEG	5184 x 3456	460	52 x 35	20.7 x 13.8

[1] With a 16GB memory card installed
[2] Approximate size when printed at 99 pixels per centimeter (ppcm)
[3] Approximate size when printed at 250 pixels per inch (ppi)

more images before the card fills, but your postproduction adjustment options and the size of acceptable quality prints will be more constrained. The upside of using a lower quality, lower resolution image setting—apart from smaller files sizes—is that the maximum burst when shooting continuously will be increased. See the grid above for more information.

› Beep

When set to **Enable**, the Rebel T6/EOS 1300D will beep to confirm focus lock and whenever the self-timer is activated. However, silence is sometimes preferable (when shooting at a wedding, for instance) and on these occasions **Disable** is a more useful option.

» BLANK CANVAS

The liberating aspect of shooting Raw is that you have greater freedom to put your own stamp on an image. Because you never overwrite the basic information in a Raw file, it's possible to produce multiple interpretations of the same image, each with its own visual atmosphere.

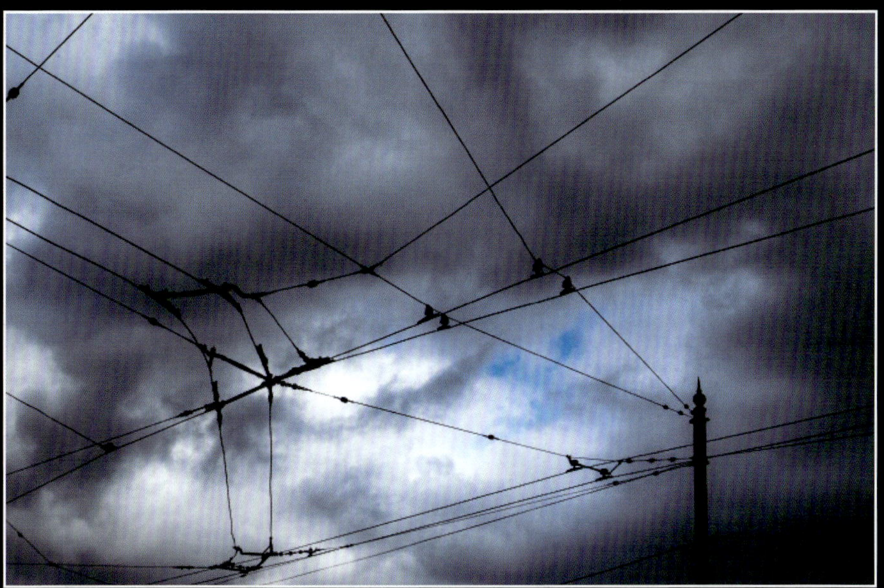

Settings
> Focal length: 35mm
> Aperture: f/13
> Shutter speed: 1/160 sec.
> ISO: 200

› Release shutter without card

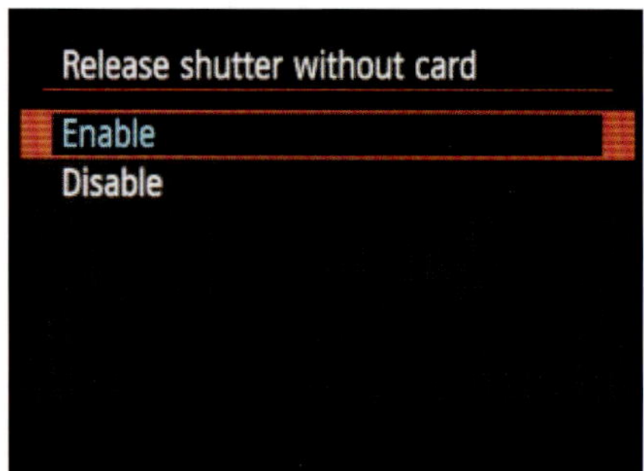

Set **Release shutter without card** to **Enable** and you can fire the shutter even if there's no memory card installed in your Rebel T6/EOS 1300D. The image shot will be displayed briefly on the LCD, but will not be saved (and therefore lost). If you're not paying attention you may not realize what's happening until it's too late.

To prevent this happening it's much safer to set **Release shutter without card** to **Disable**. Then, when there's no memory card in the camera, pressing down on the shutter-release button prompts a warning message and the shutter won't fire.

Setting **Release shutter without card** to **Enable** is only necessary for one specific technique: tethered shooting. This is achieved by connecting your Rebel T6/ EOS 1300D to a computer via a USB cable. When shooting this way the images are automatically transferred to the computer for saving to its hard drive. Tethered

shooting is most useful in studio setups, but with a suitable laptop or tablet it's also a feasible option outside as well. To use the tethered shooting technique you'll first need to install Canon's EOS Utility software (see chapter 9). You'll also need image-editing software such as Canon's Digital Photo Professional or Adobe Lightroom to view and process the captured images.

› Image review

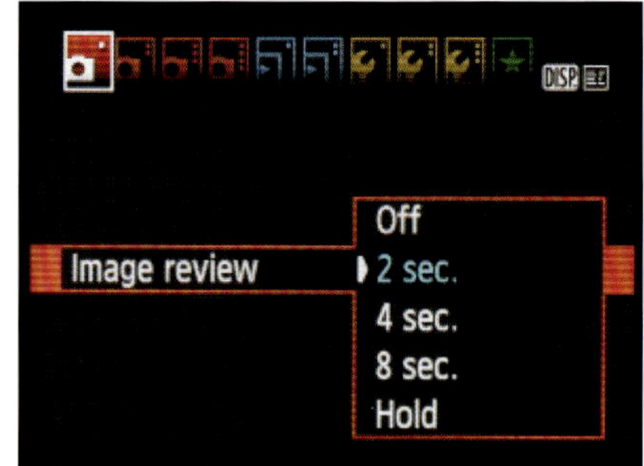

After making an exposure, the resulting image will be displayed on the rear LCD screen for a set period of time. The default is **2 sec.** but this can be altered to **Off**, **4 sec.**, or **8 sec.**. When set to **Hold**, the image will remain on screen until you press any of the controls or until the camera automatically powers down. As the LCD screen is one of the biggest drains on a camera's battery, it's a good idea to select a setting that's useful, but power efficient.

› Peripheral illumin. correct.

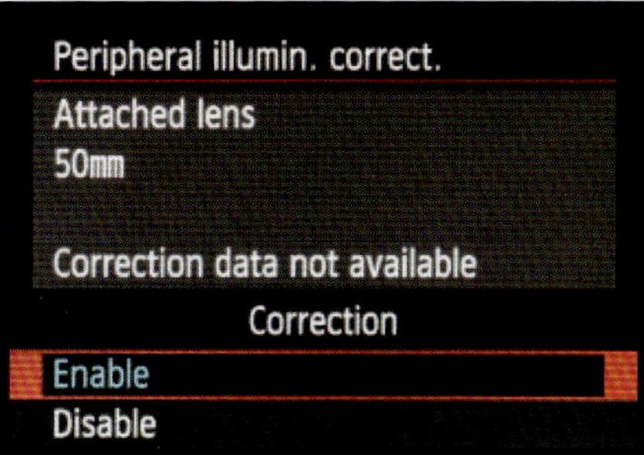

There's no such thing as a perfect lens, although some lenses are better than others. Fortunately the flaws of a specific lens design can be quantified to produce a "profile" for that lens, which can be used as a reference to remove or reduce the flaws.

Peripheral illumin. correct. tackles a lens problem known as fall-off or vignetting, which results in a darkening at the corners of an image compared to the center. Most lenses display a certain amount of vignetting at maximum aperture, but this is usually reduced as the aperture is made smaller, and may not be noticeable anyway, unless you're shooting very bright scenes.

When set to **Enable, Peripheral illumin. correct.** automatically lightens the corners of images to reduce the amount of vignetting. However, it requires that a profile for the lens fitted to your Rebel T6/EOS 1300D is installed on the camera.

By default there are profiles for over 25 Canon lenses pre-installed, including the kit lenses commonly sold with the camera. You can add or delete lens profiles using Canon's Lens Registration software, although only Canon lenses are supported.

One downside to using **Peripheral illumin. correct.** is the potential for an increase in the visibility of noise in the corners of your images. For this reason the amount of correction applied is reduced the higher the ISO value you use.

If your lens isn't supported (or you don't mind slight vignetting) set **Peripheral illumin. correct.** to **Disable**.

Notes
To change the registered lenses install **Lens Registration Tool** and then connect the Rebel T6/ EOS 1300D to your computer (see chapter 9 for details).

Raw files only have the light fall-off correction data appended to the image; the corrections applied can be removed in postproduction.

See chapter 5 for information about **Red-eye reduction** and **Flash control** (also found on the Shooting 1 ◙ menu).

› Auto Lighting Optimizer

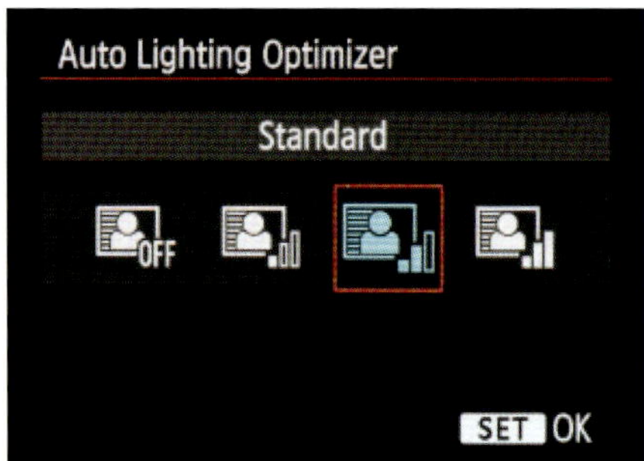

Although **Auto Lighting Optimizer** is useful in certain situations, it should be set to ⬛OFF if the scene you're shooting is relatively low in contrast or when you want a backlit subject recorded as a silhouette. **Auto Lighting Optimizer** can also undo changes made to the exposure using exposure compensation (see page 37), so when **Auto Lighting Optimizer** is activated you may find you need to dial in a higher exposure compensation value than usual.

High-contrast scenes are commonly faced by photographers, generally resulting in images with dark and dense shadows. If you shoot Raw, contrast can (to a degree) often be rectified during postproduction. However, choose JPEG and there's less scope for adjustment (at least without reducing image quality).

To aid JPEG users, the Rebel T6/EOS 1300D offers **Auto Lighting Optimizer**. Switched to any setting other than ⬛OFF **Off**, **Auto Lighting Optimizer** will analyze your images as you shoot. If it determines that high contrast is a problem, the shadows are lightened to make an image more tonally balanced. You can control the effect by choosing between ⬛ **Low**, ⬛ **Standard**, and ⬛ **Strong** (with ⬛ applying the most correction to your images).

> **Notes**
> Auto Lighting Optimizer cannot be used at the same time as Highlight tone priority.
>
> Auto Lighting Optimizer is fixed at ⬛ **Standard** when you use a Basic Zone mode.

› Custom White Balance

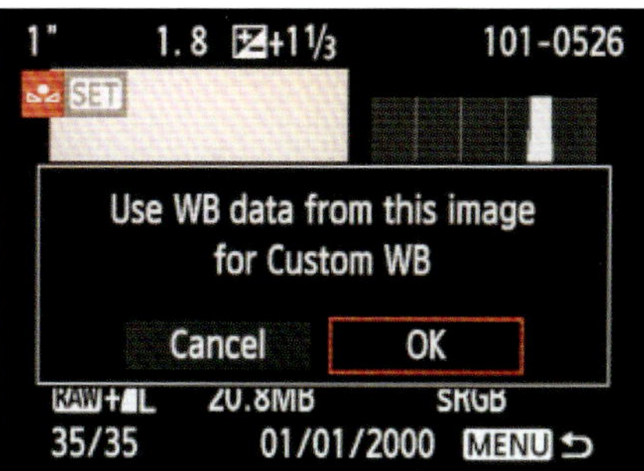

AWB is a convenient way to let the camera decide the WB adjustment required, but it isn't perfect. For example, it can be fooled into overcompensating if there is a single color that is naturally predominant in a scene, such as green in woodland. Therefore, if you need accurate color, creating a custom white balance is a far better option.

To set the custom white balance you must first take a reference shot of a neutral white surface. The white surface should fill the viewfinder and be lit by the same light as your subject. Switch your lens to MF (it doesn't matter whether the white surface is in focus or not) and adjust the exposure so that the white surface is almost clipping the right edge of the histogram.

Setting the custom white balance

1) Select **Custom White Balance** from the ◙ menu.

2) The image you've just shot should be displayed (press ◄ / ► if it's not, or if you want to use a different image to create the custom WB). Press SET.

3) Select **OK** to create the custom WB, or **Cancel** to return to step 2.

4) Once you've created your custom white balance, select the ◣ custom WB preset from the **Q** or screen or by pressing ▼/WB.

> **Note**
> A custom white balance setting is specific to one particular scene. As soon as you shoot under different lighting the custom WB will need to be updated.

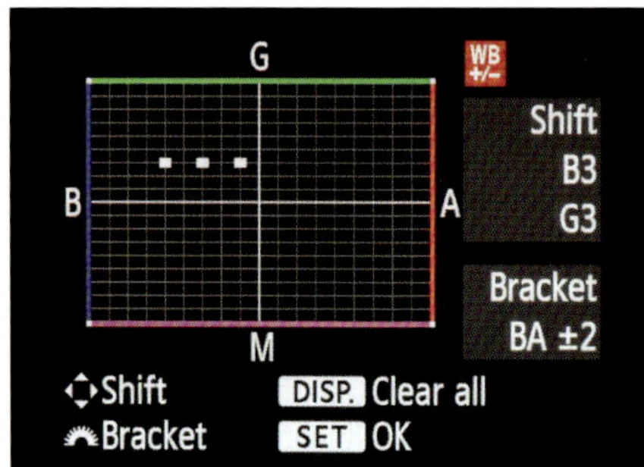

The WB presets generally make it fairly straightforward to set a pleasing white balance, but you may encounter light sources that aren't quite a perfect match for any of the presets. In this case, **WB Shift/Bkt.**, lets you tweak the currently selected preset by adding more **G** (green), **M** (magenta), **B** (blue), or **A** (amber/red). You can also choose to set bracketing so that three shots are taken using three variations of the selected color adjustment.

> **Note**
> When WB Shift has been set, WB will be displayed on the viewfinder and on the LCD.

Setting WB Shift

1) Select **WB Shift/Bkt.**.

2) Move the WB adjustment point around the displayed grid using ✛. Move the point to the right to increase the amber bias (making the image warmer) or to the left to add more blue (making it cooler). If you're shooting under fluorescent lighting you may find that adjusting the green/magenta bias improves color accuracy: move the point up and down to add more green and magenta respectively. Re-centering the adjustment point removes the color correction.

3) To set WB bracketing turn ⛭. Turning ⛭ to the left sets the G/M bracketing; turning ⛭ to the right sets the B/A bracketing. If you choose to bracket WB, the next three shots will use the current WB preset setting followed by either a blue then amber bias, or a magenta then green bias. The cycle then repeats until WB bracketing is cancelled.

4) Press (SET) to set the WB adjustment and return to the main 📷 menu screen, or press **DISP.** to clear the WB adjustments and return to step 2.

› Color space

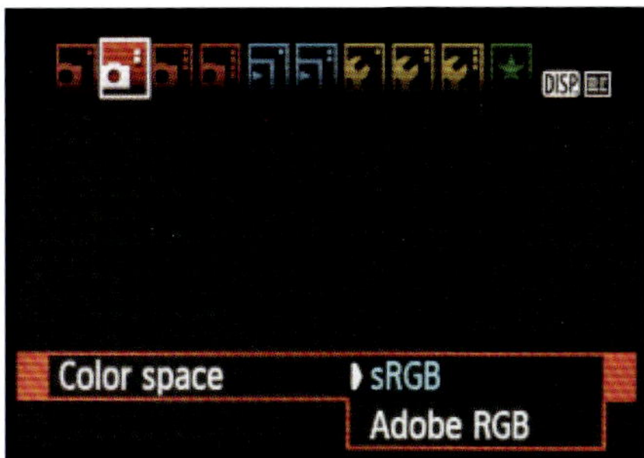

Your images can be tagged either with the **sRGB** color space or **Adobe RGB**. **Adobe RGB** encompasses a larger and richer range of colors than **sRGB**, which makes it the better option if you plan to modify your images in postproduction, but **sRGB** is preferable if you intend to use your images straight out of the camera, as devices such as monitors and printers use smaller color spaces. Internet browsers also prefer images to be **sRGB**.

Your choice of **Color space** is particularly important if you use JPEG—Raw files can be tagged with a different color space during postproduction, without a loss of image quality.

> **Note**
> **sRGB** is used automatically when the mode dial is set to a Basic Zone mode.

› Picture Style

Picture Style gives you control over certain visual qualities of an image, including the vividness (saturation) of colors, sharpness, and contrast. You can select from one of a number of **Picture Style** presets (see the grid on page 102) or create your own custom styles by modifying the presets in-camera or using Canon's EOS Utility software.

Choosing the right **Picture Style** is more important when shooting JPEG than Raw; when you shoot Raw you can unpick the settings in postproduction. This means that you can use a dramatic **Picture Style** like **M Monochrome** and undo its effects later (even reverting to color). This cannot be done when shooting JPEGs.

Setting the Picture Style

1) Select **Picture Style**.

2) Highlight the required **Picture Style** by pressing ▲ / ▼. Press (SET) to select the **Picture Style** and return to the main 📷 menu (or MENU to cancel your selection).

You can download more Picture Styles from Canon's Japanese website at *www.canon.co.jp/imaging/picturestyle/file/index.html*. These can be added to your Rebel T6/EOS 1300D using Picture Style Editor (see chapter 9).

> **Notes**
> **Picture Style** can also be set via the Ⓠ screen.

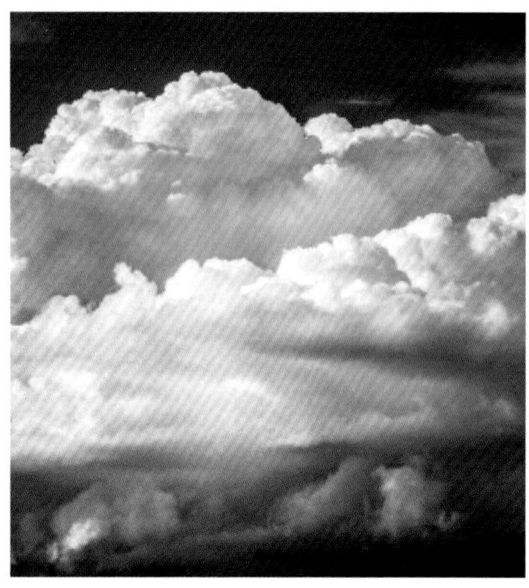

MONOCHROME
High-contrast subjects, such as this cloud bank, often work as well in black and white as they do in color.

Preset	Description
Automatic	Picture Style is automatically modified by the Rebel T6/EOS 1300D according to the shooting situation.
Standard	Suitable for general photography; produces images with reasonably saturated colors.
Portrait	Sharpness is set lower than Standard; colors adjusted to produce sympathetic skin tones.
Landscape	Greens and blues are more saturated; image sharpness is increased.
Neutral	Natural colors with lower saturation and contrast.
Faithful	Lower saturation still; produces the most accurate colors when shooting under normal daylight conditions of all the presets.
Monochrome	Converts images to black and white.
User Defined 1–3	–

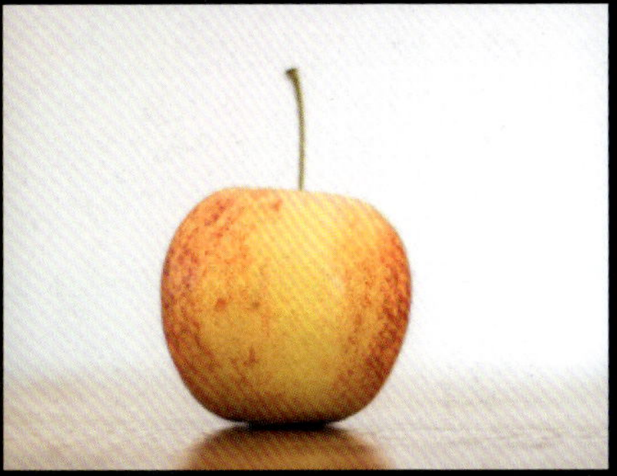

Automatic

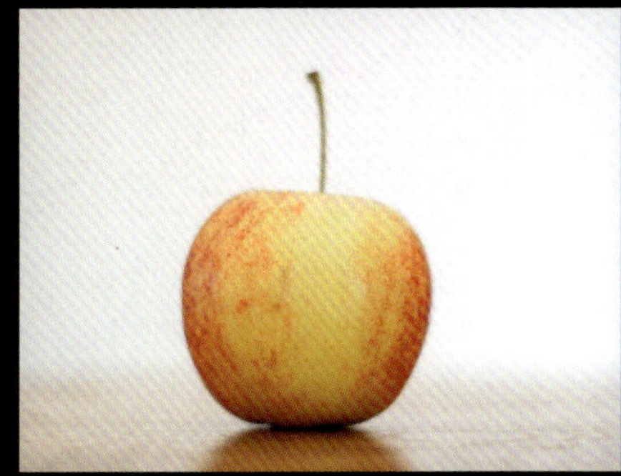

Standard

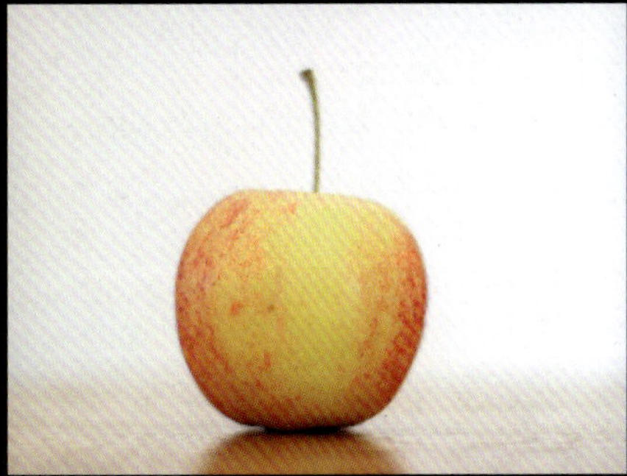

Portrait

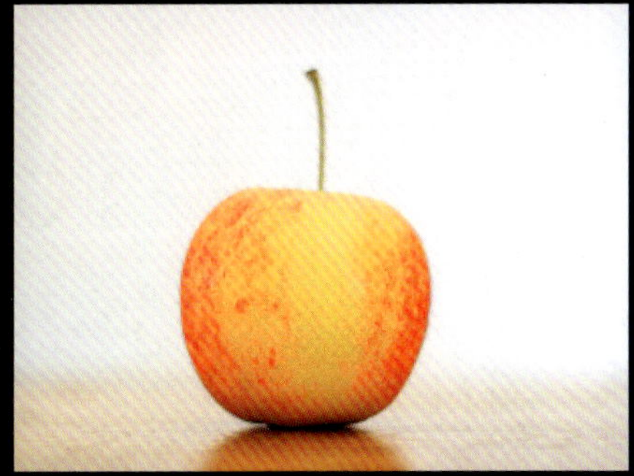

Landscape

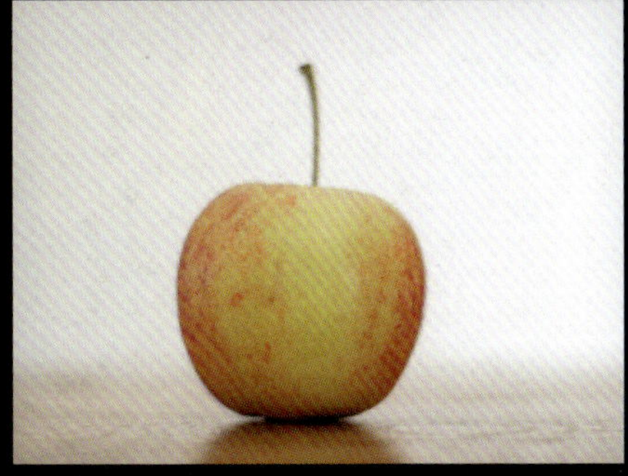

Neutral

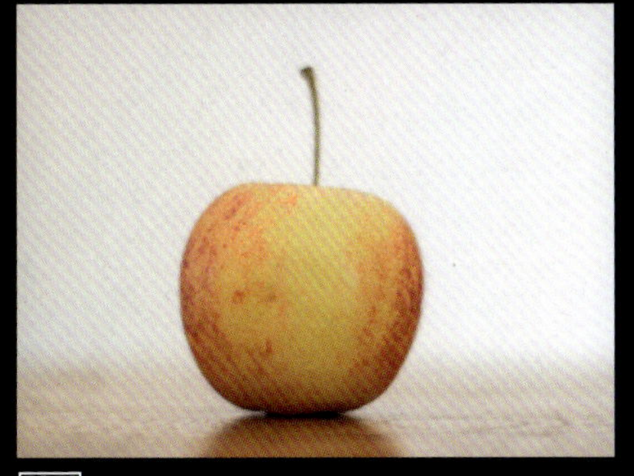

Faithful

Detail Settings

With the exception of M, Picture Styles are defined by four parameters: **Sharpness**, **Contrast**, **Saturation**, and **Color Tone**.

The Picture Styles can be modified by adjusting one or all of these parameters. To do this, highlight the Picture Style you wish to alter and press SET. Select the desired parameter and press ◀ to decrease the effect of the setting or ▶ to increase it. Press SET when you're happy with the adjustments you've made.

To clear your adjustments, highlight **Default set.** at the bottom of the screen and press SET.

When you're done, press MENU to return to the main **Picture Style** screen.

Presets	Description
Sharpness	0: No sharpening applied / 7: Maximum sharpening
Contrast	- Low contrast / + High contrast
Saturation	- Low color saturation / + High color saturation
Color tone	- Skin tones more red / + Skin tones more yellow

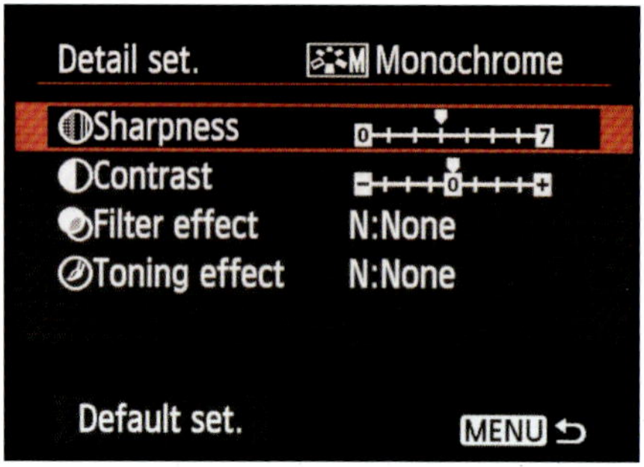

M Monochrome

When M is adjusted, Saturation and Color Tone are replaced by **Filter effect** and **Toning effect**. Filter effect mimics the use of colored filters when shooting with black-and-white film, while Toning effect adds a color wash to your monochrome images (you can choose between **N: None**, **S: Sepia**, **B: Blue**, **P: Purple**, and **G: Green**).

Filter effect	Description
N: None	No filter effect applies
Ye: Yellow	Blues darkened; greens and yellows lightened
Or: Orange	Blues darkened further; yellows and reds lightened
R: Red	Blues very dark; reds and oranges lightened
G: Green	Purples darkened; greens lightened

Detail set.	User Def. 1
Picture Style	Auto
Sharpness	0 +++++++ 7
Contrast	- ++++0++++ +
Saturation	- ++++0++++ +
Color tone	- ++++0++++ +
	MENU ↩

User Defined Picture Style

You can modify and permanently save three Picture Style preset modifications as **User Def. 1**, **2**, or **3**. There are many good reasons for creating user-defined Picture Styles, the first of which is that it's an excellent way to personalize your images.

In addition, when shooting JPEGs, creating a subdued Picture Style (one that is low in contrast and saturation) will give you more scope to make postproduction alterations. It's still not as flexible as Raw, but adding contrast and saturation in postproduction is less likely to cause image quality issues than trying to remove them. This applies most strongly to sharpening.

In fact, sharpening is almost impossible to remove once it's been applied to an image, so if you think you'll want to increase the resolution of an image later on (to make a large print, for example) set sharpening to **0**. You'll have to sharpen your images later, but they will be far easier to resize without a visible drop in quality.

Creating a User Defined Picture Style

1) Highlight **User Def. 1**, **2**, or **3** and press DISP..

2) Select **Picture Style**. Press ▲ / ▼ to find the **Picture Style** preset you want to modify, then press (SET).

3) Select and alter the four **Picture Style** parameters as described previously. When you're finished, press MENU to return to the main **Picture Style** menu.

Tip

*In playback, Raw images are displayed with the Picture Style selected at the time of shooting. This means that the histogram may not necessarily be accurate, especially when a vivid, contrasty Picture Style such as has been used. For greater accuracy create a custom Picture Style that has the **Contrast** and **Saturation** set at the lowest levels. The image will appear flat and dull on playback, but it will give a more accurate indication of the tonal range of the Raw file. You would then adjust the image in postproduction.*

› Dust Delete Data

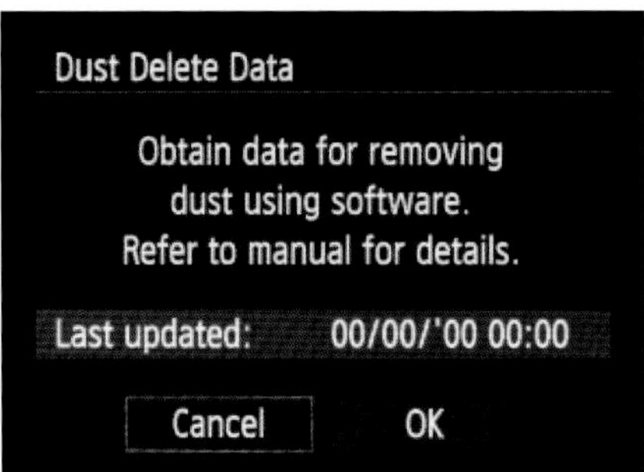

The sensor in your camera generates an electrical charge that attracts dust, which will be seen as small black blobs in images (particularly when smaller apertures are used). There are two ways of dealing with dust: either physically clean it off the sensor, or remove it from the image during postproduction. The former requires the use of cleaning tools and is described in more detail later in this chapter.

Dust Delete Data is an aid to removing dust during postproduction (for still images only—postproduction dust removal from movies is complicated and time consuming, so it's better to clean the sensor physically before shooting movies). **Dust Delete Data** lets you shoot a reference image that's used to create a map of the location of any dust on the sensor. This information is then appended to images as you shoot. When the image is imported into Digital Photo Professional, the software uses this data to clone dust automatically from the images.

However, it is not foolproof, and you may find important details are removed from your images at the same time. Therefore, it's important to check your image carefully once the dust removal process is complete.

Setting Dust Delete Data

1) Attach a lens longer than 50mm to your Rebel T6/EOS 1300D, switch it to manual focus and set the focus at Infinity (∞).

2) Press MENU, navigate to 📷, and select **Dust Delete Data**.

3) Select **OK** to continue or **Cancel** to return to the 📷 menu.

4) Aim your camera at a clean, white surface—such as a sheet of paper—from a distance of approximately 12 inches (30cm). The white surface should fill the viewfinder entirely.

5) When *Fully press the shutter-release button, when ready* is displayed, press the shutter-release button down. Once the reference image has been captured it will be processed.

6) When **OK** is displayed press (SET). If the data is not obtained correctly, follow the instructions on screen and reshoot.

7) Once the data has been recorded you can shoot as normal. Both JPEG and Raw files will have Dust Delete Data added.

8) Switch on your computer, import any photos shot after obtaining Dust Delete Data, and then launch DPP. Select one of your photos in the main DPP window and click on the **Stamp** button. The photo will redraw itself and any dust will be removed automatically using the Dust Delete Data. Once this process is finished, click on **Apply Dust Delete Data**.

9) Click **OK** to return to the main DPP window.

> **Note**
> **Dust Delete Data** will become out of date over time. Reshoot periodically, particularly if you're working in a dusty environment.

› ISO Auto

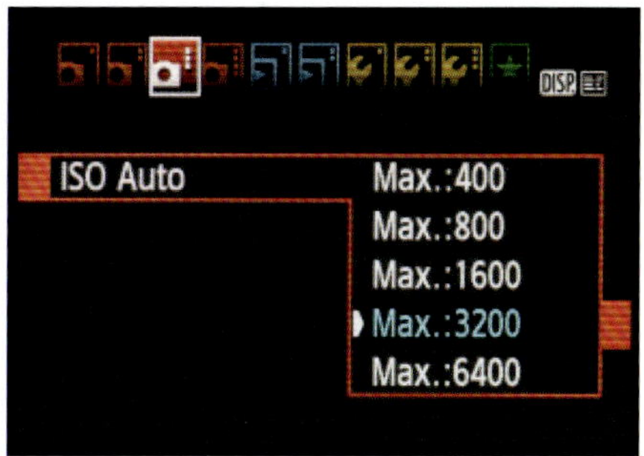

When you set the ISO to AUTO, the ISO value will change to suit the lighting conditions (increasing as light levels drop). **ISO Auto** allows you to set the maximum ISO value that will be chosen by your Rebel T6/EOS 1300D; you can choose between **Max.:400**, **Max.:800**, **Max.:1600**, **Max.:3200**, or **Max.: 6400**.

Increasing the ISO is usually done to enable you to use a faster shutter speed, which is particularly useful when handholding a camera. However, if you want to maximize image quality—at the increased risk of camera shake—you might prefer to choose a lower maximum ISO value.

› Live View shooting

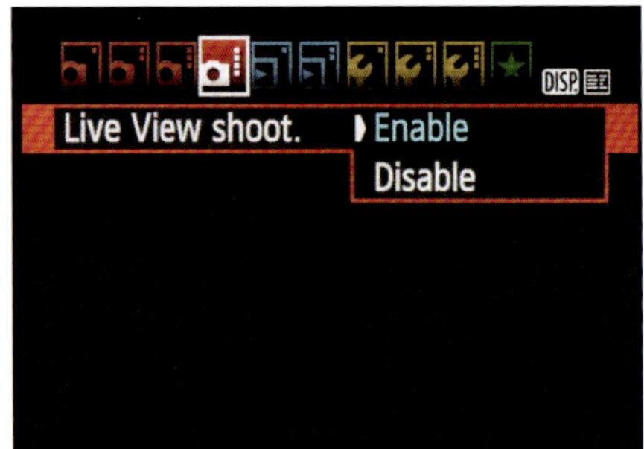

› Grid display

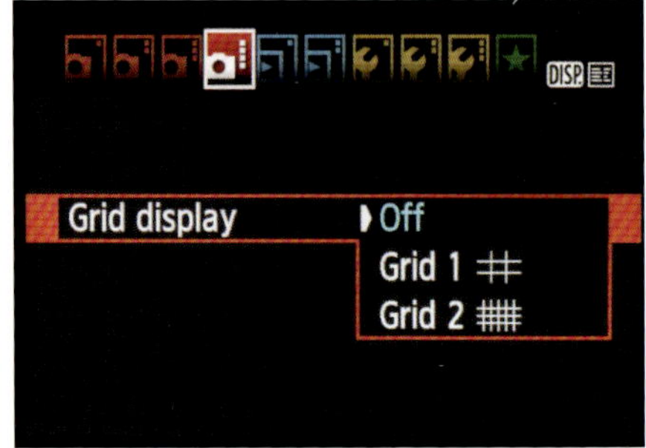

In order to use the Rebel T6/EOS 1300D's Live View facility you must have **Live View shoot.** set to **Enable**. When **Disable** is selected, you can't switch to Live View; you'll only be able to use the viewfinder to compose an image. There's no real advantage to disabling Live View, other than to prevent it from being activated if the button is pressed accidentally.

> **Note**
> See chapter two for information about **AF method**.

The **Grid display** function overlays two different grid types on the LCD when Live View is activated. These grids can be used as an aid to composition or as a visual check that elements in the scene are straight relative to the camera.

Grid 1 divides the screen into nine equal rectangles using two equally spaced vertical lines and two equally spaced horizontal lines.

Grid 2 divides the screen into 24 squares, which is useful when shooting architectural subjects that need to be square to the camera.

Off turns the grid function off entirely.

› Aspect ratio

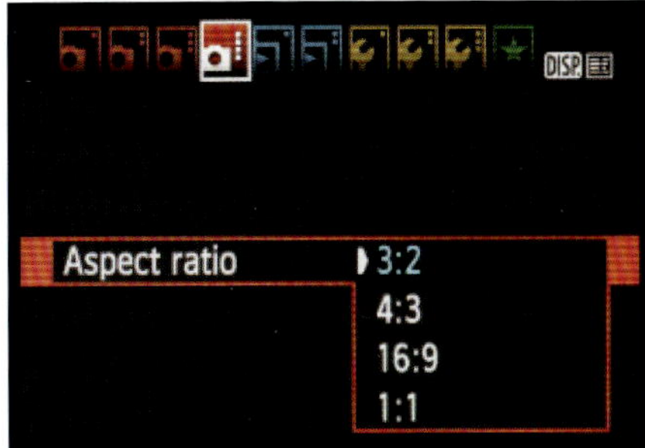

Note

Aspect ratio can be set when you shoot Raw files, but the cropping information is only appended to the file. DPP can read the appended cropping information as an aid to cropping in postproduction, or the information can be ignored.

The aspect ratio of an image is the ratio of its width to its height. The Rebel T6/EOS 1300D lets you create JPEG images with an aspect ratio of **3:2**, **4:3**, **16:9**, or **1:1**.

The default setting is **3:2**, which matches the aspect ratio of the sensor inside the Rebel T6/EOS 1300D. The **16:9** aspect ratio is more "panoramic" and matches the standard aspect ratio used for HD video. **4:3** is the standard shape of an analog television and the Micro Four Thirds camera system. Finally, **1:1** is square—a shape commonly used when shooting medium-format film.

It's worth noting that when you use an aspect ratio other than **3:2**, the full resolution of the sensor is not used. In fact, shooting at **3:2** and cropping in postproduction will achieve the same effect as using any of the other aspect ratios (and give you scope for cropping in a less constrained way).

Image quality	Aspect ratio and resolution (pixels)			
	3:2	4:3	16:9	1:1
L / RAW	5184 x 3456	4608 x 3456	5184 x 2192	3456 x 3456
M	3456 x 2304	3072 x 2304	3456 x 1944	2304 x 2304
S1	2592 x 1728	2304 x 1728	2592 x 1456	1728 x 1728
S2	1920 x 1280	1696 x 1280	1920 x 1080	1280 x 1280
S3	720 x 480	640 x 480	720 x 405	480 x 480

› Metering timer

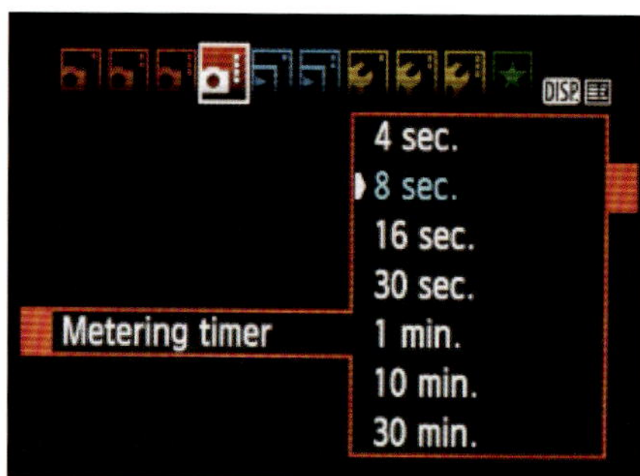

› Movie exposure

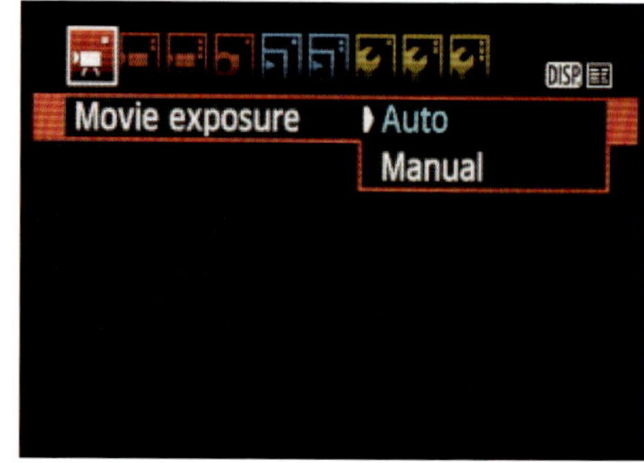

Metering timer specifies the length of time that the exposure information is displayed in the viewfinder for and how long AE lock is maintained after pressing ✱. The options are 4, 8, 16, and **30 sec.**, and **1**, **10**, and **30 min.**. **Metering timer** is automatically set to **8 sec.** when a Basic Zone mode is used and cannot be altered.

Movie exposure lets you select whether the exposure for movies is **Auto** or **Manual**. **Auto** is by far the easier option, but you are locked out of the exposure process (as with shooting still images, this is an important part of movie making).

Manual lets you set the ISO, shutter speed, and aperture when shooting movies—see chapter two for more details.

› AF w/ shutter button during 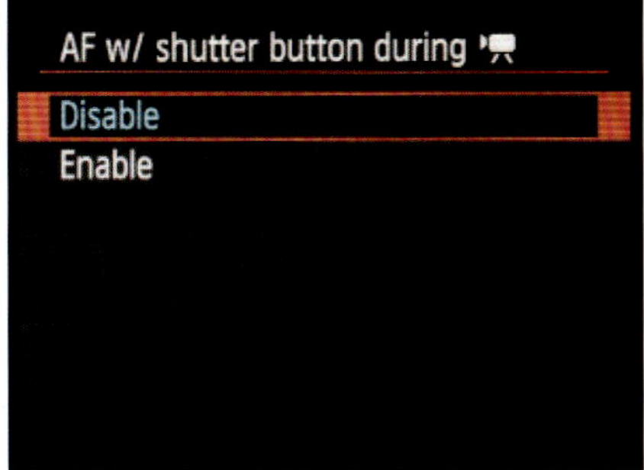

Note

See chapter two for information about **AF method**; see page 136 for information about **Highlight tone priority**; and page 138 for information about **Shutter/ AE lock button**—these are also found on the Movie Shooting 1 menu.

If you set **AF w/ shutter button during** to **Enable**, you can use single-shot AF during movie recording (continuous AF isn't possible). However, for most lenses this is not recommended, as the microphone in the Rebel T6/EOS 1300D can pick up the noise of the lens' AF motor.

A better option is to set **AF w/ shutter button during** to **Disable** and to focus manually during movie recording. The exception to this is if you are using one of Canon's STM lenses, which are designed to focus in near silence.

» MOVIE SHOOTING 2 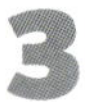

› Movie rec. size

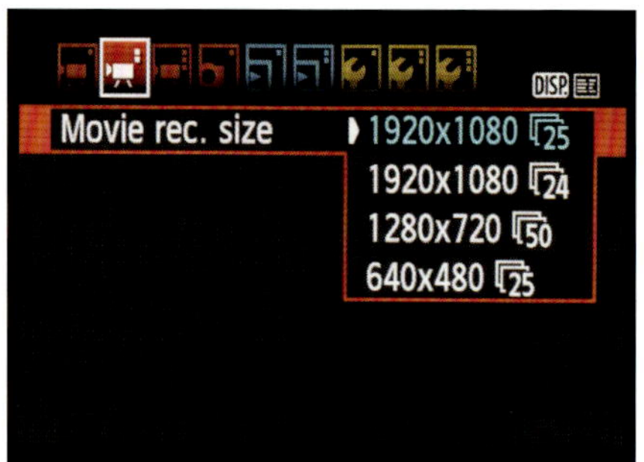

Movie rec. size lets you set the resolution and frame rate of your movies. The options that are shown will vary depending on whether **Video System** (further down the menu) is set to **PAL** or **NTSC**.

Resolution	
1920	Full HD recording at 1920 x 1080 pixels, with an aspect ratio of 16:9.
1280	HD recording at 1280 x 720 pixels, with an aspect ratio of 16:9.
640	Standard definition recording at 640 x 480 pixels, with an aspect ratio of 4:3 (suitable for analog TV and Internet use).

Frame rate	
30 / 60	For use in NTSC TV standard areas (North America/Japan). With its faster frame rate, 60 will allow more scope for slowing footage during editing.
25 / 50	For use in PAL TV standard areas (Europe/Australia). 50 allows greater scope for slowing footage during editing.
24	For conversion to motion picture/film standard.

› Sound recording

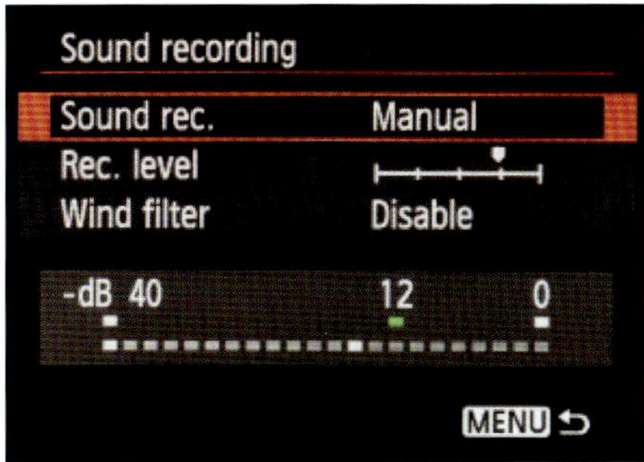

Sound recording is where the recorded volume of your movie's soundtrack is controlled. When **Sound rec.** is set to **Auto**, the soundtrack volume is adjusted automatically as it's recorded, whereas **Manual** lets you set the volume level between 1 and 64.

After selecting **Manual**, select **Rec. level** and press ◀ / ▶ to set the required volume. You should aim to have your peak (loudest) sound level reach no more than the -12 dB level. Any higher and the sound may be distorted.

No sound is recorded with your movie when **Sound rec.** is set to **Disable** (you would use this option when recording audio to a separate audio recorder).

When **Wind filter** is set to **Enable**, your Rebel T6/EOS 1300D will eliminate the interference noise caused by wind blowing across the microphone during recording. This achieves the same effect digitally as fitting a foam windshield on an external microphone. If you're shooting indoors or in calm conditions you should set **Wind filter** to **Disable**.

› Video snapshot

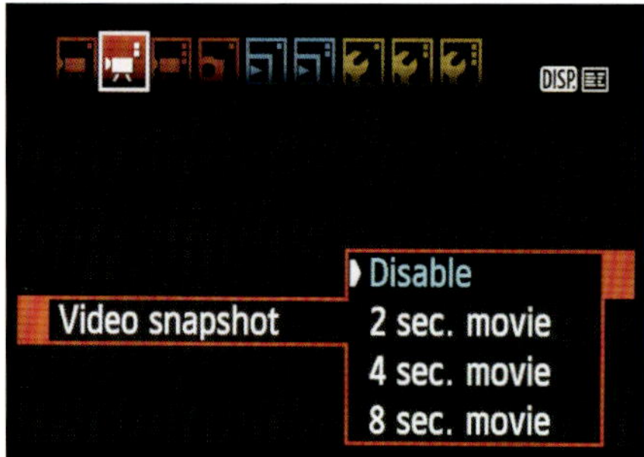

A snapshot is a short video clip that can be a **2 sec. movie**, **4 sec. movie**, or **8 sec. movie**. Snapshots are saved in albums, which let you group similar snapshots together and view them as a continuous sequence.

When you have chosen the clip length, press half way down on the shutter-release button to return to movie shooting. When you press ● / ◻, a clip is recorded at the specified length (a blue bar at the bottom of the LCD screen shows the time elapsed).

When recording has finished, you have the choice to 🎬 **Save as album** (if this is the first snapshot you've created), 📹 **Playback video snapshot** (which lets you play the snapshot you've just created), or ✖ **Do not save to album** (which erases the recorded snapshot and returns you to movie shooting).

The second time you shoot a snapshot you can 🎬 **Add to album** (which adds the new snapshot to a previously created album) or 📹 **Save as new album** (which creates a new and separate album to one previously created).

When you've added several snapshots to an album you can view them together by pressing ▶. An album is distinguished from a standard movie by the 🎬 **SET** icon at the top left corner of the LCD.

> **Note**
> **Metering timer** and **Grid display**—also found on the Move Shooting 2 🎥 menu—work in the same way as they do when shooting still images. For details, see pages 110 and 108.

› Video system

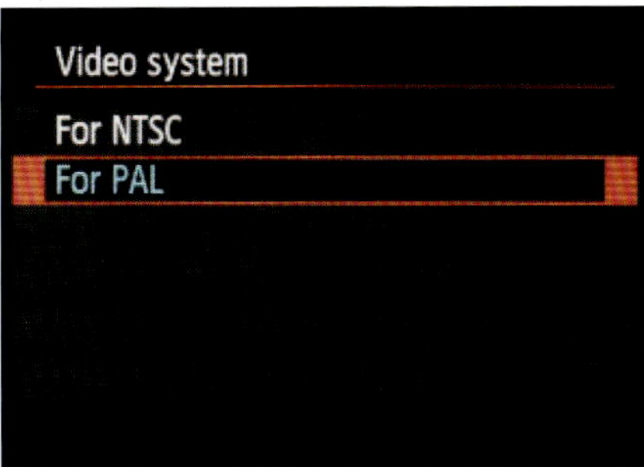

There are two main television standards in use around the world. If you want to connect your Rebel T6/EOS 1300D to a TV you should select the standard that is appropriate for your location: **NTSC** is used in North America and Japan, while **PAL** is used mainly in Europe, Russia, and Australia. The choice you make here will determine the frame rates available in **Movie rec. size** (see page 112).

Note

Movie shooting 3 duplicates **Exposure comp, Auto Lighting Optimizer, Custom White Balance,** and **Picture Style** described previously. However, settings adjusted via this menu don't affect still image shooting.

› Rotate

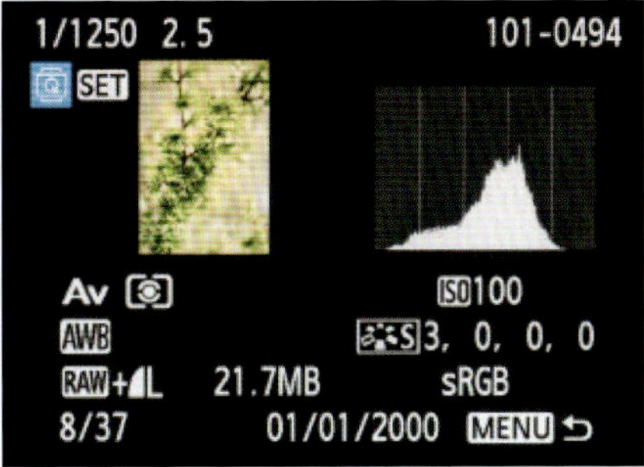

Through no fault of its own, the Rebel T6/EOS 1300D can sometimes get confused about the orientation it was held when you took a shot (happening most often when you shoot straight up or down). In playback this can result in images being displayed in the wrong orientation. **Rotate** fixes this problem. After selecting **Rotate**, navigate to the image that needs rotating and press (SET) to rotate it 90° clockwise; press (SET) a second time to rotate it a further 180°. Pressing (SET) a third time restores the image to its original orientation.

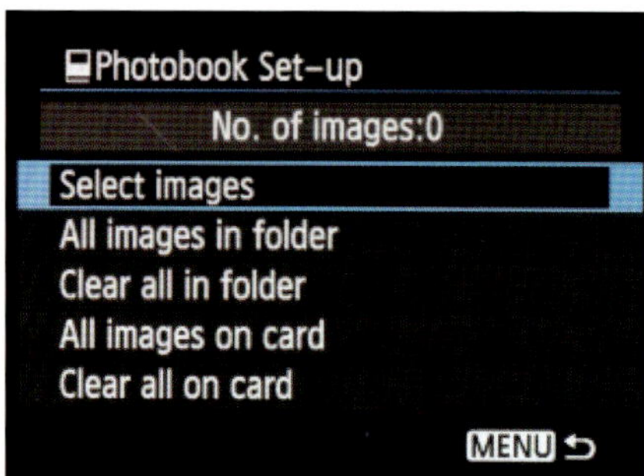

One of the big changes brought about by digital photography is the ability to create photobooks packed with your own images. These books can be ordered online in quantities of one copy upward.

Photobook Set-up lets you select up to 998 images for use in a photobook. You can then transfer the selected images to your computer using EOS Utility, where they'll be saved into a dedicated folder. The procedure for choosing images is very similar to choosing images for protection. You can: **Select images, All images in folder, Clear all in folder, All images on card**, and **Clear all on card**.

The key to creating a satisfying photobook is in the images you choose. The impact of a photobook will be reduced if you add repetitive imagery or photographs that are technically lacking, so be ruthless in your selection—don't be tempted to add images purely to fill pages.

Notes
Raw files cannot be added to a photobook selection.

See chapter two for information about **Protect images** and **Erase images**, and see chapter nine for more information about **Print order**: these options are also found on the Playback 1 ▶ menu.

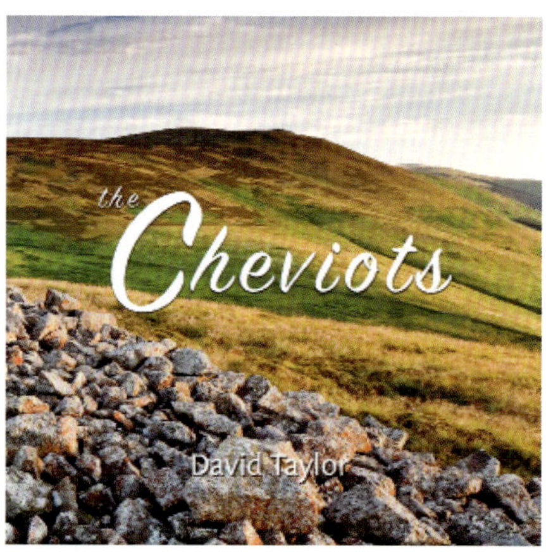

INTEREST ⌃
Creating a book after completing a long-term photographic project is an excellent way of commemorating your achievement.

› Creative Filters

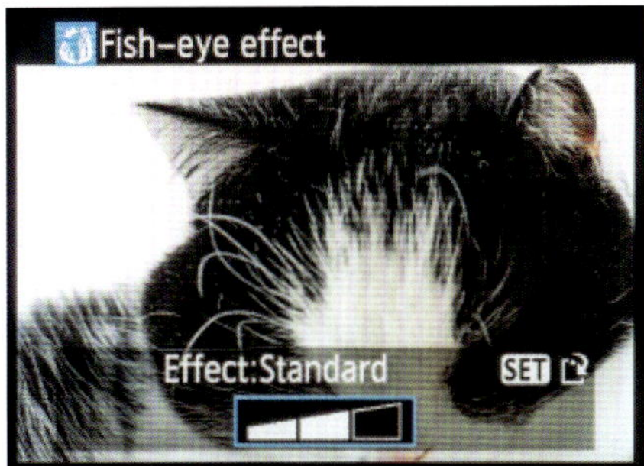

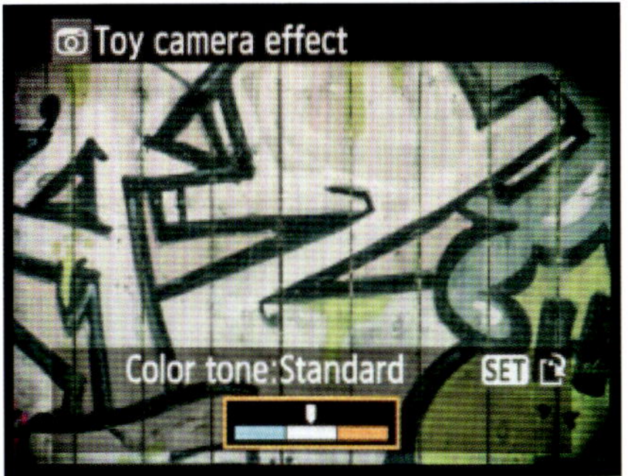

Creative Filters lets you apply simple postproduction effects to your images in-camera. It's not as sophisticated as dedicated software, but it's convenient and it's fun. You can choose from: **Grainy B/W**, **Soft focus**, **Fisheye effect**, **Toy camera effect**, and **Miniature effect**. The strength of each effect can be modified, allowing you more scope for personalization.

In each case, the original image file isn't overwritten; every time you apply an effect to an image you're forced to save a new file so that your original always remains safe. You can apply Creative Filters to both Raw and JPEG images, but the result will always be saved as a JPEG.

Effect name	Results	Options
Grainy B/W	Creates a high-contrast, grainy, black-and-white image.	Low; Standard; High
Soft focus	Adds a soft-focus glow to an image for a more romantic feel.	Low; Standard; High
Fisheye effect	Distorts the image so that it looks as if it was shot with a fisheye lens.	Low; Standard; Strong
Toy camera effect	Adds a vignette around the edges of the image, as well as altering the color palette.	Color tone: Cool tone; Standard; Warm tone
Miniature effect	Makes the image look like a miniature model by adjusting the apparent plane of focus.	Move the bar up and down or left and right to set the focus point.

› Resize

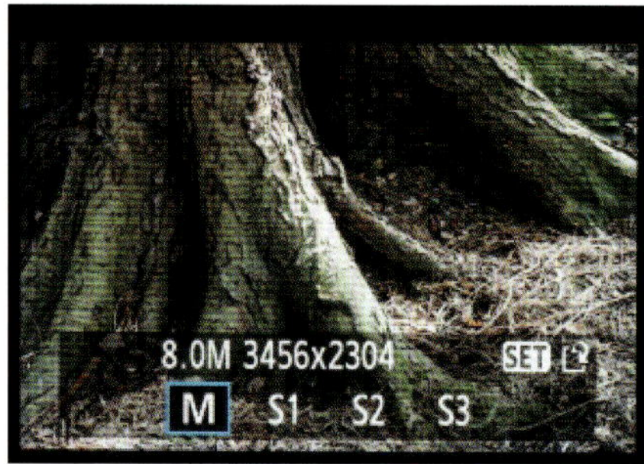

› Histogram display

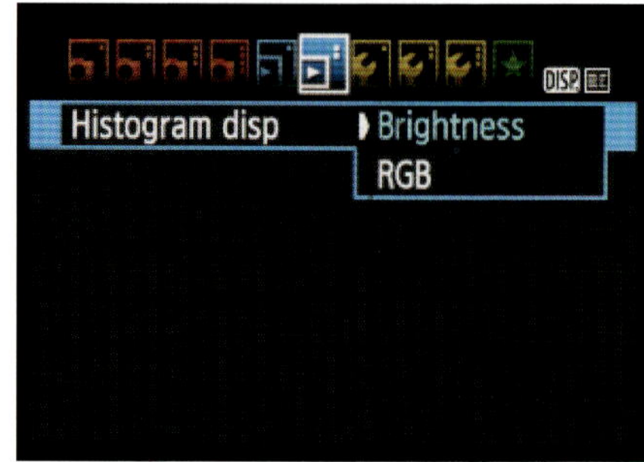

The Rebel T6/EOS 1300D's **Resize** option lets you reduce the resolution of JPEG images on the memory card and save the resized image as a new file. Note, however, that the smaller the original image is, the fewer options you have to make it smaller.

When you call up detailed shooting information in playback mode, the Rebel T6/EOS 1300D can display a **Brightness** or **RGB** histogram (and both together with the loss of some useful shooting information). **Histogram disp** lets you choose which histogram you'd prefer.

Original size	Sizes available for resizing			
	M	S1	S2	S3
L	Yes	Yes	Yes	Yes
M	–	Yes	Yes	Yes
S1	–	–	Yes	Yes
S2	–	–	–	Yes
S3	–	–	–	–

› Image jump w/

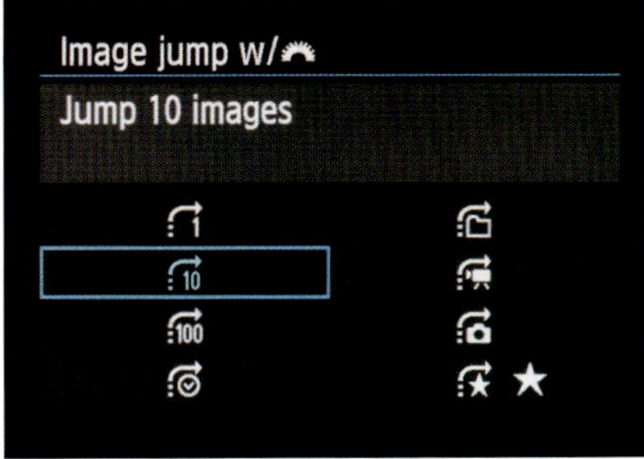

Symbol	Description
	Display one image at a time
	Jump 10 images at a time
	Jump 100 images at a time
	Display images by date
	Display images by folder
	Display movies only
	Display still images only
	Display by rating

Image jump w/ sets how you skip through images when turning in single image playback. When there are only a few images on the memory card, **Image jump w/** is relatively unimportant. However, once you've shot a good number of images **Image jump w/** can prove very useful.

The **Image jump w/** choice you make will either speed up skipping through images or filter the types of images shown. Filtering by an image's rating is particularly useful if you carefully rate images by type (such as landscape or portrait), or by project.

Once you've set how you'd like the images to jump, press ▶ to enter playback and then turn .

Note

If you haven't rated any of your images, you cannot use to jump through them using .

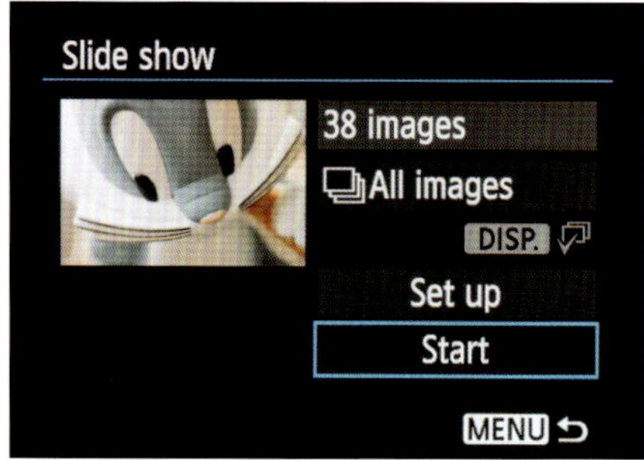

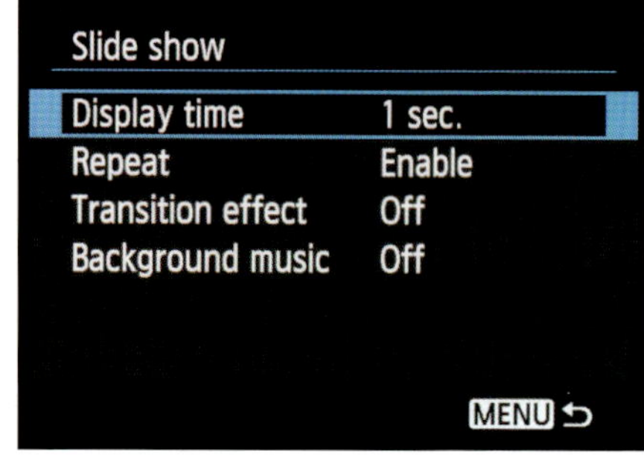

Slide show turns your Rebel T6/EOS 1300D into a digital "slide projector" that you can use to display a slide show of your images on the LCD or, for more impact, on a TV (see chapter 9).

Using Slide show
1) Select **Slide show**.

2) On the main **Slide show** screen select ⬛ **All images**. Press ▲ / ▼ to change this to ⬛ **Date**, ⬛ **Folder**, ⬛ **Movies**, ⬛ **Stills**, or ★ **Rating** as required. If ⬛ **Date**, ⬛ **Folder**, or ★ **Rating** are selected you can view and alter options that refine what's viewed during the slide show by pressing **DISP.** (there are no options for ⬛ **All images**, ⬛ **Movies**, or ⬛ **Stills**). Press ⬛ when you're finished.

3) Select **Set up**. **Display time** lets you choose how long each image will remain on screen during the slide show, while **Repeat** can be set to either **Enable** or **Disable** depending on whether you want your slide show to repeat once it's run through the selected images.

Transition effect lets you set how one image replaces another during the slide show.

Background music lets you choose what music to play during the slide show (the music must be copied to the memory card of your Rebel T6/EOS 1300D using EOS Utility). Having made your changes, press MENU to continue.

4) Select **Start** to begin the slide show.

5) To pause and restart the slide show press ⬛, and press MENU to stop the slide show and return to the main slide show screen. If you're playing movies, turning ⬛ will alter the volume during playback.

› Rating

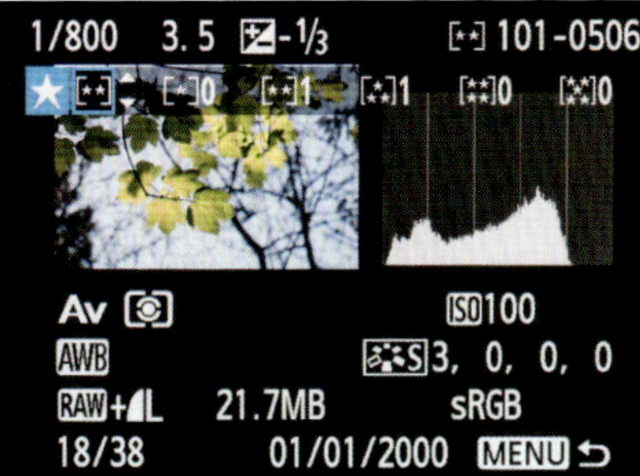

Rating lets you tag individual images with one to five stars (★) or no stars—**Off** (the default). The rating you set is then embedded in the selected image's metadata and can be used as a filter for **Image jump w/**, **Slide show**, or on your computer when they're viewed in Digital Picture Professional.

The most obvious use of **Rating** is to rank images according to their technical or esthetic success. However, it can also be used more imaginatively—you could use **Rating** to sort images into categories, for example, with 1 ★ for portraits, 2 ★ for landscapes, and so on.

CATEGORIZED »
Using Rating imaginatively means you can create interesting Slide show collections as you shoot.

Changing the rating

1) Select **Rating**.

2) Press ◀ / ▶ to skip through the images on the memory card. To view three photographs on screen at once press ▦ / ⊖; to view a single image press ⊕.

3) Press ▲ / ▼ to decrease or increase the **Rating** value when the image that you want to rate is displayed. Repeat steps 2–3 to add **Rating** values to other images.

4) When you've finished, press MENU to return to the main ▶ menu screen.

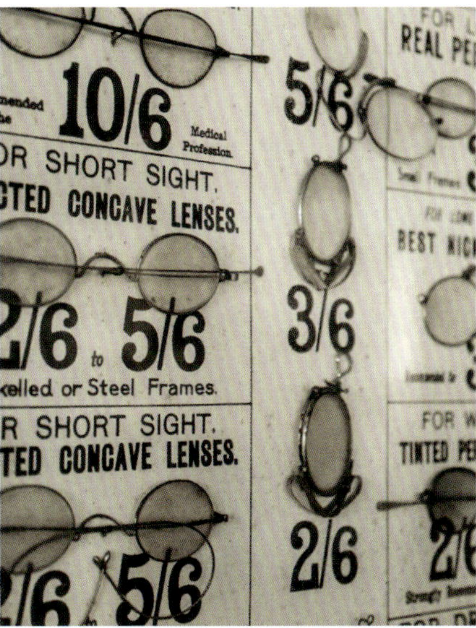

› Auto power off

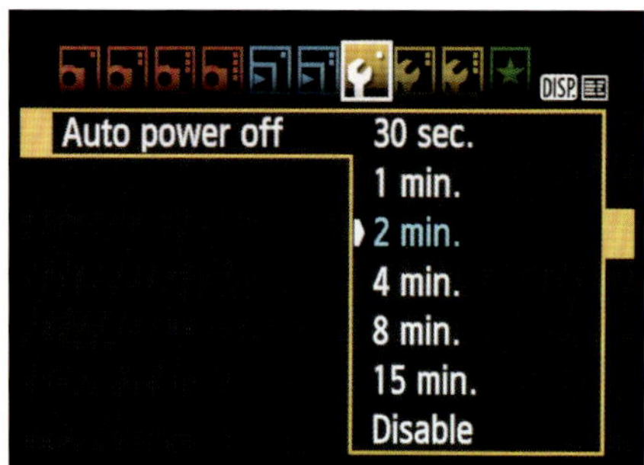

› Auto rotate

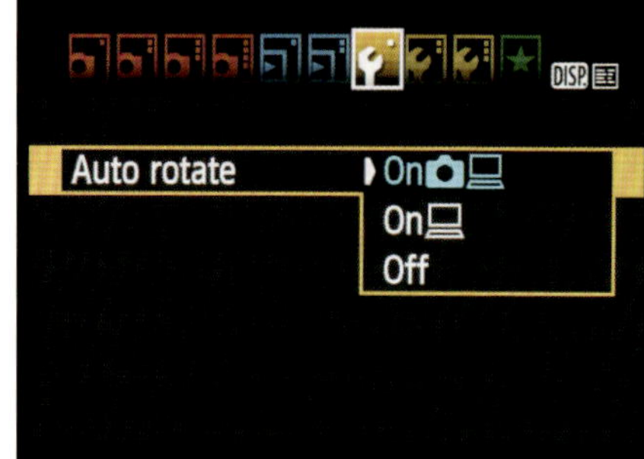

If you leave your Rebel T6/EOS 1300D switched on, but don't touch it, it will eventually power down to conserve the battery. You can use **Auto power off** to specify the length of time before this happens, choosing between **30 sec.**, and **1**, **2**, **4**, **8**, or **15 min**. When the camera is powered down it can be woken by lightly pressing on the shutter-release button, MENU, **DISP.**, ▶, or ◻.

When **Auto power off** is set to **Disable**, the camera will not power down, although the LCD screen will switch off after 30 minutes of inactivity (or if you press **DISP.**).

> **Note**
> See chapter two for information about **Format card**.

Auto rotate lets you choose whether vertical still images you shoot are rotated or not during playback.

On rotates the images so that they remain vertical on the LCD and on your computer (once they've been copied there from your memory card). This means that vertical images will appear relatively small on the camera's LCD screen.

On doesn't rotate the images when you view them on the camera's LCD, but it does rotate them "behind-the-scenes" so they're in the correct orientation when copied to your computer.

Off does not rotate the images, either on your camera or when copied to your computer; you will need to use image-editing software to rotate them to the correct orientation.

› File numbering

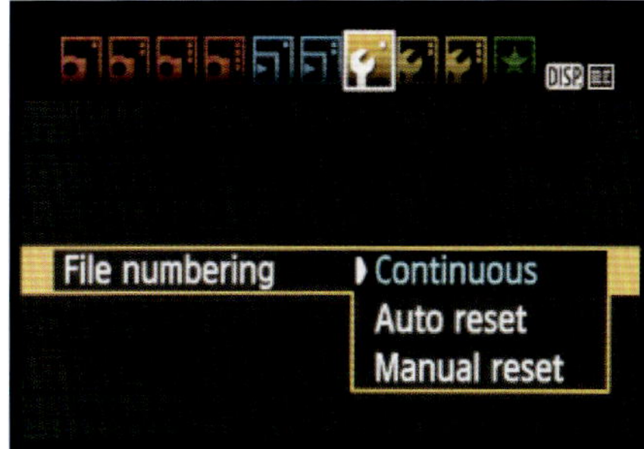

› Select folder

Every time a file is written to the memory card it's assigned a file name. The last four characters before the file type suffix are numbers—a count of the number of images you've created starting from 0001.

Select **Continuous** and the count continues up to 9999 before cycling round to 0001 again, no matter how many different folders you create or memory cards you use.

However, select **Auto reset** and your Rebel T6/EOS 1300D will reset the count to 0001 every time you create a new folder or swap to an empty memory card.

If you begin a new photographic project and you want to keep those images separate, **Manual reset** is useful. When this option is selected, a new folder is created on the memory card and the file name count is reset to 0001.

Every still image or movie you shoot on your Rebel T6/EOS 1300D is stored in a folder on the memory card. When you format a memory card a new, default folder is created automatically. You can also create new folders and use those instead. There are a variety of reasons for doing this. You could, for example, create a new folder for a particular shooting session, which will keep those images separate from all the others on the memory card.

To create a new folder choose **Select folder** followed by **Create folder**. Confirm the creation of the folder by selecting **OK** (or **Cancel** to return to **Select folder** screen). Folders created on the Rebel T6/ EOS 1300D use a three number system starting with 100 and continuing up to 999. The numbers are followed by the word

CANON. The new folder number will be one more than the highest folder number already on the memory card.

To swap between folders, choose **Select folder** and then highlight and select the desired folder name. Until you choose or create a new folder, the Rebel T6/EOS 1300D will save all subsequent images and movies shot into this folder.

> **Notes**
>
> The first four characters of still images are IMG_ (or _IMG when **Color Space** is set to **Adobe RGB**). Movie files use MVI_.
>
> A folder can hold 9999 images. A new folder is automatically created when you reach this number. You can have 999 folders. However once you reach image 9999 in folder 999 you won't be able to add any more images to the card even if it's not full.
>
> You can create new folders on the memory card whenever it's attached to your computer. If you do this you must use the naming convention described above. The five-letter word part of the name can only use alphanumeric characters (a–z, A–Z, or 0–9) or an underscore "_." No other characters (including "space") are allowed. The new folder must be within the DCIM folder.

› Screen color

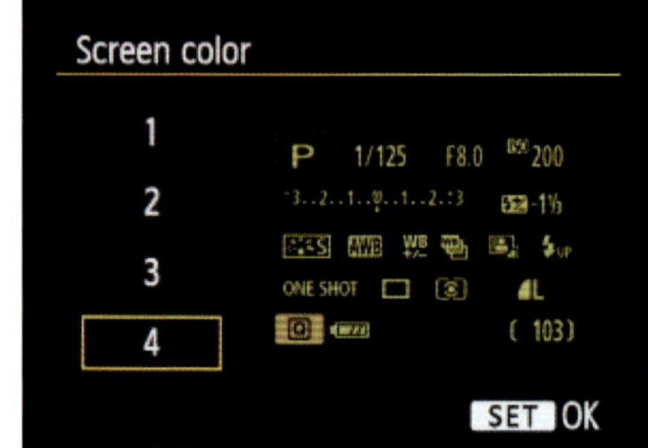

By default, the background color of the Rebel T6/EOS 1300D's shooting setting and **Q** screens are black with white text. **Screen color** lets you choose between one of four different colors: **1** (black), **2** (light gray with black text), **3** (brown with white text), or **4** (dark green with mid-green text). There's no right or wrong answer to which is preferable—it's purely down to personal taste.

» SET UP 2

› LCD brightness

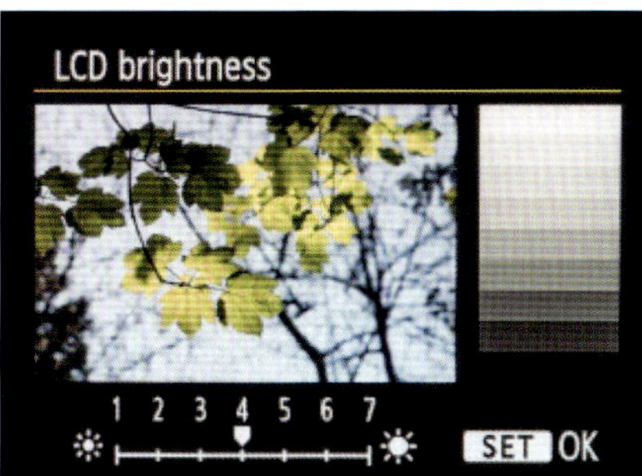

› LCD off/on btn

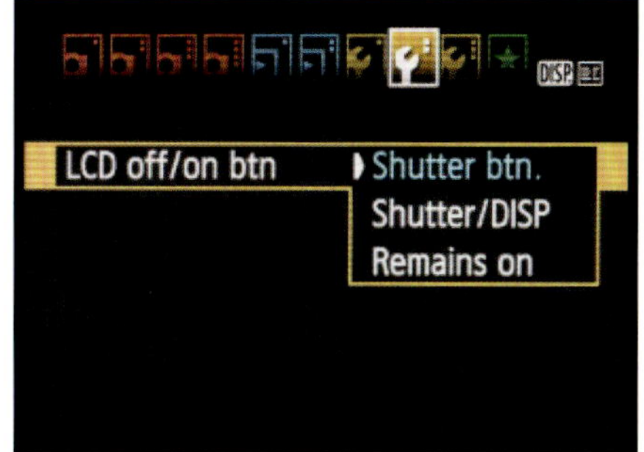

Clearly seeing a camera's LCD screen can be difficult in bright light, especially when the sun's shining on it. Creating a shade with your hands is one solution (although only really practical when your camera is mounted on a tripod); another solution is to temporarily adjust the **LCD brightness**.

Select **LCD brightness** and then press ◀ to darken the LCD or ▶ to brighten it. Ideally you should be able to distinguish all eight of the gray bars on the right of the screen. Press (SET) when you've adjusted the brightness to the level you desire.

The detailed shooting settings screen is a useful way to check the current settings of your camera. By default, when **LCD off/ on btn** is set to **Shutter btn.**, the LCD turns off when you press the shutter-release button down half way and comes back on again when you release the shutter-release button. This means the LCD isn't distracting when you look through the viewfinder.

However, select **Shutter/DISP.** and the LCD won't turn back on again until you press **DISP.** after releasing the shutter-release button.

Selecting **Remains on** will mean the LCD will stay on permanently, even when you press down on the shutter-release button. This arguably makes the LCD a distraction when looking through the viewfinder, but it also means you'll always know which shooting settings are in use.

a good choice: the subdued color scheme won't affect your night vision as much as the other options (particularly if you also reduce the LCD brightness to its minimum).

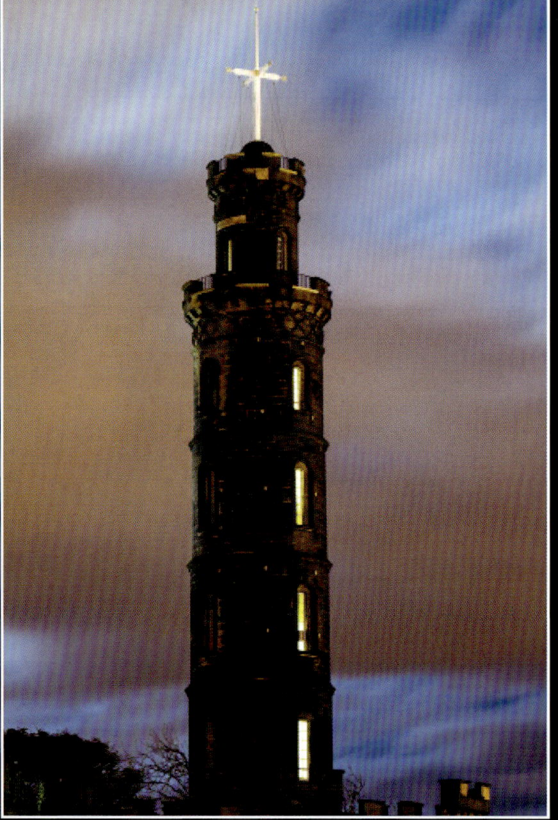

› Language

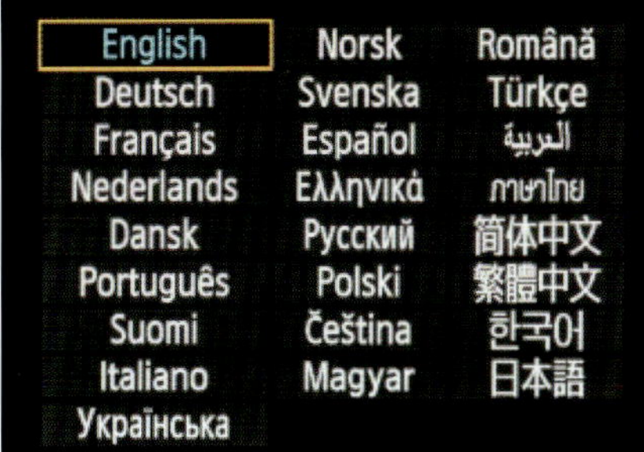

The Rebel T6/EOS 1300D can display the menu and shooting options in the following languages: English; German; French; Dutch; Danish; Portuguese; Finnish; Italian; Ukrainian; Norwegian; Swedish; Spanish; Greek; Russian; Polish; Czech; Hungarian; Romanian; Turkish; Arabic; Thai; Simplified Chinese; Chinese (traditional); Korean; Japanese.

Note
See page 28 for information about changing **Date/Time/Zone**.

› Clean manually

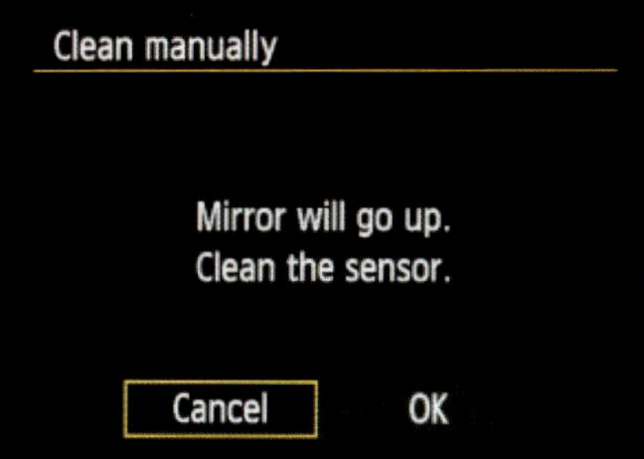

Unlike some of Canon's other DSLRs, the Rebel T6/EOS 1300D doesn't offer automatic sensor cleaning. If dust starts to become a problem you can send your camera to an approved Canon service center for cleaning (and be charged for the privilege), or select **Clean manually** and clean it yourself.

The simplest cleaning tool is a blower, which can be used to blow the dust from the sensor. However, care must be taken not to touch the surface of the sensor with the tip of the blower, otherwise the sensor could be scratched.

For more persistent dust (such as pollen, which often adheres to sensors) you'll need to use a wet-cleaning system. This usually involves brushing a swab, moistened with a cleaning agent, across the sensor. Most photography stores offer a sensor-cleaning service or will advise on the cleaning system you require.

Manual cleaning with a blower

1) Select **Clean manually** and the mirror will swing up and the shutter will open. Remove the lens from your camera.

2) Hold your camera so that the front is facing downward. Place the tip of your blower inside the lens mount and squeeze it, taking care not to touch the sensor as you blow it.

3) When you've finished, replace the lens and turn the camera off.

Warning!

Only use a freshly charged battery when cleaning the camera manually. If in doubt, use the optional DC Coupler DR-E10 and Compact Power Adaptor CA-PS700 or ACK-E10 AC Adaptor to power your camera during the cleaning process.

› Feature guide

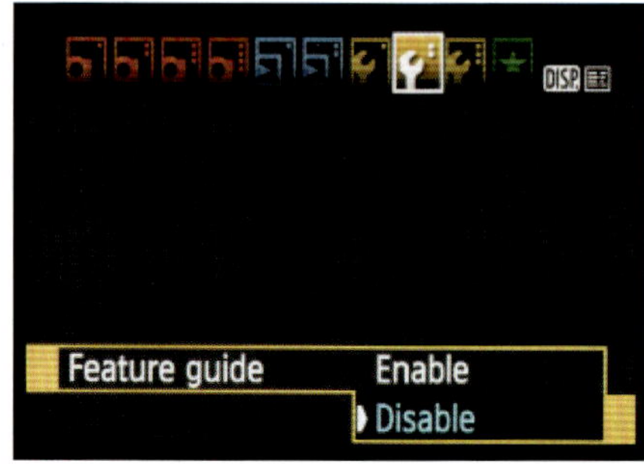

Setting **Feature guide** to **Enable** displays short, but useful, notes on the LCD screen. These notes are simple explanations of the various shooting functions as you select them. Once you feel confident about using your camera, selecting **Disable** will turn these notes off. This will marginally speed up the operation of your camera and make the menus feel less cluttered.

› GPS device settings

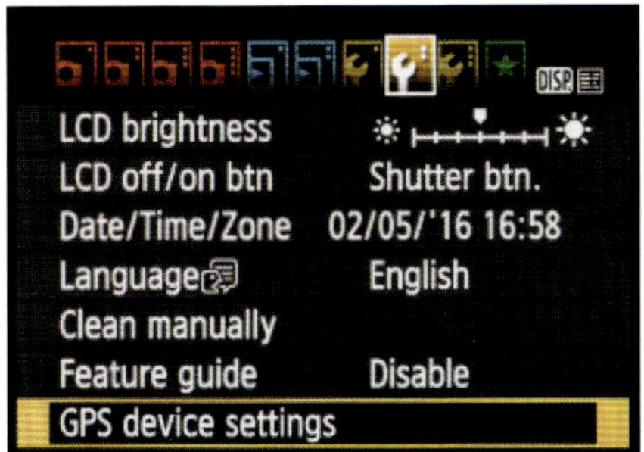

Access settings specific to Canon's optional GP-E2 GPS unit (this menu is only available when the GPS unit is fitted to your Rebel T6/EOS 1300D).

Note
See pages 235-237 for information about **Wi-Fi/NFC** and **Wi-Fi function**.

» SET UP 3

› Certification Logo Display

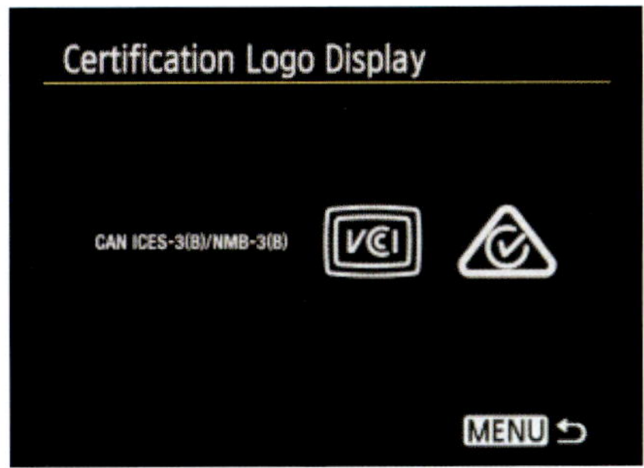

Certification Logo Display is a slightly eccentric menu option. When selected all you can do is view a series of graphics and logos indicating that your Rebel T6/EOS 1300D has been passed as fit for purpose by certain standards organizations. This information is irrelevant to how you use your camera, so **Certification Logo Display** is an option you may look at once (if at all) and then never view again.

› Custom Functions (C.Fn)

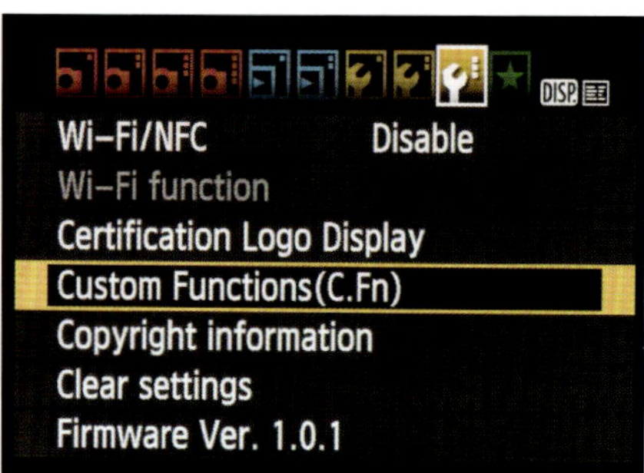

Custom functions let you fine tune certain shooting functions, so you can customize the camera to your personal way of working. There are 11 custom functions in total, divided into four groups based on the function type: C.Fn I: Exposure, C.Fn II: Image, C.Fn III: Autofocus/Drive, and C.Fn IV: Operation/Others.

If you select **Clear Settings > Clear all Custom Func. (C.Fn)** (found lower down

C.Fn I: Exposure		📷 shooting
1	Exposure level increments	Yes
2	ISO expansion	Yes
3	Flash sync. speed in **Av** Mode	Yes
C.Fn II: Image		
4	Long exp. noise reduction	Yes
5	High ISO speed noise reduct'n	Yes
6	Highlight tone priority	Yes
C.Fn III: Autofocus/Drive		
7	AF-assist beam firing	With AFQuick
C.Fn IV: Operation/Others		
8	Shutter/AE lock button	Yes
9	Assign (SET) button	Yes (except option 3)
10	Flash button function	Yes
11	LCD display when power ON	–

the 🔧 menu) then any custom functions you change will revert to their default settings. Custom functions only apply to still images and not to movie shooting.

Setting Custom Functions

1) Select **Custom Functions (C.Fn)**.

2) Press ◄ / ► to skip between the 11 custom function screens. Press (SET) when you reach the custom function you want to alter—the current custom functions settings are displayed below their respective numbers, at the bottom of the LCD screen.

3) Press ▲ / ▼ to highlight the desired option, followed by (SET) to select it.

4) Repeat steps 2 and 3 if there are additional functions that you wish to alter. If not, press MENU to return to the main 🔧 screen.

› C.Fn I-1 Exposure level increments

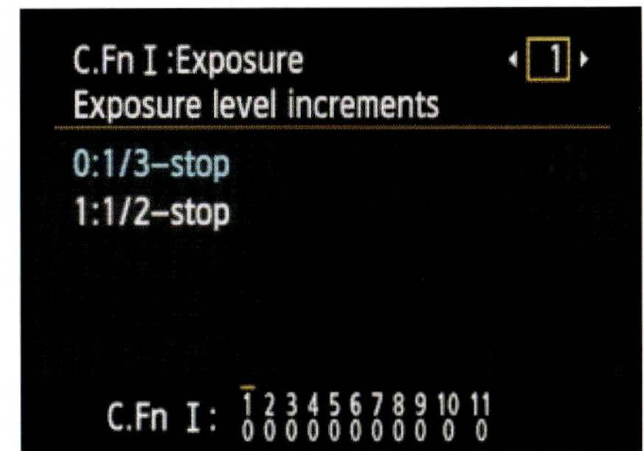

This option allows you to set either **0: 1/3-stop** or **1: 1/2-stop** increments for exposure operations such as shutter speed, exposure compensation, and so on. When set to **1: 1/2-stop**, the exposure controls will be coarser, making it less easy to set the exact exposure (although the very small difference between ½ stop and ⅓ stop is not noticeable in most situations).

The main advantage of setting **1: 1/2-stop** over **0: 1/3-stop** is that setting the exposure parameters will be speeded up slightly as there will be a smaller range of options to choose from.

› C.Fn I-2 ISO expansion

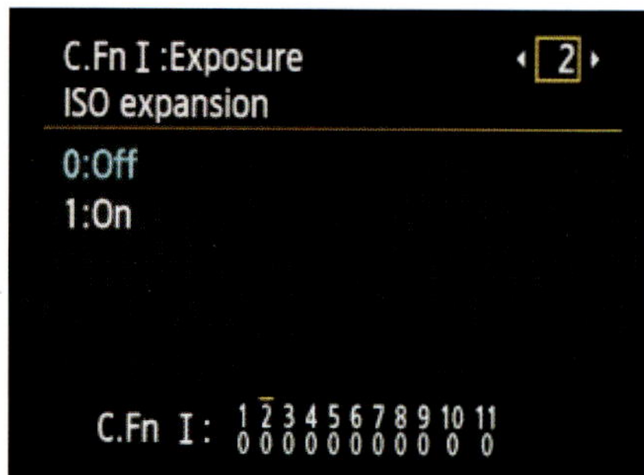

When **ISO expansion** is set to **1: On**, an extra option is added to the ISO selection screen—**H**—which is equivalent to ISO 12800. However, although this may seem a useful option, noise when **H** is selected will be very high, so it should only be used if you desperately need to maintain a certain exposure setting in low light.

If you set **ISO expansion** to **0: Off**, **H** won't appear on the ISO selection screen.

H cannot be used when **Highlight tone priority** is enabled.

› C.Fn I-3 Flash sync. speed in Av mode

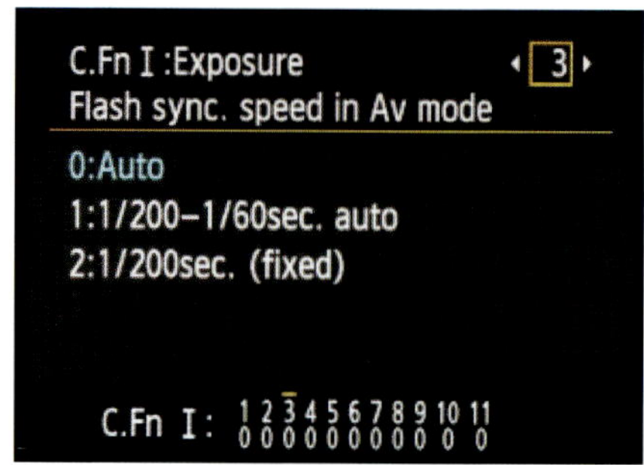

The fastest shutter speed your Rebel T6/ EOS 1300D can use with flash is 1/200 sec. (an exception to this rule is high speed sync [HSS] flash—described in chapter 5). However, there's no reason why 1/200 sec. should be the only shutter speed selected when using flash; slower shutter speeds can be used too.

If you're shooting in low light you may find that 1/200 sec. is too fast to record details in areas that are not illuminated by flash. The technique of using a longer shutter speed than the sync speed is known as "slow sync flash."

Slow sync flash lets you accurately expose parts of a scene lit only by ambient light (which would typically be the areas behind your subject and therefore at a greater distance to the flash).

When using **Av** mode, you normally have no choice over the shutter speed that is selected automatically by the Rebel T6/EOS 1300D. **Flash sync. speed in Av mode** lets you exert some influence over the range of shutter speeds automatically selected by the Rebel T6/EOS 1300D.

Slow sync is most effective when the ambient light is low but still present. However, the lower the ambient light levels the longer the shutter speed will need to be. This means you'll need to use a tripod or run the risk of camera shake marring your images. See chapter 5 for more information about using flash.

Option	Result
0: Auto	The Rebel T6/EOS 1300D is free to select any shutter speed between 30 sec. and 1/200 sec., according to the ambient light level. This means that the risk of camera shake is high if a slow shutter speed is selected. However, areas of an image not illuminated by flash are more likely to be correctly exposed. High speed sync with a compatible Speedlite is still possible.
1: 1/200–1/60sec. auto	To minimize the risk of camera shake, the Rebel T6/EOS 1300D will only select a shutter speed between 1/60 sec. and 1/200 sec. This may result in underexposure of any areas not illuminated by flash.
2: 1/200sec. (fixed)	Only the sync speed of 1/200 sec. is available. Non-flash-lit areas may be grossly underexposed, but the risk of camera shake is minimized.

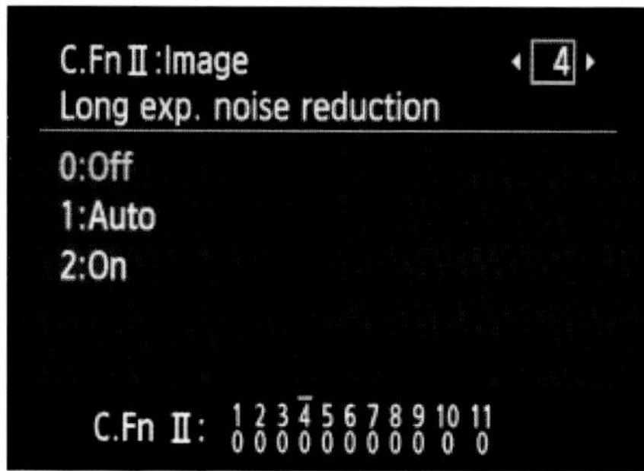

Electronic circuitry generates heat, and the longer an electronic device is active for, the hotter it becomes. This applies to the digital sensor inside your Rebel T6/EOS 1300D, and the heat caused when a sensor is on and exposed to light creates a type of noise in an image known as "thermal noise." Typically, the risk of thermal noise increases when exposures greater than 30 sec. are used.

If you set **Long exp. noise reduction** to **1: Auto**, your Rebel T6/EOS 1300D will—if necessary—suppress thermal noise if there's a risk that it may be visible when exposure times longer than 1 sec. are used.

When **Long exp. noise reduction** is set to **2: On**, the camera will always perform noise reduction on exposures of 1 sec. or longer.

Thermal noise is difficult to remove in postproduction, so dealing with it in-camera (even when shooting Raw)

is advisable. However, there is a downside: because of the processing involved, your long exposures will take twice as long as the shutter speed (so a 1 sec. exposure will take 2 sec. to shoot and process with noise reduction, and so on). This can make using long exposures a drawn-out affair, particularly as you cannot shoot more images until the camera has finished processing the image.

Using **Long exp. noise reduction** also increases the risk that the batteries in your Rebel T6/EOS 1300D will deplete before the exposure is finished (which means that you'll lose your photograph).

When **Long exp. noise reduction** is set to **0: Off**, no noise reduction will be performed when shooting long exposures. This will shorten the exposure times though it may lead to the need for extensive remedial work during postproduction.

› C.Fn II-5 High ISO speed noise reduct'n

High ISO speed noise reduct'n lets you decide whether your Rebel T6/EOS 1300D will try to tackle high ISO noise and to what degree.

The greatest amount of noise reduction is applied when this function is set to **2: Strong**. Unfortunately, **2: Strong** doesn't just remove noise—it's just as effective at removing some of the desirable fine detail in your images too. **0: Standard** and **1: Low** offer a better compromise between noise and loss of detail.

Your Rebel T6/EOS 1300D will not perform any noise reduction when **Disable** is set, so if there's noise in your images you'll need to tackle it in postproduction.

Note

Your camera has more work to do when it's processing an image with **High ISO speed noise reduct'n** set to **2: Strong**. This will cause a noticeable drop in the burst rate when shooting using Continuous drive mode.

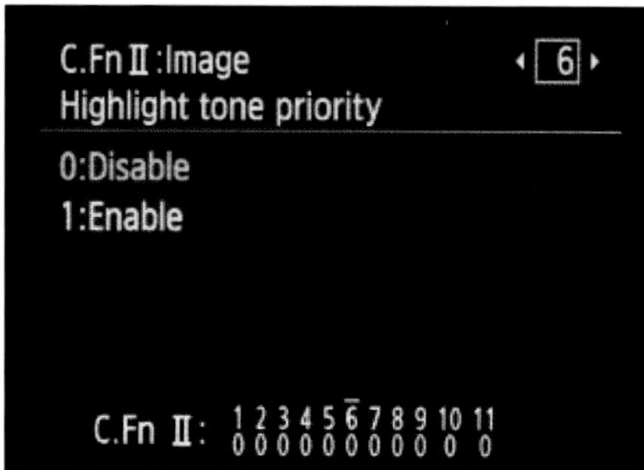

Note

Although you can enable **Highlight tone priority** when shooting Raw, you can achieve the same result by underexposing your images by 1 stop and then adjusting the image's tone curve during postproduction to increase the exposure. This would make the retention of highlight detail more likely (and let you set the required level of brightness for the highlights).

High-contrast lighting is often problematic, and usually requires you to keep detail in the highlights or shadows but not both. When shooting JPEG, **Highlight tone priority** is a useful way to tackle this.

When set to **1: Enable**, **Highlight tone priority** works to prevent the overexposure (or clipping) of highlights. However, it can't work miracles and there are limits; highlights are still likely to be lost in very high contrast lighting. **Highlight tone priority** will also increase the risk that noise will be visible in the shadow areas of your images.

Other drawbacks are that **Highlight tone priority** restricts the usable ISO range to 200–6400 and it cannot be used at the same time as **Auto Lighting Optimizer**.

When **Highlight tone priority** is active, **D+** is displayed in the viewfinder and on the LCD.

› C.Fn III-7 AF-assist beam firing

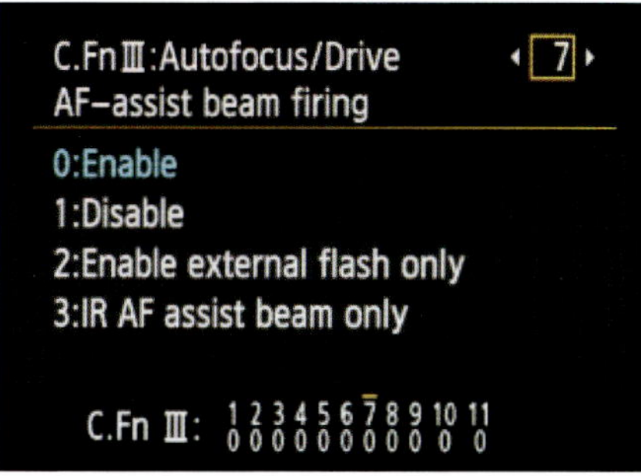

The Rebel T6/EOS 1300D's AF system can start to struggle in low light, particularly when a lens with a relatively small maximum aperture is fitted.

When **AF-assist beam firing** is set to **0: Enable**, the built-in flash (or attached Speedlite) will pulse light when needed to provide illumination to focus with.

However, this can be distracting if you're shooting wildlife or documentary imagery, in which case **1: Disable** will be the preferable option.

The other options allow you to use a Speedlite as an AF assist lamp. **2: Enable external flash only** will ignore the built-in flash, and only use the Speedlite; **3: IR AF assist beam only** uses the infrared beam available on certain Speedlite models to assist the autofocus.

› C.Fn IV-8 Shutter/AE lock button

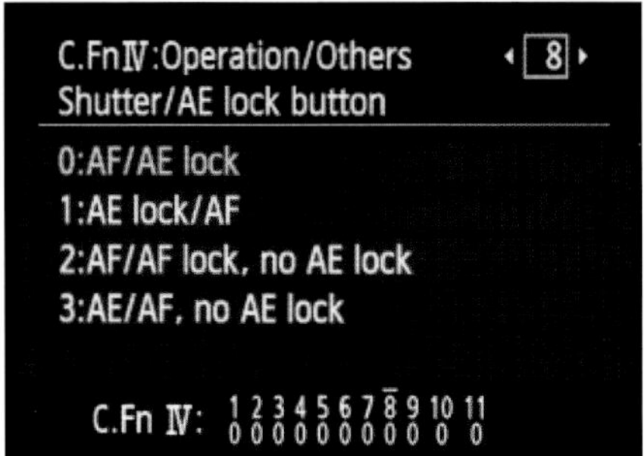

This custom function sets how focus and exposure are activated or locked using the shutter-release button and ✳ button.

0: AF/AE lock activates and locks both the metering and AF when the shutter-release button is pressed down half way (exposure can also be locked using ✳).

When **1: AE lock/AF** is selected, ✳ activates autofocus, while pressing the shutter-release button down half way activates and locks the exposure.

If you're using AI Servo mode, **2: AF/ AF lock, no AE lock** lets you temporarily pause AF by pressing and holding down ✳. Exposure is not set until the shutter-release button is pressed down fully.

3: AE/AF, no AE lock lets you turn AI Servo on or off by repeatedly pressing ✳. Exposure is again not set until the shutter-release button is pressed down fully.

› C.Fn IV-9 Assign ⒮ button

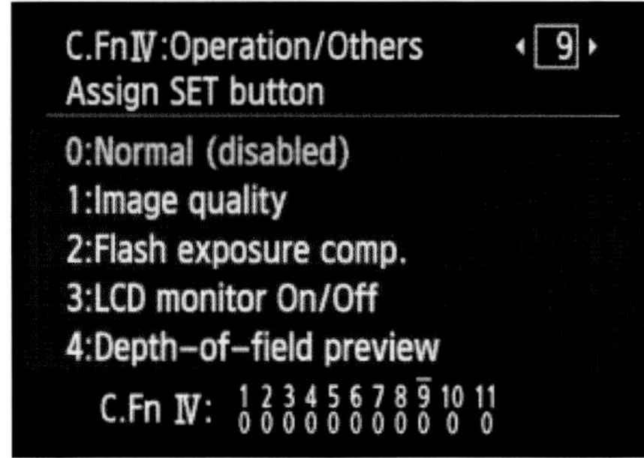

⒮ is a "soft" button that can be reprogrammed to perform one of a number of different functions in shooting mode. Which you choose is largely dependent on your personal shooting needs. The default setting is **0: Normal (disabled)** so that ⒮ has no function.

Select **1: Image Quality** and you can view the **Image quality** screen by pressing ⒮ allowing you to swap quickly between JPEG and Raw.

If you're a regular flash user, you may prefer **2: Flash exposure comp.**, which displays the flash exposure screen instead.

3: LCD monitor On/Off toggles the LCD on and off whenever ⒮ is pressed. However, this duplicates the **DISP.** button, so is arguably less useful.

If you're a landscape photographer you may find **4: Depth-of-field preview** preferable. Select this option and when ⒮ is held down the aperture in the lens is closed to its set value. This lets you see how the selected aperture affects depth of field, both in the viewfinder and on the LCD. The only downside to this is that the viewfinder may darken considerably (you may need to wait a few seconds for your eyes to adjust) or the Live View display may look more grainy than normal. However, this is a small price for a function that gives you a more accurate preview.

Notes
The aperture is normally held open at its maximum setting when you view your scene through the viewfinder or on the rear LCD screen. This makes for a brighter viewfinder image and crisper Live View display, but it also means you always see depth of field at its minimum extent.

Depth-of-field preview is particularly useful for landscape photography, which typically requires the use of small apertures to maximize depth of field (the effects of which aren't visible unless the depth-of-field preview is selected).

› C.Fn IV-10 Flash button function

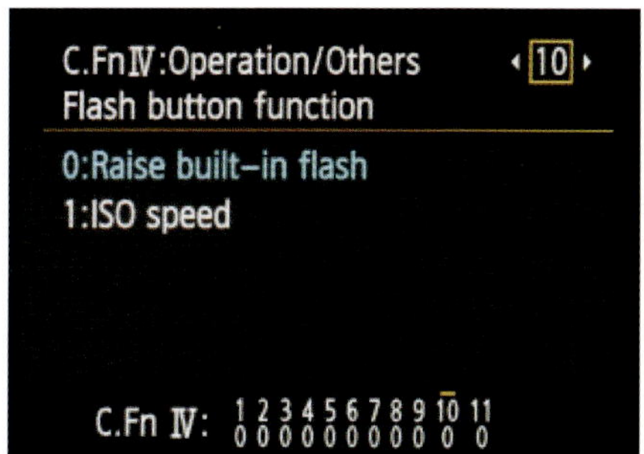

The ⚡ button is another "soft" button. By default, pressing ⚡ will raise the flash (**0: Raise built-in flash**), but if you set **IV-10 Flash button function** to **1: ISO speed**, the button is re-purposed so that the ISO screen is displayed instead (which means there's no way to raise the flash).

This may seem like a restriction, but if you rarely use flash (and frequently use Live View) it's worth doing. This is because in Live View the ▲/ISO button is used to move the AF point around the screen; it can't be used to set ISO (that can only usually be done via the **Q** screen).

Depth of field is at its smallest extent when a lens is set at its maximum aperture. Focusing therefore needs to be precise, as there's less depth of field to hide focusing errors. For this shot I switched to manual focus and focused on the sheep's eye, which needed to be the sharpest part in the shot.

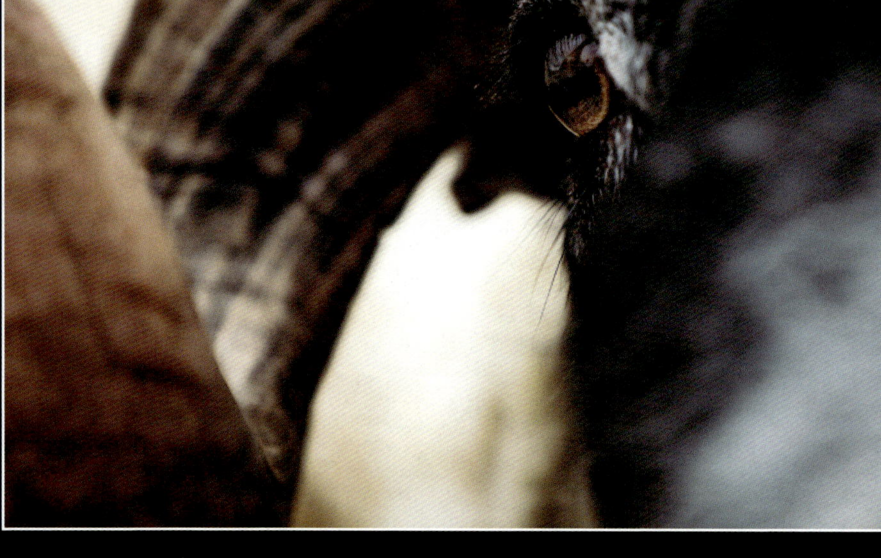

Settings

> Focal length: 50mm

> Aperture: f/2.8

> Shutter speed: 1/640 sec.

> ISO: 100

» ABSTRACT

Photography is often seen as a literal medium in that you record "reality" as you shoot (unlike painting, which is far more subjective). However, there's no need to produce conventional photos of familiar subjects. Getting in close and excluding context is a useful way to produce more abstract and visually intriguing imagery.

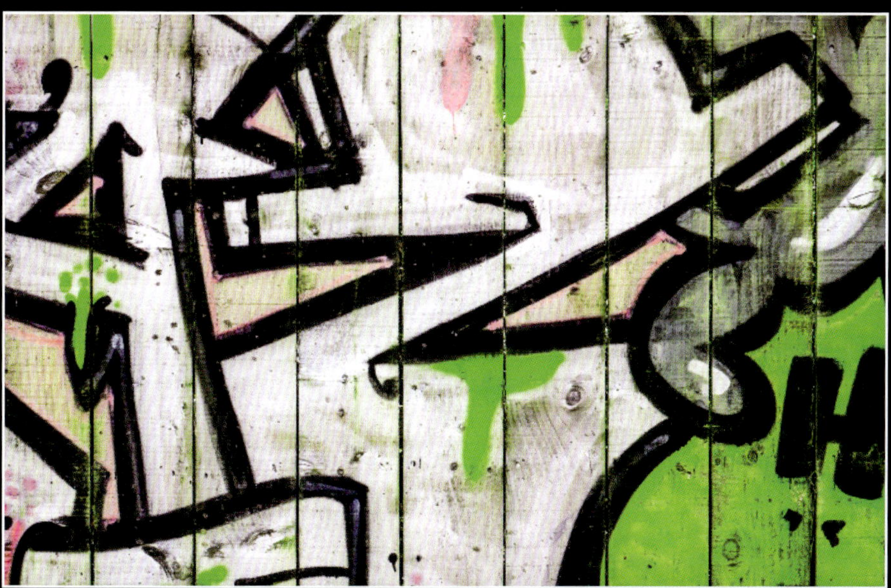

Settings
> Focal length: 50mm
> Aperture: f/5.6
> Shutter speed: 1/80 sec.
> ISO: 100

› C.Fn IV-11 LCD display when power ON

› Copyright information

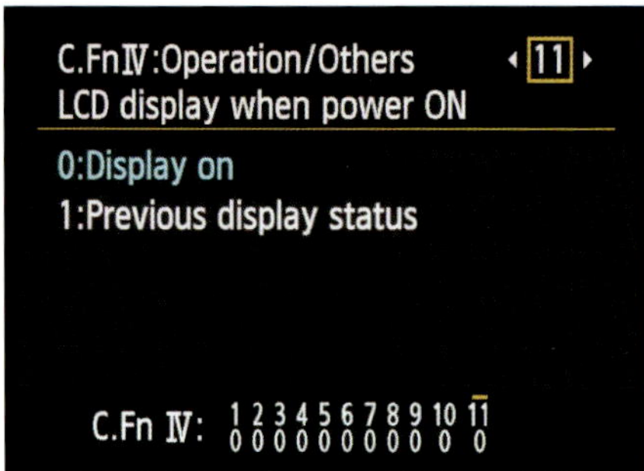

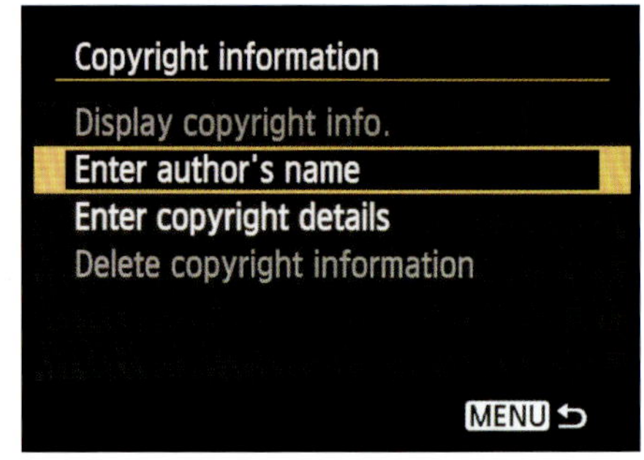

This option sets the status of the LCD when you first switch your Rebel T6/EOS 1300D on. Select **0: Display on** and the shooting settings screen is always displayed initially. However, select **1: Previous display status** and, if you turn off the LCD by pressing **DISP.** and then turn off the camera, the LCD will stay blank when you turn the camera back on again. You can only view the shooting settings screen by pressing **DISP.**. This is a useful, albeit minor, way to save battery power.

Copyright protects the rights of anyone who creates something. This means that every image you shoot on your Rebel T6/ EOS 1300D belongs to you and no one else—you have the right to request some form of payment should someone use one of your images without permission. The first step toward verifying your ownership of an image is to automatically add **Copyright information** to the metadata of your images as you shoot.

Setting copyright information
1) Select **Copyright information**.

2) Select either **Enter author's name** or **Enter copyright details**.

3) On the text entry screen press Q to jump between the text entry box and the rows of alphanumeric characters below. Press ✛ or turn ⚙ to highlight

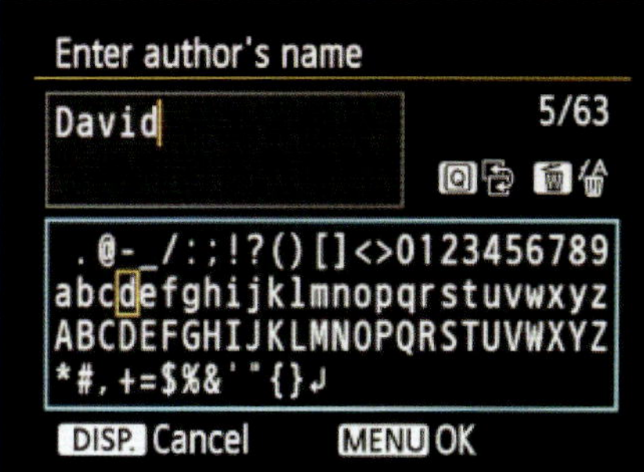

the required character and then press (SET) to add it to the text entry box. If you accidentally select the wrong character, press 🗑/Av⊞ to delete it.

4) Press MENU and then select **OK** when you've completed the text entry. This will save the details and return you to the main **Copyright Information** menu (press **DISP.** to return to the main **Copyright Information** screen without saving).

Other Copyright information settings

Selecting **Display copyright info.** displays the currently set copyright information. If no copyright information is set the option is grayed out and cannot be selected.

Selecting **Delete copyright information** will remove the current copyright information saved on the camera (but does not remove copyright details added to the metadata of images

Notes

You would generally set the same information for **Enter author's name** and **Enter copyright details**. However, copyright in an image (or any created work) can be assigned to anyone, so you could enter someone else as the copyright owner (your employer if the photographs are being taken for work purposes, for example).

Some social media web sites strip out the copyright information from images when they're uploaded to the site. Adding a subtle copyright watermark to images intended for use on social media is a good habit to develop (don't add the watermark to the originals though—use copies of those images).

already saved on the memory card). Again, if no copyright information is set, the option is grayed out.

› Clear settings

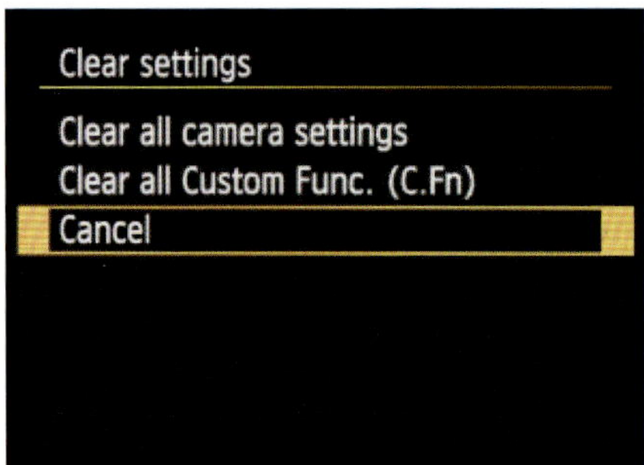

› Firmware Ver.

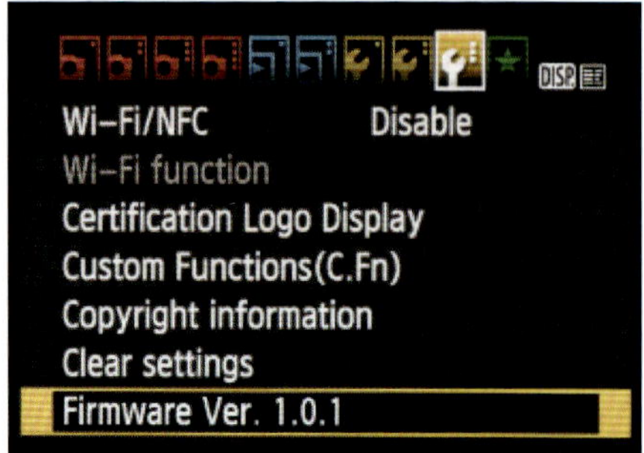

Choosing this option allows you to either **Clear all camera settings** on your Rebel T6/EOS 1300D, restoring them to their original factory settings, or **Clear all Custom Func. (C.Fn)** you may have set. Once you commit yourself to this you cannot undo your decision!

Clearing settings

1) Select **Clear settings**.

2) Select **Clear all camera settings** or **Clear all Custom Func. (C.Fn)**. Select **OK** to reset your camera, or **Cancel** to return to the **Clear settings** sub-menu without clearing the settings.

Underpinning the operation of the Rebel T6/EOS 1300D is firmware, which ensures your camera runs smoothly. However, no firmware is entirely free of problems. At the time of writing, there are no reported issues with the Rebel T6/EOS 1300D, but that doesn't mean there aren't any waiting to be discovered. Canon will occasionally release new firmware to cure bugs that have been found.

More happily, firmware is also sometimes released to radically improve a camera by adding new features. Canon will announce on its web site when a firmware update is available, as well as by email to registered users.

Full instructions on how to update your camera will be included with the firmware update, but if you're not confident about doing this yourself you can get the firmware updated at a Canon Service Center (for a fee).

» MY MENU ★

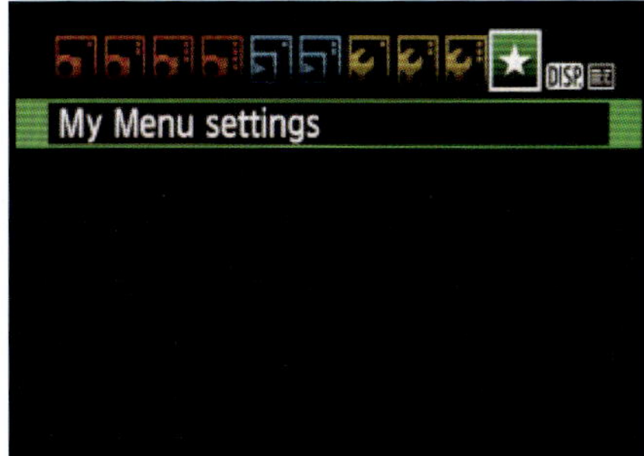

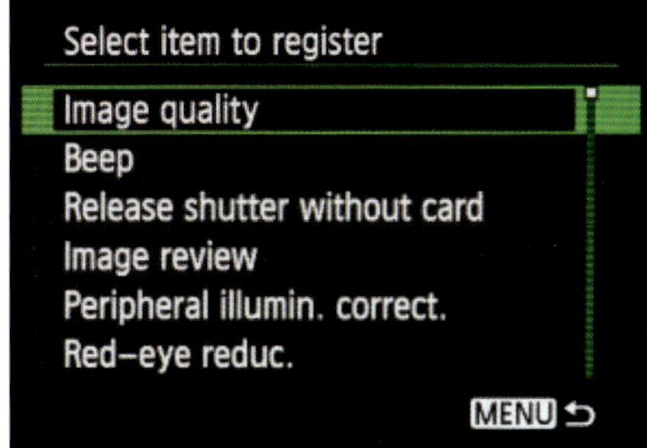

My Menu allows you to group together six menu settings onto one screen, letting you find and alter them both quickly and easily. It's worth leaving ★ until you're familiar with your Rebel T6/EOS 1300D, so you can make an informed decision about which menu settings you use most often.

Adding options to My Menu

1) Press MENU and navigate to the ★ tab.

2) Select **My Menu settings**, followed by **Register to My Menu.**

3) Press ▲ / ▼ to move up and down the function list.

4) Press (SET) when an option you want to add to My Menu is highlighted. Select **OK** to continue, or **Cancel** to return to the **Register to My Menu** screen without adding the function. When a function has been added to My Menu it will no longer be selectable.

5) Continue to add functions (up to six) as required and then press MENU to return to the **My Menu settings** menu.

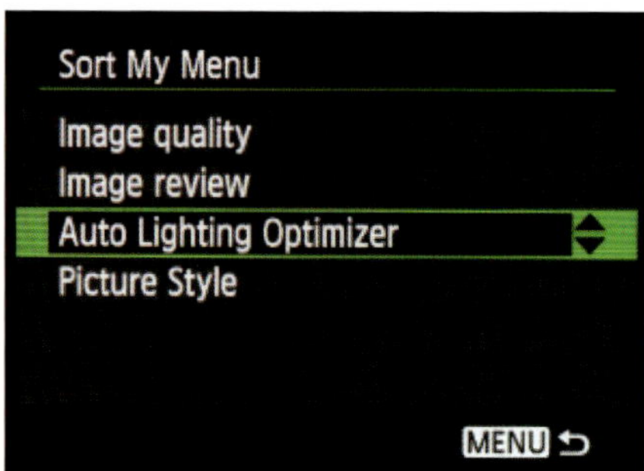

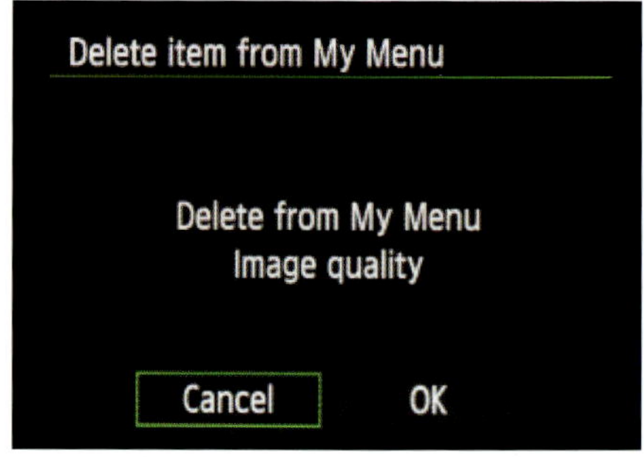

Altering the order of options registered to My Menu

1) Select **My Menu settings**, followed by **Sort**.

2) Highlight the item that you want to move and press (SET). Use ▲ / ▼ to move the item up and down the list. Press (SET) you're happy with the positioning of the selected item in the function list.

3) Repeat step 2 to move other items up or down the list.

4) Press MENU to return to the main **My Menu** screen.

Deleting options registered to My Menu

1) Select **My Menu settings**.

2) To delete individual options from the list, select **Delete item/items**. Highlight the option you want to delete, press (SET), and then select **OK** to delete the option (or **Cancel** to return to the option list).

3) To delete every option on the list, select **Delete all items**. Select **OK** to clear the My Menu list (or **Cancel** to return to the main **My Menu** screen).

Note
Select **Enable** on **Display from My Menu** so that My Menu is always the first menu shown when you press MENU.

» SPEED

Configuring My Menu to suit your needs is useful when you have to work quickly. It's also useful when you want to minimize the number of button presses as you use your camera. In cold weather, the less time taken with gloves removed to change camera settings is always welcome.

Settings
> Focal length: 200mm
> Aperture: f/14
> Shutter speed: 2.5 sec.
> ISO 100

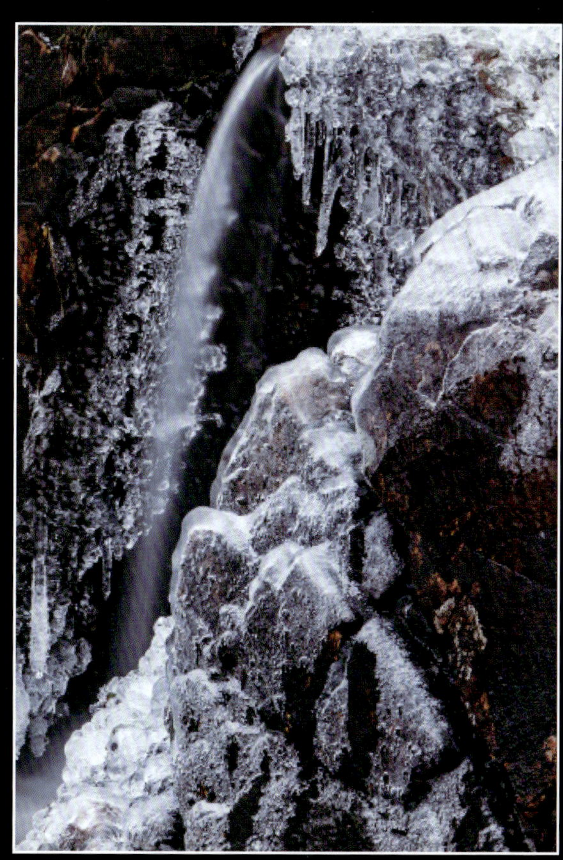

LENSES

Canon's lens range is extensive, with lenses to suit all pockets and styles of photography. If you factor in third-party lenses, you're spoilt for choice when it comes to lenses that are compatible with the Rebel T6/EOS 1300D.

Canon's EOS (Electro-Optical System) autofocus lens system was introduced in 1987. There are—at the time of writing—more than 80 Canon lenses that are compatible with the Rebel T6/EOS 1300D.

However, you don't have to stick to Canon lenses, as there are plenty of third-party lenses that have the advantage of being cheaper (sometimes by a wide margin), yet still capable of delivering great results. There are even types of third-party lenses that Canon doesn't manufacture. The three main third-party lens manufacturers are Sigma, Tamron, and Tokina.

This chapter is an introduction to lenses, covering some of the concepts you'll need to understand in order to make an informed decision about lenses you may want to add to your camera bag.

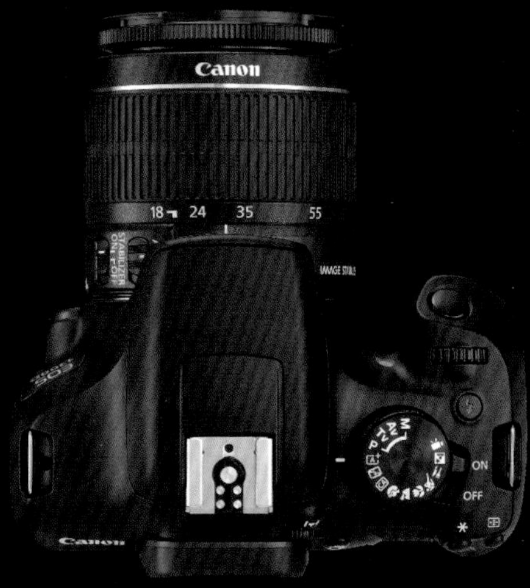

SLOW ⌃
The 18–55mm kit lens that is commonly sold with the Rebel T6/EOS 1300D is a good starting point, but it is limited in terms of reach and has a relatively slow maximum aperture.
© Canon

FAST »
There's an argument to be made that the lens you use is more important than the camera. Certainly, the lenses you own will constrain the types of images you shoot. This image, shot with a fast prime lens set at maximum aperture, wouldn't be possible with the slower kit lens.

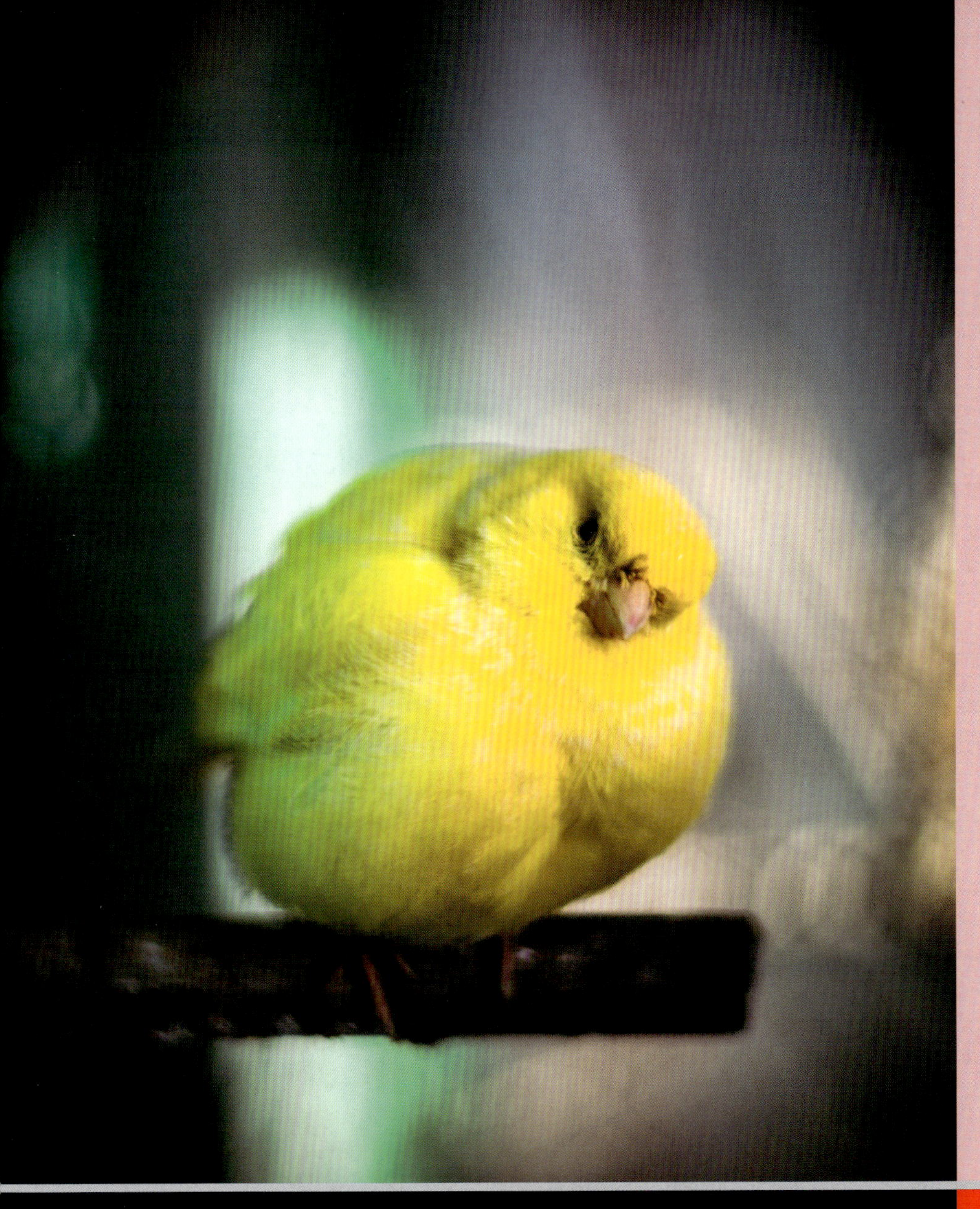

» LENS NAMING

Canon produces two ranges of lenses: EF-S and EF. EF-S lenses, such as the kit lenses commonly sold with the Rebel T6/EOS 1300D, will only fit on Canon's APS-C (cropped sensor) cameras, whereas Canon's EF lenses are compatible with all EOS cameras, with the exception of Canon's new mirrorless M-series models.

The EF range can be further subdivided into L-series lenses and non-L-series lenses. L-series lenses are the best lenses that Canon produces and their price reflects this; currently there are no EF-S L-series lenses available.

The S in EF-S stands for "short back focus." This refers to the fact that the rear element of the lens projects further inside the camera than an EF lens. It is this characteristic that makes them incompatible with full-frame cameras (the rear element would catch on the reflex mirror if you were able to fit an EF-S lens to a full-frame camera). If you think you might purchase a full-frame camera at some point it's a good idea to keep your EF-S lens collection to a minimum.

EF lenses make up the bulk of Canon's lens range, with a lineage stretching back to 1987. There are numerous discontinued EF lenses that are compatible with your Rebel T6/EOS 1300D and if you're prepared to buy pre-owned equipment, your lens choices will be far wider.

Note
Lenses are often referred to as either "fast" or "slow." A fast lens is one with a large maximum aperture (f/2.8 or larger), while a slow lens is one with a relatively small maximum aperture (f/4 or smaller). Prime lenses are generally "faster" than zooms.

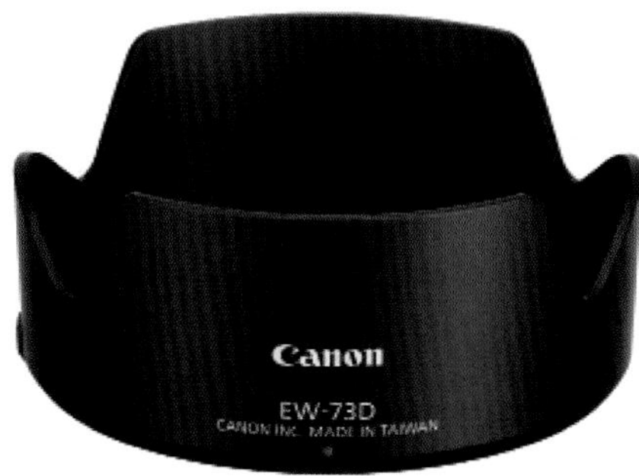

SHADED ⌃
One useful accessory for any lens is a lens hood. This fits onto the front of a lens and shades the front element from light sources that are just outside the field of view, which might otherwise cause lens flare.
© Canon

» ANATOMY OF A LENS

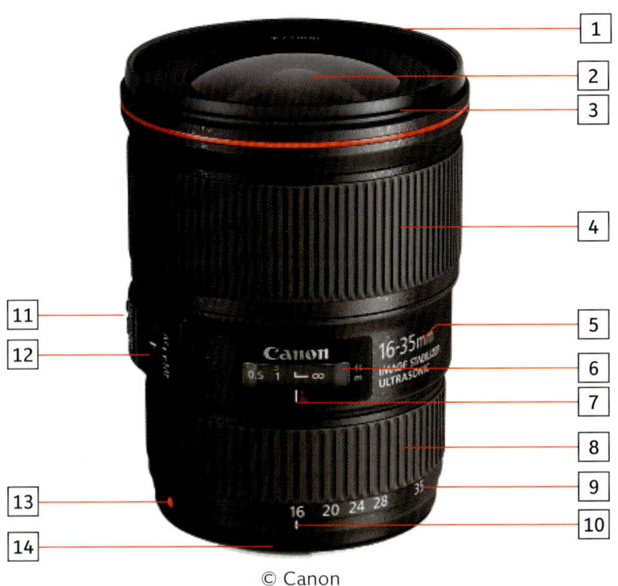

© Canon

1	Filter thread	9	Focal length range
2	Lens front element	10	Focal length index mark
3	Lens hood mount	11	Image Stabilization switch
4	Focus ring	12	AF/MF switch
5	Lens information (model/focal length/features)	13	Lens mount index
6	Focus distance window[1]	14	Lens mount
7	Focus distance index		
8	Zoom ring		

[1] Not every Canon lens features a distance scale; EF-S lenses often don't have a focus distance indicator.

» LENS TECHNOLOGY

Beneath the metal or plastic skin of a lens is a number of different technologies that help to improve the handling, focusing speed, and optical performance of that lens. The following is a short list of some of these technologies, their purpose, and the relevant abbreviations used by Canon in its lens descriptions.

Autofocus stop feature (AF-S)

If a lens has an AF-S button you can press it down to temporarily stop AF. AF will not resume again until the button is released.

Diffractive Optics (DO)

DO lenses are smaller and lighter than an equivalent conventional lens, yet still boast high optical quality. This is achieved through the use of special—and expensive—glass elements. To date there are only two DO lenses produced by Canon: a 70–300mm zoom and a 400mm prime. They can be distinguished by a green band around the lens barrel.

Dust and water resistance (DW-R)

Some of Canon's lenses are fitted with thin rubber seals around the periphery of the lens mount. This creates a dust-resistant, watertight seal when the lens is attached to a camera. DW-R is typically found on L-series lenses.

Fluorine Coating

Fluorine is used to provide a micro-thin, anti-static coating on the external glass elements of some Canon lenses. The coating is water repellent and makes cleaning the glass easier.

Full-time manual focusing (FT-M)

FT-M allows you to override AF at any point without switching AF off permanently. Canon achieves this using either electronic or mechanical manual focusing.

Electronic manual focusing detects that the focus ring is being turned and uses the focusing motor to move the lens elements; mechanical manual focusing relies entirely on the manual focus ring being moved to adjust the focus.

Image Stabilization (IS)

A growing number of Canon lenses are equipped with Image Stabilization. An IS lens can detect the slight movements that naturally occur when you handhold a camera, and an optical system in the lens is then adjusted to compensate for this movement. The most up-to-date iteration of Canon's IS system, Hybrid IS, can compensate for shutter speeds that are 5-stops slower than would normally cause camera shake. It can also compensate for angular velocity and shift.

Internal/Rear focusing (IF/RF)

A lens with internal focusing can focus without the need to extend its physical length. Rear focusing is similar, but in this instance only the lens elements near the rear of the camera are moved. A benefit with both systems is that the front lens element does not rotate during focusing, which is useful when you are using filters that need to be set in a certain orientation.

IMAGE STABILIZATION

IS systems take a second or two to settle and stabilize, so shouldn't be relied on if you're moving around and shooting quickly.

Stepper Motor (STM)

An STM is a type of autofocus motor that's designed to make focusing smoother than a USM (see below). Although slightly slower in operation, an STM is useful if you regularly shoot movies.

Ultrasonic Motor (USM)

A USM is an AF motor that provides fast, quiet, and accurate focusing. Canon currently uses two types of USM—ring-type and micro. The big advantage of a ring-type USM is that it allows full-time manual focusing in AF mode.

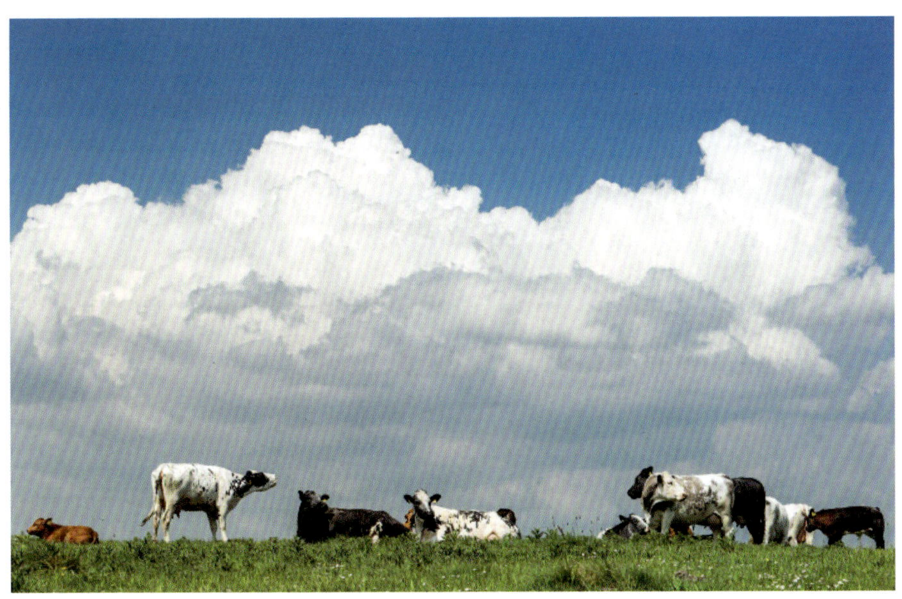

› Focal length

Parallel rays of light converge to a point when they enter a lens that is focused on infinity (∞). This point is known as the focal point. The focal length of a lens is the distance in millimeters from the optical center of the lens to the focal point (also referred to as the focal plane). The sensor in the Rebel T6/EOS 1300D is placed at the focal plane, which is indicated by the ⊖ symbol at the left of the viewfinder housing on top of the camera.

The focal length of a lens has a number of effects. Shorter focal length lenses have a wider angle of view (which is why they're commonly known as wide-angle lenses), whereas long focal length lenses (or telephotos) reduce the angle of view and magnify an image, making a subject appear larger in the frame.

› Angle of view

The angle of view is a measurement—in degrees (°)—of the extent of a scene that is projected by the lens onto the sensor. The angle of view can refer to either the horizontal, vertical, or diagonal coverage, but if just one figure is used it's generally safe to assume that it's referring to the diagonal measurement.

There are two factors that affect the angle of view of a lens: the focal length of the lens, and the size of the sensor used in the camera.

WIDE 
This image was shot with a 24mm lens fitted to a full-frame camera, which delivers a wide, 84° angle of view. To match that angle of view on the Rebel T6/EOS 1300D you would need to use a 16mm lens.

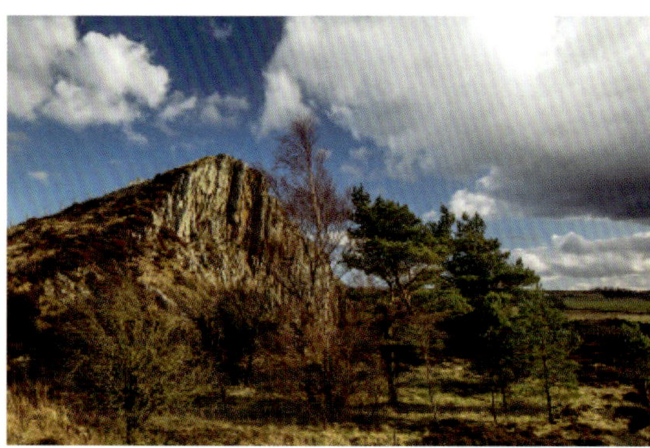

› Crop factor

Because the Rebel T6/EOS 1300D uses an APS-C sized sensor, a "crop factor" must be taken into account when working out the angle of view of a lens. The Rebel T6/EOS 1300D has a crop factor of 1.6x, which means a lens will appear to have a focal length that is 1.6x longer than it would be on a camera with a "full frame" sensor. As a result, wide-angle lenses will not appear to be as wide, and telephoto lenses will appear (usefully) longer.

However, the focal length hasn't changed, just the angle of view, which narrows simply because the sensor records less of the scene projected by the lens. All other aspects of the lens—such as the available depth of field at a particular combination of aperture and subject-to-camera distance—is the same, regardless of sensor size.

Note
Canon uses EF-S to indicate that a lens can only by used on an APS-C camera, such as the Rebel T6/EOS 1300D. Sigma uses the letters DC to indicate the same thing; Tamron uses Di II and Tokina uses DX.

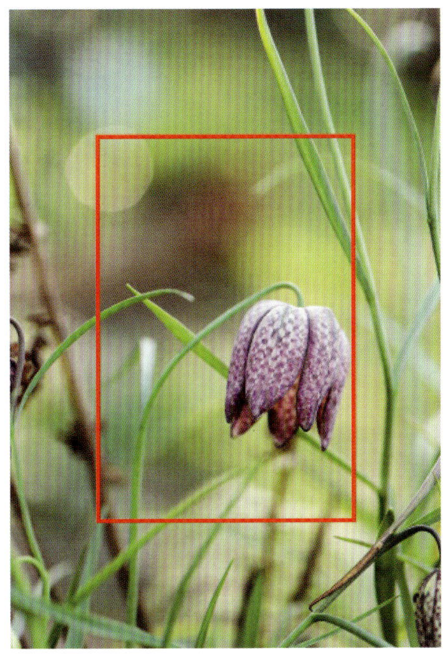

CROPPED ⌃
This image was shot with a 100mm lens fitted to a full-frame camera. If the same lens were fitted to the Rebel T6/EOS 1300D only the area within the red box would be recorded.

» LENS TYPES

› Primes versus zooms

A prime lens is one with a fixed focal length, such as 35mm or 100mm, while a zoom lens covers a range of focal lengths (such as 18–55mm or 70–200mm). Zooms are far more convenient, as just one or two lenses can cover a very wide focal length range. This means you don't need to change lenses as often (if at all) to get the shot you are after—you can simply zoom in and out to refine your composition.

However, primes do have certain advantages. By their very nature, prime lenses are mechanically and optically less complicated than zooms, which makes it easier to optimize their design. So, while modern zooms are generally excellent, they still can't match a good prime for ultimate image quality. Prime lenses also generally have larger maximum apertures, such as f/1.8, f/1.4, or even f/1.2, making them ideal when a restricted depth of field is required or you are shooting in low light.

ZOOM

Some of Canon's high-end zooms—such as the 100-400mm shown here—are large and heavy. However, one large zoom will still take up less room in a kit bag than multiple prime lenses covering the same focal length range.
© Canon

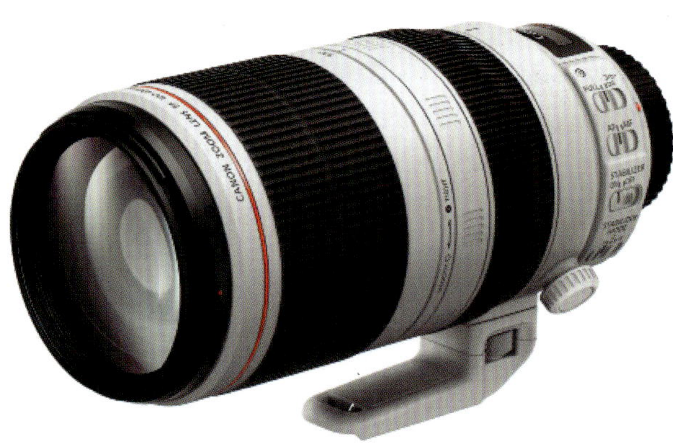

› Wide-angle lenses

A wide-angle lens is generally thought of as any lens with an angle of view that's wider than a standard lens. On the Rebel T6/EOS 1300D, a lens with a focal length of less than 22mm could be considered wide-angle, so the 18mm end of the 18–55mm IS II kit lens is wide-angle.

However, it's possible to go wider than this. Both Canon and third-party manufacturers produce wider prime and zoom lenses. Canon's widest EF-S lens is the 10–22mm f/3.5–4.5 USM (equivalent to a 16–35mm lens on a full-frame camera). If you wish to go wider still (into the realms of fisheye lenses) Canon also produces the EF 8–15mm f/4L USM.

The wider the focal length of a lens, the closer you will need to get to your subject, and the more unnatural the perspective of an image will look. Spatial relationships between elements in a scene are stretched, and distant objects will appear far smaller in the image than expected. This is useful for landscape photographers, who often use wide-angle lenses to create a sense of space in an image.

However, wide-angle lenses are not flattering for head-and-shoulder portraits, as the exaggerated perspective created when you get close to your subject applies equally to a person's facial features.

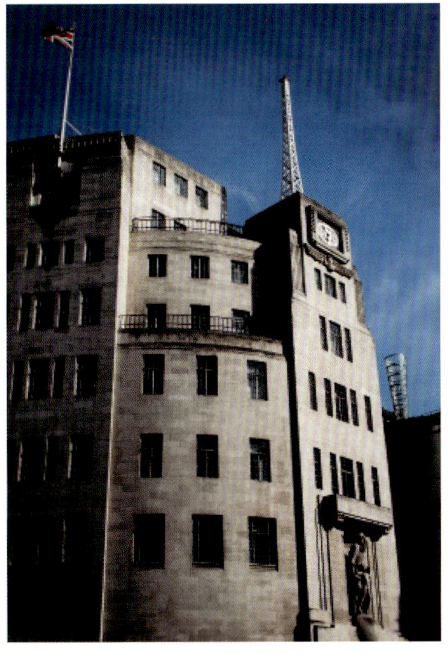

ROOM »
Wide-angle lenses are useful when you're shooting a large subject and don't have much room to move backward to fit it in. However, despite using a wide-angle lens for this shot I still had to tip the camera backward to include the flag and radio mast.

› Standard lenses

A standard lens is one with a focal length that approximately matches the diagonal measurement of the camera's sensor. As the diagonal measurement of the sensor inside the Rebel T6/EOS 1300D is 26.7mm, a 28mm focal length is considered the "standard" focal length.

Typically, standard lenses are thought of as prime lenses, and Canon produces three 28mm prime lenses. The least expensive is an f/2.8 variant; next in specification and price is a faster (and weightier) f/1.8 lens; and the newest lens is a 28mm f/2.8 featuring USM focusing and 4-stop IS.

Although the 18–55mm IS II kit lens doesn't have a 28mm focal length marked on its barrel, it effectively becomes a "standard" lens when the focal length is set midway between 24mm and 35mm.

Notes

The diagonal width of a full-frame sensor (in cameras such as the EOS 5D MkIII) is 43mm, although 50mm is widely seen as the standard focal length for these cameras.

Using a 50mm lens on a Rebel T6/ EOS 1300D is like using an 80mm lens on a full-frame camera. 50mm prime lenses also have wide maximum apertures (typically in the region of f/1.2–f/1.8) making them excellent portrait lenses.

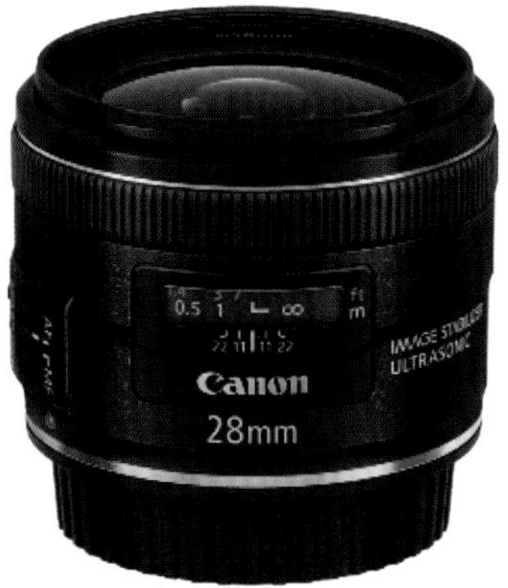

CANON 28MM F/2.8 〈〈
Canon's latest 28mm prime lens features USM focusing and 4-stop IS.
© Canon

› Telephoto lenses

A telephoto lens is generally regarded as any lens with a focal length longer than "standard." On the Rebel T6/EOS 1300D, this means that any lens with a focal length greater than 28mm could be regarded as a telephoto lens.

Telephoto lenses magnify the image projected onto the sensor, which appears to bring distant objects closer. One effect of this magnification is that the angle of view is narrowed, so less of the scene is captured. Longer focal length telephoto lenses are popular with wildlife photographers who generally need to keep a reasonable distance from their subject, while shorter telephoto lenses (such as the 55mm end of the kit zoom lens) work well as portrait lenses. As you have to stand back from your subject, the perspective for facial features is more pleasing than when using a wide-angle lens.

As long telephoto lenses are often large and cumbersome, they are often difficult to handhold, and as the image is magnified, any movement will be exaggerated, increasing the risk of camera shake. Image Stabilization can help, but IS telephoto lenses are more expensive than their non-stabilized equivalents.

EXTREME ⌄
The longest lens currently produced by Canon is the EF 800mm f/5.6L IS USM. This is an extreme lens in all respects: reach, size, weight, and price. © Canon

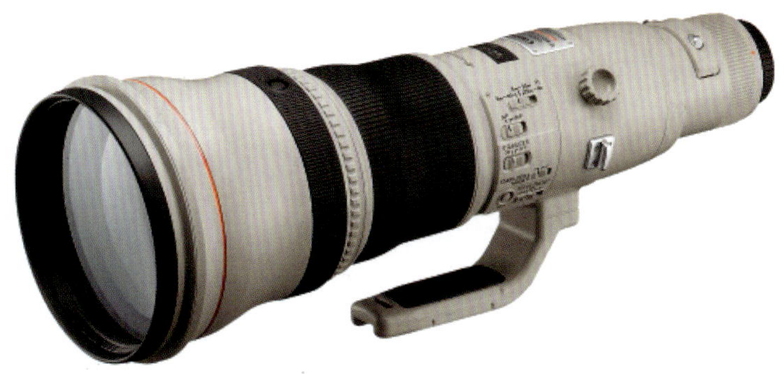

» STANDARD

Images created with a standard lens have a pleasing, natural perspective that is neither "stretched" like a wide-angle lens, nor "compressed" like a telephoto lens. This makes them ideal for subjects that suit a less dramatic visual style, such as reportage or documentary photography.

Settings
> Focal length: 28mm
> Aperture: f/2.8
> Shutter speed: 1/13 sec.
> ISO: 200

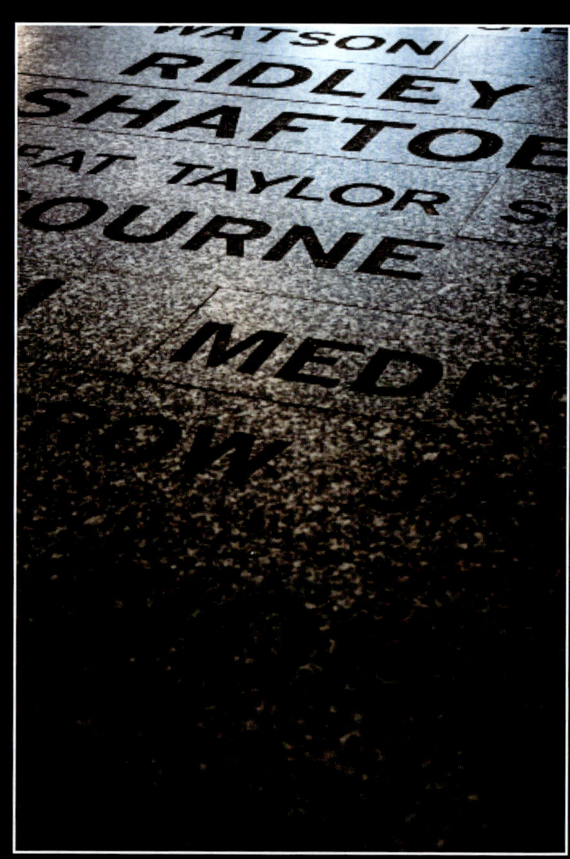

» COMPRESSED

A peculiar visual quirk of telephoto lenses is spatial compression, which is seen as objects in a scene appearing closer together than they do in reality. This is purely because telephoto lenses tend to be used from a greater distance than wide-angle lenses, but it's a useful "trick" if you want to imply an intimate connection between the various elements in your photograph.

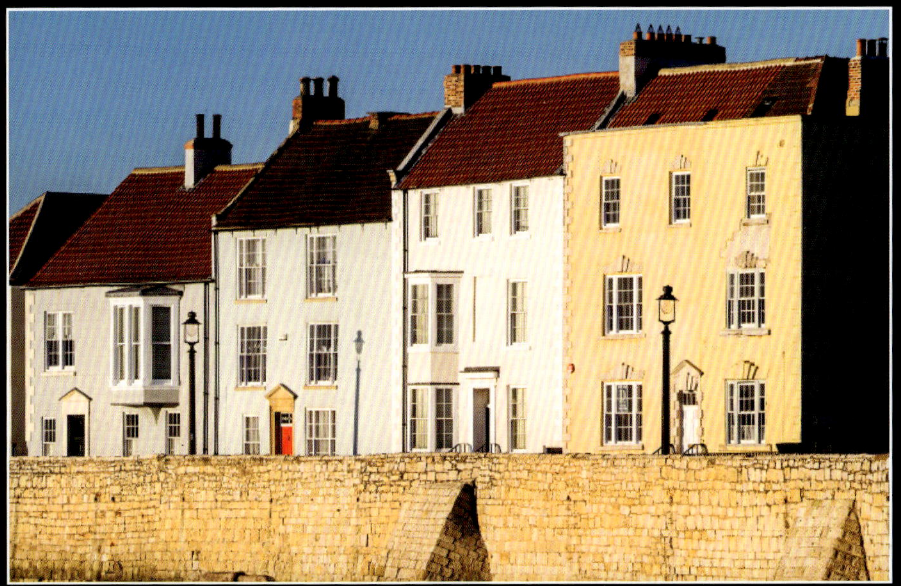

Settings
> Focal length: 160mm
> Aperture: f/10
> Shutter speed: 1/30 sec.
> ISO: 100

4   › Teleconverters

A teleconverter (or "Extender," as Canon calls it) is a secondary lens that fits between a camera body and the main (usually telephoto prime) lens to increase the focal length by a given factor. Canon currently makes two teleconverters: a 1.4x model that increases the focal length by a factor of 1.4, and a 2x model that doubles focal length.

Teleconverters are a good way to increase the reach of telephoto lenses in a relatively inexpensive way, but they do have their drawbacks, not least a reduction in image quality. Nor can all Canon lenses be used with a teleconverter—some lenses may even be damaged if they are used with an Extender. A teleconverter also reduces the amount of light passing through to the sensor, effectively making the lens slower. In low light this can reduce the camera's AF performance considerably, as well as making the viewfinder darker. A 1.4x Extender loses 1 stop of light; a 2x teleconverter loses 2 stops.

EXTENDER EF 2X III

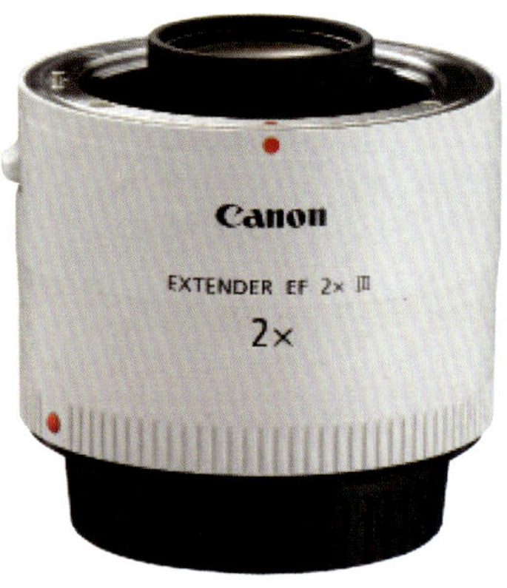

© Canon

EXTENDER EF 1.4X III

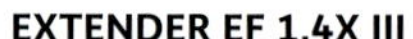

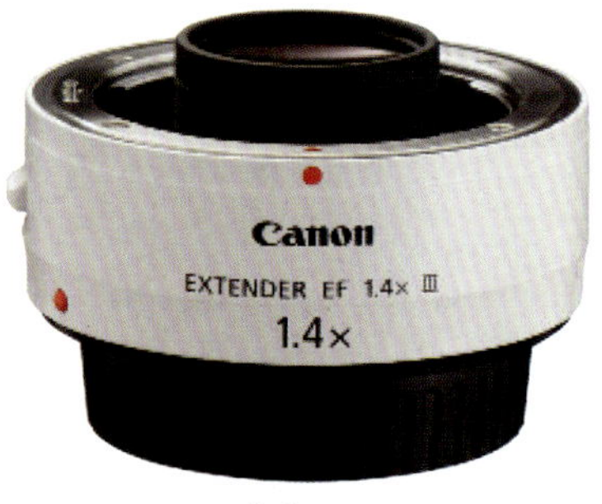

© Canon

Teleconverter	Specifications	Dimensions	Weight
Extender EF 1.4x III	7 elements in 3 groups	2.8 x 1.1 in. 72 x 27mm	7.9 oz 225g
Extender EF 2x III	9 elements in 5 groups	2.8 x 2.1 in. 72 x 53mm	11.5 oz 325g

» CANON EF/EF-S LENSES

Lens	35mm equiv.	Filter size	L x W (mm)	Weight (grams)
EF 8–15mm f/4L USM	12.8–24mm	67mm	83 x 79	540
EF-S 10–18mm f/4.5–5.6 IS STM	16–28mm	67mm	72 x 74	240
EF-S 10–22mm f/3.5–4.5 USM	16–35mm	77mm	90 x 84	385
EF 11–24mm f/4L USM	18–38mm	–	132 x 108	1180
EF 14mm f/2.8L II USM	22mm	rear	94 x 80	645
EF 15mm f/2.8 Fisheye	–	rear	62 x 73	330
EF-S 15–85mm f/3.5–5.6 IS USM	22–136mm	72mm	88 x 82	575
EF 16–35mm f/2.8L II USM	25–56mm	82mm	112 x 89	635
EF 16–35mm f/4L IS USM	25–56mm	77mm	113 x 83	615
TS-E 17mm f/4L	27mm	n/a	107 x 89	820
EF 17–40mm f/4L USM	27–64mm	77mm	97 x 84	500
EF-S 17–55 f/2.8 IS USM	27–88mm	77mm	111 x 83	645
EF-S 17–85mm f/4–5.6 IS USM	27–136mm	67mm	92 x 78	475
EF-S 18–55mm f/3.5–5.6 III	28–88mm	58mm	70 x 69	195
EF-S 18–55mm f/3.5–5.6 IS STM	28–88mm	58mm	75 x 69	205
EF-S 18–55mm f/3.5–5.6 IS II	28–88mm	58mm	70 x 69	200
EF-S 18–135mm f/3.5–5.6 IS	28–216mm	67mm	101 x 75	455
EF-S 18–135mm f/3.5–5.6 STM	28–216mm	67mm	96 x 77	480
EF-S 18–135mm f/3.5–5.6 IS USM	28–216mm	67mm	96 x 77	515
EF-S 18–200mm f/3.5–5.6 IS	28–320mm	72mm	102 x 79	595
EF 20mm f/2.8 USM	32mm	72mm	77 x 71	405
EF 24mm f/1.4L II USM	38mm	77mm	93 x 87	650
EF 24mm f/2.8 IS USM	38mm	58mm	68 x 56	280
EF-S 24mm f/2.8 STM	38mm	52mm	68 x 23	125
TS-E 24mm f/3.5L II	38mm	82mm	107 x 89	570
EF 24–70mm f/2.8L II USM	38–112mm	82mm	113 x 88	805
EF 24–70mm f/4L USM	38–112mm	77mm	93 x 83	600
EF 24–85mm f/3.5–4.5 USM	38–136mm	77mm	73 x 69	380
EF 24–105mm f/3.5–5.6 IS STM	38–168mm	77mm	104 x 83	525

Lens	35mm equiv.	Filter size	L x W (mm)	Weight (grams)
EF 24–105mm f/4L IS USM	38–168mm	77mm	107 x 83	670
EF 28mm f/1.8 USM	45mm	58mm	73 x 56	310
EF 28mm f/2.8 IS USM	45mm	58mm	68 x 51	280
EF 28–90mm f/4–5.6 II USM	45–144mm	58mm	71 x 67	190
EF 28–90mm f/4–5.6 III	45–144mm	58mm	71 x 67	190
EF 28–105mm f/3.5–4.5 II USM	45–168mm	58mm	75 x 72	375
EF 28–105mm f/4.0–5.6 USM	45–168mm	58mm	68 x 67	210
EF 28–135mm f/3.5–5.6 IS USM	45–216mm	72mm	97 x 78	540
EF 28–200mm f/3.5–5.6 USM	45–320mm	72mm	90 x 78	500
EF 28–300mm f/3.5–5.6L IS USM	45–480mm	77mm	184 x 92	1670
EF 35mm f/1.4L USM	56mm	72mm	86 x 79	580
EF 35mm f/1.4L II USM	56mm	72mm	105 x 80	760
EF 35mm f/2	56mm	52mm	67 x 42	210
EF 40mm f/2.8 STM	64mm	52mm	68 x 27	130
TS-E 45mm f/2.8	72mm	72mm	90 x 81	645
EF 50mm f/1.2L USM	80mm	72mm	86 x 65	580
EF 50mm f/1.4 USM	80mm	58mm	74 x 50	290
EF 50mm f/1.8 II	80mm	52mm	68 x 41	130
EF 50mm f/1.8 STM	80mm	49mm	69 x 39	160
EF 50mm f/2.5 Compact Macro	80mm	52mm	67 x 63	280
EF 55–200mm f/4.5–5.6 II USM	88–320mm	77mm	184 x 92	1670
EF-S 55–250mm f/4–5.6 IS II	88–400mm	58mm	108 x 70	390
EF-S 55–250mm f/4–5.6 IS STM	88–400mm	58mm	111 x 70	375
EF-S 60mm f/2.8 Macro USM	96mm	52mm	73 x 70	335
MP-E 65mm f/2.8 1–5x Macro	104mm	58mm	98 x 81	730
EF 70–200mm f/2.8L IS II USM*	112–320mm	77mm	199 x 89	1490
EF 70–200mm f/2.8L USM*	112–320mm	77mm	194 x 76	1310
EF 70–200mm f/4L IS USM*	112–320mm	67mm	172 x 176	760
EF 70–200mm f/4L USM*	112–320mm	67mm	172 x 176	705
EF 70–300mm f/4.5–5.6 DO IS USM	112–480mm	58mm	99 x 82	720

Lens	35mm equiv.	Filter size	L x W (mm)	Weight (grams)
EF 70–300mm f/4–5.6 IS USM	112–480mm	58mm	143 x 76	630
EF 70–300mm f/4–5.6L IS USM	112–480mm	67mm	143 x 89	1050
EF 75–300mm f/4–5.6 III	120–480mm	58mm	122 x 71	480
EF 75–300mm f/4–5.6 III USM	120–480mm	58mm	122 x 71	480
EF 80–200mm f/4.5–5.6 II	128–320mm	52mm	79 x 69	250
EF 85mm f/1.2L II USM	136mm	72mm	91 x 84	1025
EF 85mm f/1.8 USM	136mm	72mm	91 x 84	1025
TS-E 90mm f/2.8	144mm	58mm	88 x 74	565
EF 100mm f/2 USM	160mm	58mm	75 x 73	460
EF 100mm f/2.8 Macro USM	160mm	58mm	119 x 79	600
EF 100mm f/2.8L Macro IS USM	160mm	67mm	78 x 123	625
EF 100–400mm f/4.5–5.6L IS USM*	160–640mm	77mm	189 x 92	1380
EF 100–400mm f/4.5–5.6L IS II USM*	160–640mm	77mm	193 x 94	1570
EF 135mm f/2.8 soft focus	216mm	52mm	98 x 69	390
EF 135mm f/2L USM*	216mm	72mm	112 x 82	750
EF 180mm f/3.5L Macro USM*	288mm	72mm	186 x 82	1090
EF 200mm f/2L IS USM*	320mm	52mm+	208 x 128	2520
EF 200mm f/2.8L II USM*	320mm	72mm	136 x 83	765
EF 200–400mm f/4L IS*	320–640mm	58mm	122 x 73	3620
EF 300mm f/2.8L IS II USM*	480mm	52mm+	248 x 128	2400
EF 300mm f/4L IS USM*	480mm	77mm	221 x 90	1190
EF 400mm f/2.8L IS II USM*	640mm	52mm+	343 x 163	3850
EF 400mm f/4 DO IS USM*	640mm	52mm+	233 x 128	1940
EF 400mm f/4 DO IS II USM*	640mm	52mm+	233 x 128	1200
EF 400mm f/5.6 L USM*	640mm	77mm	257 x 90	1250
EF 500mm f/4L IS USM*	800mm	52mm+	146 x 383	3190
EF 500mm f/4L IS II USM*	800mm	52mm+	449 x 168	3920
EF 600mm f/4L IS USM*	960mm	52mm+	448 x 168	3920
EF 800mm f/5.6L IS USM*	1280mm	52mm+	461 x 163	4500

* Indicates that a lens is compatible with Canon's Extenders   + Drop-in filter size

5 FLASH

Flash is useful when the light levels are low and extra illumination is needed. The Rebel T6/EOS 1300D has a built-in, pop-up flash and is also compatible with all of Canon's Speedlites and many third-party alternatives.

Flash is often seen as complicated, but it's perhaps simpler than you might think—once a few key concepts have been grasped, illumination (both literally and metaphorically) soon follows.

There are two main problems that can trip you up when using flash. The first is that flash is a relatively weak light source, particularly in comparison to sunlight. This means that flash has a limited range: even the most powerful Canon Speedlite can't illuminate distant objects, such as a performer on stage at a concert.

The second problem is that flash is a frontal light (at least the built-in flash is, as is a Speedlite fitted to the camera's hotshoe, pointing directly forward). Frontal light isn't the most flattering light for most purposes, particularly when shooting portraits. This is because frontal light flattens texture and reduces shadows, which can make a three-dimensional object appear "flat" and two-dimensional in the final image.

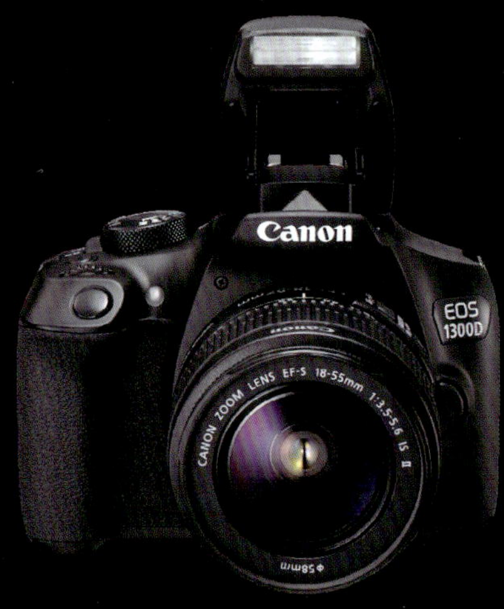

BUILT-IN FLASH ⌃
The Rebel T6/EOS 1300D's built-in flash isn't particularly powerful, but when you need it, any flash is better than none at all.
© Canon

OFF-CAMERA FLASH »
Using a Speedlite gives you more scope for creative flash, especially when you use it wirelessly, away from the camera.

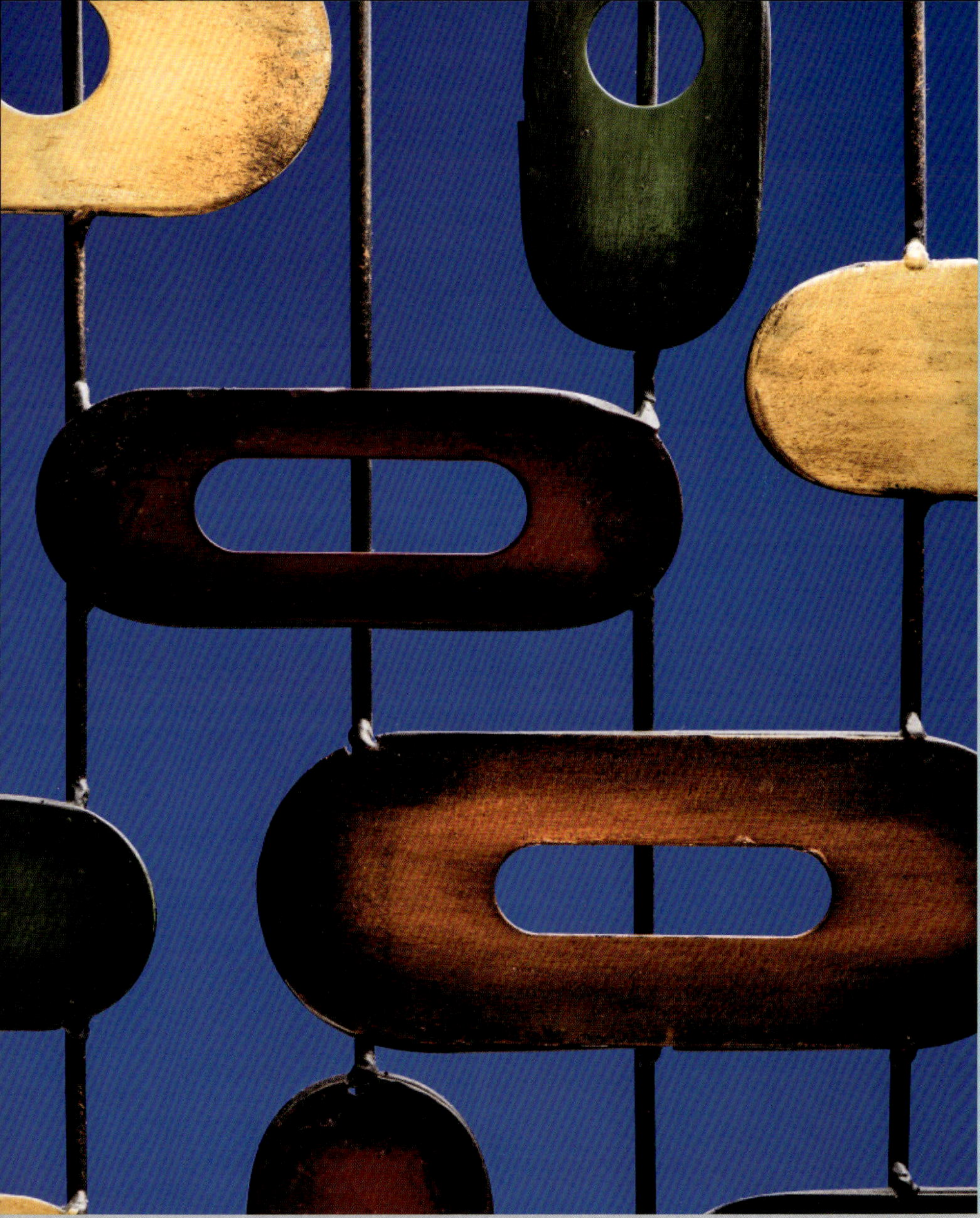

» FLASH BASICS

The light-emitting part of a flash—the flash head—is an airtight chamber filled with xenon gas. When the flash is triggered, an electrical charge is pulsed across the chamber, which causes the molecules of gas to release energy in the form of light.

The power to fire the flash head comes from a capacitor, which is recharged by a battery (or batteries) every time the flash is fired. If you fire a flash at full power, the capacitor is totally drained of energy, and needs to be recharged fully before it can fire again. However, if the flash is fired at ½ power only ½ the capacitor's charge is used, so the flash will be able to fire again at the same power before it needs to recharge. At ¼ power the flash will be able to fire four times before it needs to recharge, and so on.

The power output of a flash controls the amount of light discharged by varying the length of time that it emits light. At full power the duration of the illumination is relatively long (approximately 1/800 sec.). At ½ power the flash is "turned off" more quickly (after approximately 1/1600 sec., which results in a halving of the light emitted by the flash). At ¼ power the flash duration is halved again, and so on. Every halving of power shortens the duration of the light emission, which results in less light being emitted.

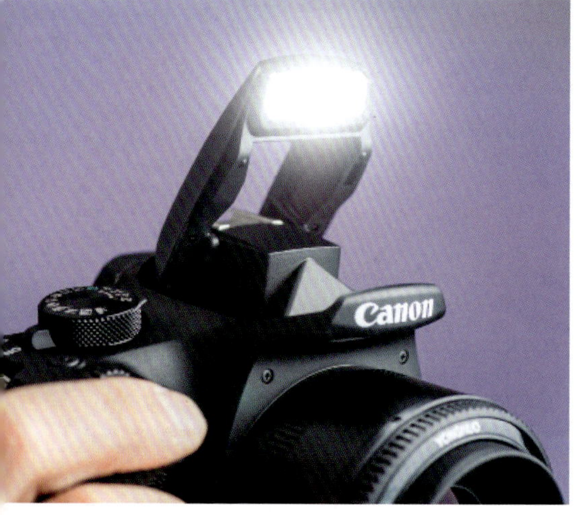

> **Note**
> Using a lower power setting makes it easier to freeze movement with flash, as the flash duration is shorter. The downside is that you need to be closer to your subject to effectively illuminate it.

BUILT-IN «
The Rebel T6/EOS 1300D's built-in flash works on exactly the principles as a Speedlite—the only difference is in the lower power and therefore the smaller effective range.

› Flash exposure

There are two ways to control flash exposure. It can either be determined automatically by the camera, or the flash can be set to manual, leaving you to adjust the flash power to suit.

To automatically determine correct flash exposure, Canon uses a proprietary exposure system known as E-TTL II. Generally, this is an accurate system, but it's not infallible. As with Evaluative metering, a very bright or very dark subject can "fool" the flash into under- or overexposing, while changes in subject brightness can lead to inconsistent exposures. For greater consistency it is better to set the flash exposure manually, although this involves more calculations before shooting.

When flash is set to manual there are two main ways to control its effective distance (the maximum distance at which the flash can illuminate a subject). Flash exposure compensation is the first control, and this can be set via the Rebel T6/EOS 1300D's **Flash control** menu or directly on a Speedlite if one is fitted.

The second exposure control is the aperture: the smaller the aperture used, the shorter the effective distance of the flash. If a subject is further than the effective flash distance for the selected aperture it will be underexposed, so you would need to use a wider aperture; if your subject is overexposed this can be remedied by setting a smaller aperture.

It's important to appreciate that the shutter speed has no influence on the flash exposure, only on the exposure of any areas of a scene that are not lit by light from the flash. However, there is one limitation placed on the shutter speed you can use with flash, and that is the camera's sync speed (or X-sync). This is the fastest shutter speed that can be set when using flash (unless a Speedlite with HSS-capability is fitted). On the Rebel T6/EOS 1300D the sync speed is 1/200 sec.

Note
You can use slower shutter speeds than the sync speed, which is useful when shooting in low light and when you want to correctly expose those areas not lit by flash. The shutter speed selected automatically by the Rebel T6/EOS 1300D when shooting with flash in **Av** mode is set using **C.Fn I-3 Flash sync. speed in Av mode**. See pages 132–133 for details.

› Guide number

The power of a flash is referred to as its guide number (GN), which determines the effective range of the flash in either meters or feet. As you increase the ISO on your camera, the GN increases also, so to avoid confusion, camera and flash manufacturers use ISO 100 as the standard reference when quoting a GN.

If you know the GN of a flash (the Rebel T6/EOS 1300D's built-in flash has a GN of 30.2ft/9.2m at ISO 100) you can calculate either the required aperture value for a subject at a given distance, or the effective range of the flash at a specified aperture. The formulae used are:

Aperture=GN/distance
Distance=GN/aperture

You can use the grid below to quickly determine the effective range of the built-in flash for a typical range of apertures and distances. There are also many apps available for smart phones that help make flash exposure calculations easier.

	Aperture					
ISO	**f/2.8**	**f/4**	**f/5.6**	**f/8**	**f/11**	**f/16**
100	10.71ft (3.29m)	7.5ft (2.3m)	5.36ft (1.64m)	3.75ft (1.15m)	2.73ft (0.84m)	1.88ft (0.57m)
200	15.15ft (4.65m)	10.71ft (3.29m)	7.5ft (2.3m)	5.3ft (1.64m)	3.75ft (1.15m)	2.73ft (0.84m)
400	21.43ft (6.57m)	15.15ft (4.65m)	10.71ft (3.29m)	7.5ft (2.3m)	5.3ft (1.64m)	3.75ft (1.15m)
800	30.3ft (9.29m)	21.43ft (6.57m)	15.15ft (4.65m)	10.71ft (3.29m)	7.5ft (2.3m)	5.36ft (1.64m)
1600	42.86ft (13.14m)	30.3ft (9.29m)	21.43ft (6.57m)	15.15ft (4.65m)	10.71ft (3.29m)	7.5ft (2.3m)
3200	60.61ft (18.59m)	42.86ft (13.14m)	30.3ft (9.29m)	21.43ft (6.57m)	15.15ft (4.65m)	10.71ft (3.29m)
6400	85.71ft (26.29m)	60.61ft (18.59m)	42.86ft (13,14m)	30.3ft (9.29m)	21.43ft (6.57m)	15.15ft (4.65m)

» GN

If a flash is used off-camera (via a sync cord or using a wireless transmitter) the distance between the flash and the camera is largely irrelevant in terms of determining the correct flash exposure. The GN is always used to calculate the effective distance between the flash and the subject only.

Settings
> Focal length: 100mm
> Aperture: f/2.8
> Shutter speed: 1/200 sec.
> ISO: 100

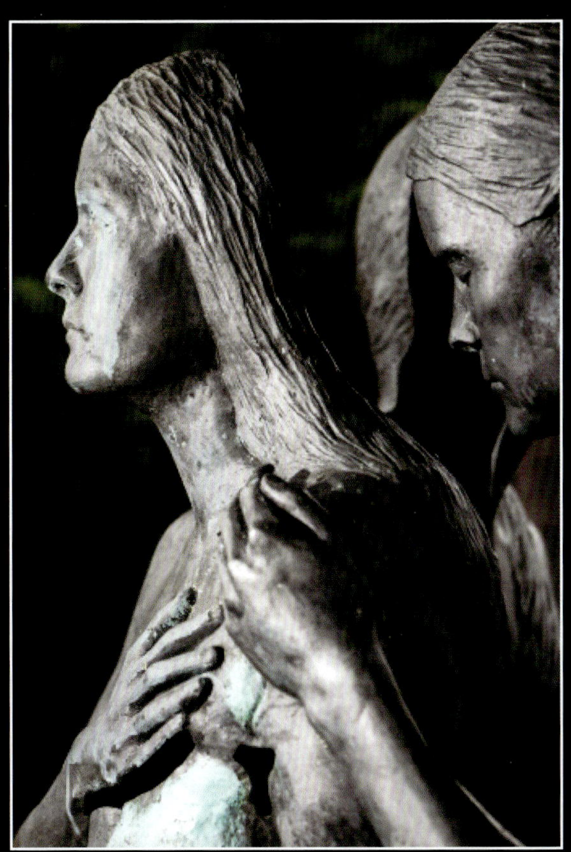

» THE BUILT-IN FLASH

When the mode dial is set to a Basic Zone mode the built-in flash will either rise and fire automatically as required, or it will not be available. Using one of the Creative Zone modes is highly recommended for more complete control over the built-in flash (including whether it's raised or not).

Raising and using the flash

1) Press the ⚡ button behind ⚙ to raise the flash.

2) Press half way down on the shutter-release button to focus. If the flash is ready for use, ⚡ will be displayed at the bottom left corner of the viewfinder (or LCD in Live View mode).

3) The flash needs to charge up after use, so there may be a short delay before the next exposure can be made. During this time, ⚡ buSY will be displayed in the viewfinder and BUSY⚡ will be shown on the rear LCD.

4) Press down fully on the shutter-release button to take the photo.

Warning!

Don't try to raise the built-in flash if you have a Speedlite fitted to the camera's hotshoe.

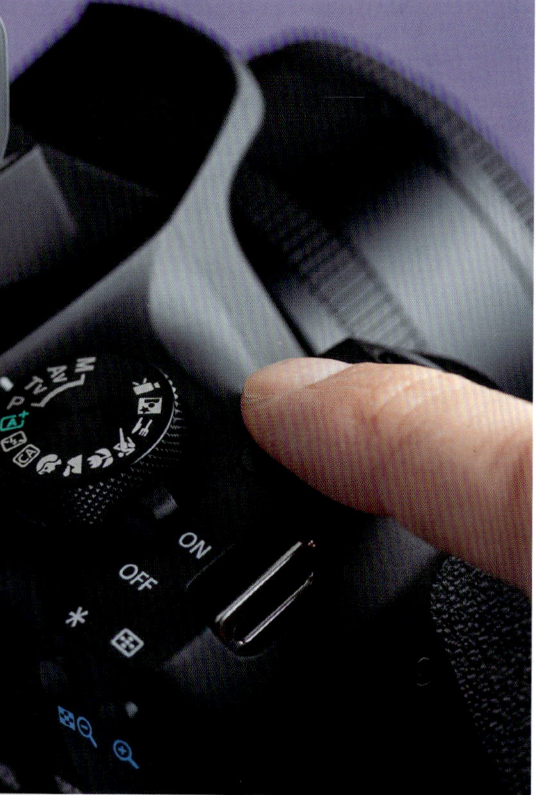

SHADOW «

If you have a lens hood or filter holder attached to your lens, remove it before you use the built-in flash, otherwise they may both cast a shadow.

› Red-eye reduction

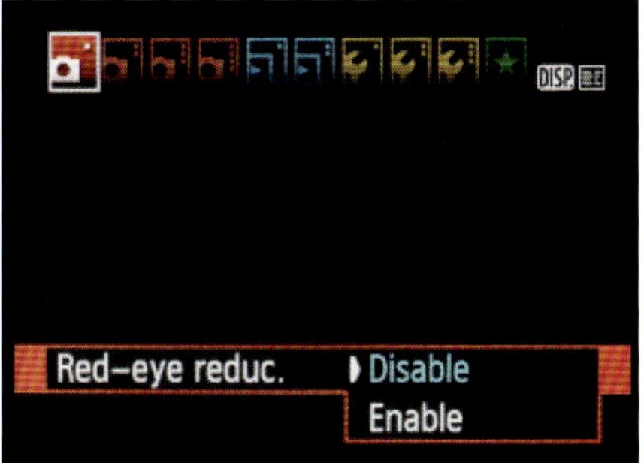

Red-eye occurs when direct flash is used to illuminate a face looking directly at the camera. Light from the flash bounces off the retina inside your subject's eye back toward the camera, picking up the color of the blood vessels in the process. The problem is made worse by the fact that flash is often used when ambient light levels are low, so your subject's pupils will be at their widest to start with.

Red-eye reduc. reduces the problem by activating the red-eye reduction lamp just before the final exposure is made. This causes the pupils of your subject's eyes to contract, and so reduces the risk of light exiting out of the eye.

Using red-eye reduction

1) Press MENU and select **Red-eye reduc.** from the ◉ menu.

2) Select **Enable** to switch red-eye reduction on. Press the shutter-release button down lightly to return to shooting mode and raise the built-in flash.

3) Press the shutter-release button down half way to focus your camera. The orange red-eye reduction lamp should now light. Look through the viewfinder: the usual exposure scale will be replaced by a line of bars. Keep your finger on the shutter-release button. As you do so, the bars will gradually disappear. When the last bar disappears, press the shutter-release button down fully to take the shot.

> **Note**
> Using off-camera flash reduces the risk of red-eye.

» FLASH CONTROL MENU

When the Rebel T6/EOS 1300D is set to a Creative Zone mode you can select **Flash control** from the ◘ menu screen. This will present you with a sub-menu of options that let you set the various shooting functions of the built-in flash and compatible Speedlites (when fitted and switched on).

› Flash firing

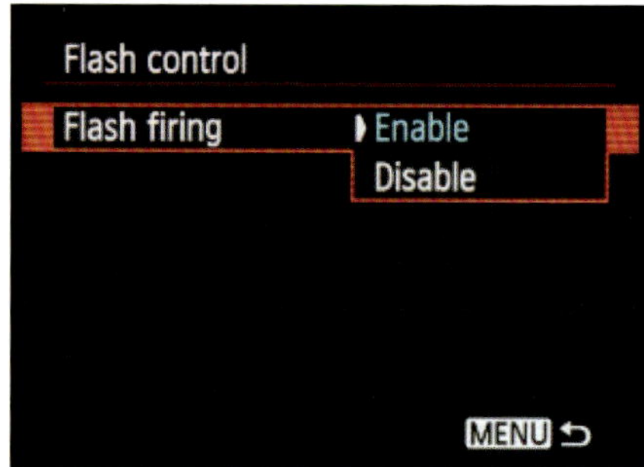

To be able to use the built-in flash or Speedlite, **Flash firing** has to be set to **Enable**; set to **Disable**, neither will fire. However, the AF assist beam on a Speedlite—if it has one—will still work, regardless of whether the flash fires or not. The AF assist beam is most useful when there is not enough ambient light for effective autofocusing.

› Built-in flash func. setting

Selecting **Built-in flash func. setting** takes you to a sub-menu where you can adjust the built-in flash function settings. These include **Flash mode**, **Shutter sync.**, **Flash exp. comp**, and **E-TTL II meter.** (described in more depth on the following pages).

› External flash func. setting

When you select **External flash func. setting** you're taken to a sub-menu of options where the function settings of compatible Speedlites can be adjusted (when the Speedlite is fitted and switched on). These function settings are described in more detail in the external flashes section of this chapter (see page 181).

› External flash C.Fn setting/ Clear ext. flash C.Fn set.

These two menu options let you set or clear the custom functions of compatible Speedlites. The custom functions available vary between Speedlite models, with higher-end Speedlites typically offering a greater level of customization.

» BUILT-IN FLASH FUNCTION SETTINGS

› Flash mode

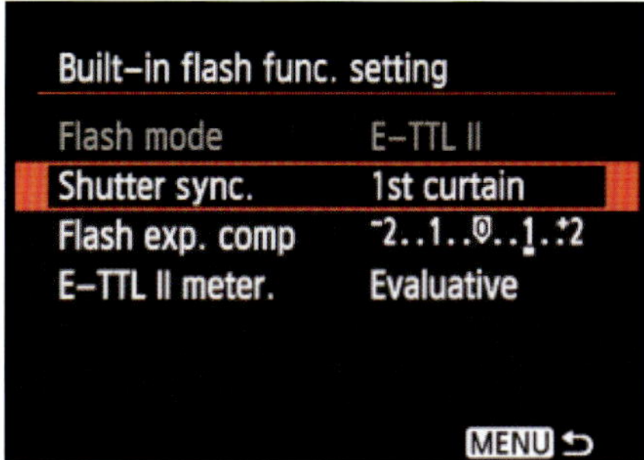

› Shutter sync.

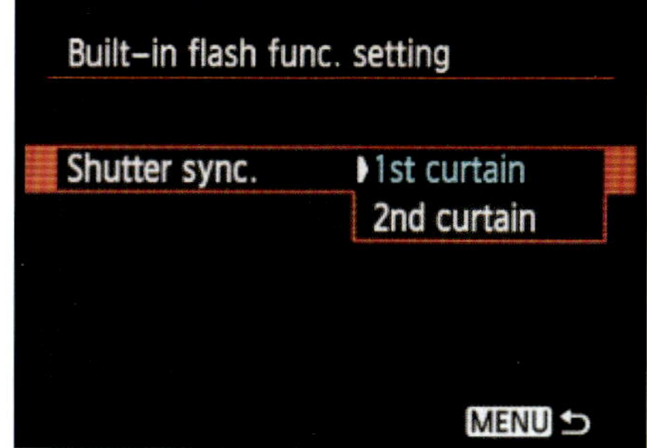

Flash mode is set permanently to **E-TTL II** when you are using the built-in flash, but fit a Speedlite and **Flash mode** (on the **External flash func. setting** menu screen) offers far more options. With a Speedlite you can either set your Speedlite to use **E-TTL II** metering (the default) or switch to **Manual**, so you have to determine the flash exposure yourself. Depending on the Speedlite, other options may also. be available, including **Multi flash**.

Shutter sync. sets whether the flash fires at the start of the exposure or at the end. If you set **Shutter sync.** to **1st curtain**, the flash is fired at the start of the exposure. If the shutter speed is sufficiently long, the subject is initially frozen by the flash. Then, as the camera continues to expose (using ambient light only), the movement of the subject is recorded as a blur, which appears in front of the subject in the final shot.

If **Shutter sync.** is set to **2nd curtain**, the flash is fired at the end of the exposure, so any subject movement is recorded as a blur until just before the shutter closes, when the flash freezes the subject. This results in the subject's movement recorded as a blur *behind* the subject. Of the two settings, **2nd curtain** usually looks more natural, although it's very much down to personal preference.

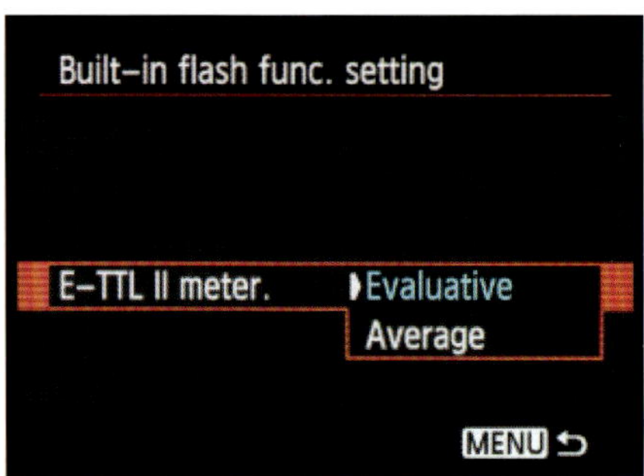

Flashes were once fitted with sensors that determined the correct exposure, but E-TTL II ("evaluative through-the-lens metering") hands responsibility for your flash exposures to the camera. If you are using a compatible lens (and all modern Canon lenses invariably are) the E-TTL II system uses the focus distance as a factor in determining the exposure, which makes your flash exposures more accurate.

The system works by firing two bursts of light from the flash. The first burst is used by the camera to evaluate the flash and ambient light exposure. Then, a second burst is used to make the actual exposure, with the power of the flash modified so that the subject is correctly exposed. This happens so quickly that neither you nor your subject will be aware that there were two bursts of flash.

The Rebel T6/EOS 1300D offers two E-TTL II metering methods. The default is **Evaluative**, which biases the flash exposure toward the subject (typically where the camera would be focused) rather than the background.

The alternative—**Average**—does exactly what you might expect: when the exposure is calculated, the flash exposure is averaged across the entire scene. This can increase the chance that a subject close to the flash will be overexposed, but if your lens doesn't supply distance information it's worth trying both settings to see which one you prefer.

› Flash exposure compensation

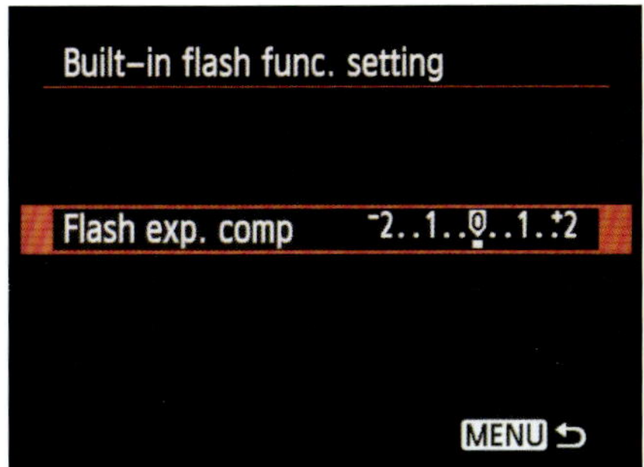

Generally, the Rebel T6/EOS 1300D's flash exposures are accurate and will produce pleasing results. But flash exposure isn't foolproof, and just like non-flash exposures, your camera can sometimes miscalculate. If this happens, you can apply flash exposure compensation of ±2 stops, which can be adjusted in one of two ways:

> **Note**
> Depending on the Speedlite you are using, you may also be able to set flash exposure compensation on the flash.

Method 1
1) In shooting mode press the Q button.

2) Highlight the flash comp icon on the Q menu screen.

3) Turn the dial to the left to decrease the flash power, or to the right to increase it. The flash comp icon will be shown in the viewfinder.

4) Press down lightly on the shutter-release button to return to shooting mode.

Method 2
1) Select **Flash exp. comp** from the **Built-in flash func. setting** menu.

2) Press ◄ to decrease the power of the flash or ► to increase it.

3) Press (SET) to apply the changes and return to the **Built-in flash func. setting** menu screen.

The Rebel T6/EOS 1300D's 1/200 sec. sync speed is relatively slow, which makes it difficult to use flash in bright conditions as a fill light to reduce contrast or, as in this shot, to use the flash as the primary light source (and deliberately underexpose the background by setting a fast shutter speed). Fortunately, there is a solution: use a Speedlite with High Speed Sync (HSS). With one important restriction (see page 181) this lets you use flash with shutter speeds faster than 1/200 sec.

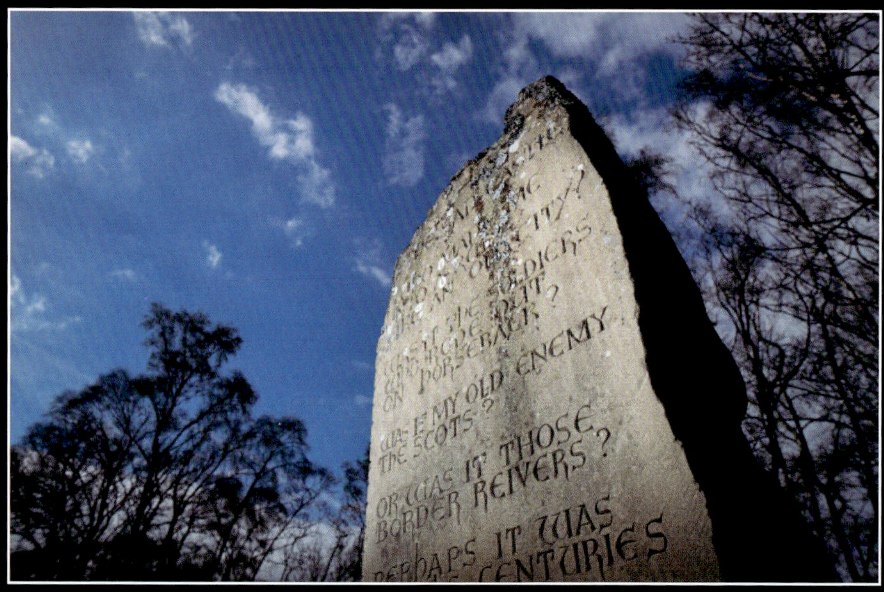

Settings

> Focal length: 16mm
> Aperture: f/5.6
> Shutter speed: 1/250 sec.
> ISO: 200

CANON REBEL T6/EOS 1300D

» FE LOCK

FE lock is the flash equivalent to AE lock, allowing you to lock the flash exposure for both the built-in flash and fitted Speedlite. A test flash must first be fired so that the flash exposure can be measured before locking. This means that FE lock isn't subtle and can easily distract a live subject (and can cause a human subject to think that you've exposed the final shot). If you don't want this distraction, don't use FE lock.

FE lock is particularly useful when the scene you want to shoot features highly reflective surfaces that would normally cause exposure problems with flash. With FE lock, you could aim the flash toward a part of the scene with more average reflectivity, lock the flash exposure, and then reframe and shoot as intended.

Notes
FE lock can't be used in Live View.

If ⚡ blinks in the viewfinder, your subject distance exceeds the effective flash distance. Either move closer to your subject, use a larger aperture, or increase the ISO setting.

The term FE lock is often shortened to FEL.

Setting FE lock

1) Raise the built-in flash or attach and switch on your Speedlite.

2) Aim the camera at your subject and press the shutter-release button down half way to focus. Check that ⚡ is displayed in the viewfinder.

3) Press ✳. The flash will fire and the exposure details will be recorded. FEL will be displayed briefly in the viewfinder and ⚡* will replace ⚡. If you press ✳ again, the process will be repeated.

4) Re-compose your shot and press the shutter-release button down fully to make the final exposure.

5) FE lock will be deactivated automatically and normal flash operation will resume.

» EXTERNAL FLASHES

Fitting an external Speedlite will open up more options for creative flash effects. Canon recommends that you do not use third-party flashes with the Rebel T6/EOS 1300D, but companies such as Metz, Nissin, Sigma, and Yongnuo all produce compatible flashes.

As with the built-in flash, the flash sync speed for external flashes is 1/200 sec., unless the flash is capable of hi-speed sync (see opposite). You can set certain Speedlite functions via **Flash control > External flash func. setting** on the 📷 menu, although you should be aware that third-party flashes may not be as adjustable using the **External flash func. setting** menu as a Canon Speedlite.

Fitting an external flash

1) Make sure that both your Rebel T6/EOS 1300D and Speedlite are switched off.

2) Slide the Speedlite shoe into the hotshoe of the camera. If your Speedlite has a locking collar, press the locking button and slide the collar round until it clicks into the "locked" position.

3) Turn the Speedlite on first, followed by the camera.

4) ⚡ will be displayed in the viewfinder or on the rear LCD if you are in Live View.

5) To remove the Speedlite, switch off the Rebel T6/EOS 1300D and Speedlite, and reverse the procedure in step 2.

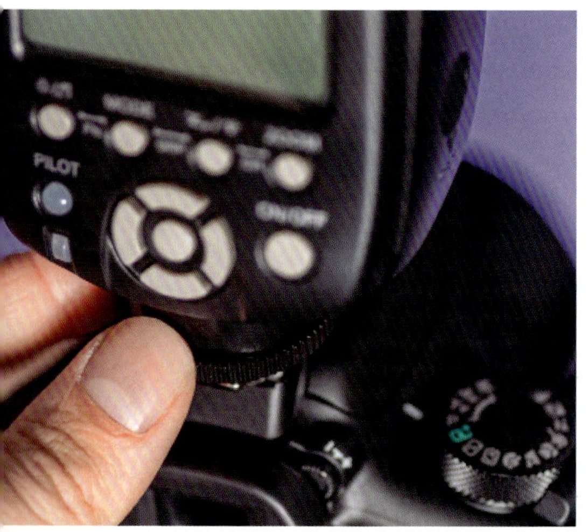

Notes

The settings available on the **Flash control** menu will differ according to the specifications of the Speedlite you are using.

The built-in flash is disabled when an external Speedlite is fitted and switched on.

› External flash func. setting

The **External flash func. setting** screen lets you set the shooting functions of compatible Speedlites in-camera rather than on the Speedlite itself. The available **External flash func. setting** options vary from Speedlite to Speedlite, but three of the more common settings you might encounter are **Zoom**, **High Speed Sync**, and **Flash exposure bracketing**.

Zoom

If your compatible flash has a zoom head, selecting **Auto** will ensure that the flash adjusts to match the focal length of the lens to ensure even coverage across the image frame. You can, however, choose to adjust the zoom head on the flash yourself. This would usually be done if you used a lens that didn't supply the necessary focal length information for **Auto** zoom, but you can also zoom the flash head for creative effect (zooming in to focus light or zooming out to spread the light more).

High Speed Sync (HSS)

The Rebel T6/EOS 1300D's relatively slow sync speed of 1/200 sec. can be limiting when you want to use flash as a fill light in bright conditions. To get around this, Canon's current Speedlites (with the exception of the 90EX) have an HSS mode, which enables you to use flash with shutter speeds of up to 1/4000 sec.

HSS works by constantly pulsing the Speedlite's output as the shutter curtains travel across the sensor during the exposure, effectively turning the flash into a continuous light source. This reduces the power of the flash (and therefore the effective distance) as the Speedlite has to discharge many times rather than once. However, as long as you keep your subject relatively close to the camera, HSS is an invaluable tool.

Flash exposure bracketing

Bracketing with a Speedlite is similar in concept to standard exposure bracketing, but it's not a feature you will find on every Speedlite—in fact, it's reserved for the high-end models. Once set, **Flash exposure bracketing** adjusts the Speedlite's output between shots rather than the shutter speed, aperture or ISO. Bracketing can usually be applied in ⅓-, ½-, or 1-stop increments.

› Speedlite range

Canon currently produces five Speedlite models that range in size, power, functions, and cost. By far the smallest and least powerful of the range is the 90EX, which was designed originally for use with Canon's EOS M camera. Unusually for such a simple Speedlite it can be used as an optical master flash to trigger other compatible flashes.

More sophisticated and better specified is the 270EX II, which features a zoom and bounce head. However, unlike the 90EX it cannot be used as a master flash to fire other Speedlites.

The 320EX is Canon's mid-range Speedlite. Unique to the 320EX is a built-in LED that provides a constant light source. This is useful when shooting video, but the LED light is relatively weak, so you need to keep your subject close to the camera for the illumination to be effective. As with the 270EX II, the 320EX can be used as a slave flash, but not as a master flash.

The Speedlite 430EX III-RT is a new professional-quality flash. The headline feature is integrated radio triggering in addition to optical triggering. Other features include HSS and 1st/2nd curtain flash sync, plus comprehensive exposure compensation options.

The 600EX-RT is the largest, heaviest, and best-specified Canon Speedlite model. Like the 430EX III-RT, it has integrated radio triggering and optical wireless flash control. The 600EX-RT also features weather sealing, High Speed Sync, and 18 custom functions.

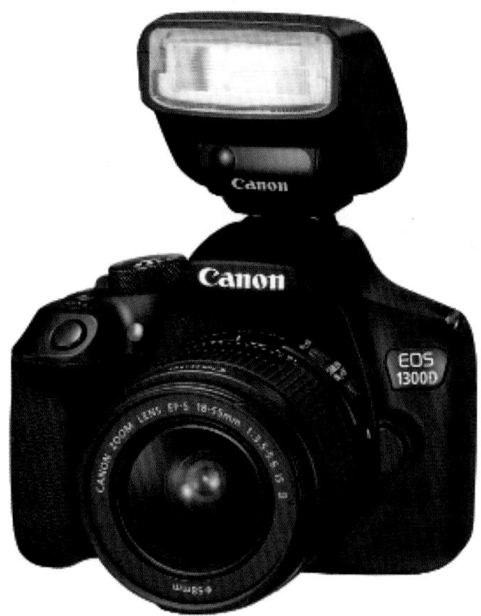

SPEEDLITE   **»**
The Rebel T6/EOS 1300D and Canon 270EX II.
© Canon

THE SPEEDLITE RANGE
© Canon (all images)

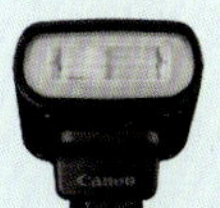 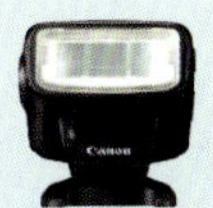 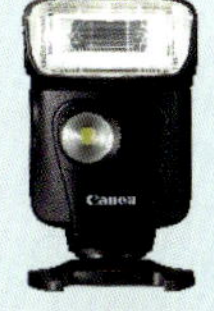 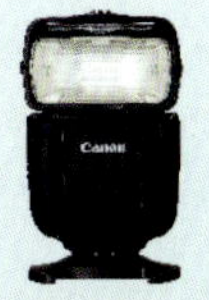 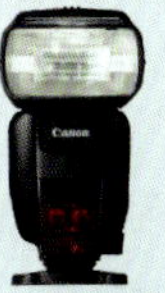

	90EX	270EX II	320EX	430EX III-RT	600EX-RT
GN @ ISO 100	29ft/9m	89ft/27m	104ft/32m	141ft/43m	196.9ft/60m
Tilt/swivel	No	Tilt only	Yes	Yes	Yes
Focal length coverage*	24mm	28–50mm	24–50mm	14–105mm	14–200mm
AF-assist beam	Yes	Yes	Yes	Yes	Yes
Flash metering	E-TTL/ E-TTL II	E-TTL/ E-TTL II	E-TTL/ E-TTL II	E-TTL/ E-TTL II	E-TTL II/ TTL/Manual
Approximate recycling time	5.5 sec.	0.1–3.9 sec.	0.1–2.3 sec.	0.1–3.5 sec.	0.1–5.5 sec. (0.1–3.3 sec. using quick flash)
Batteries	2 x AAA/LR03	2 x AA/LR6	4 x AA/LR6	4 x AA/LR6	4 x AA/LR6
Dimensions (w x h x d)	1.7 x 2 x 2.5 in./44 x 52 x 65mm	2.5 x 2.6 x 3.0 in./64 x 65 x 72mm	2.75 x 4.5 x 3.09 in./70 x 115 x 78.4mm	2.7 x 4.5 x 3.09 in./70 x 114 x 98mm	3.1 x 5.6 x 4.9 in./79.7 x 143 x 125mm
Weight (without batteries)	1.8 oz 50g	5.1 oz 155g	9.7 oz 275g	11.6 oz 320g	15 oz 425g
Other information	–	HSS	HSS	HSS, 1st and 2nd curtain sync.	HSS, 1st and 2nd curtain sync.

*Full-frame equivalent

› Bounce flash

Direct flash is a hard and unflattering light that benefits from being softened. A simple way to soften it is to reflect or "bounce" the light off another surface before it reaches your subject. This increases the area the light comes from, which makes it softer.

Bounce flash isn't possible with the built-in flash, but with the exception of the 90EX, all of Canon's Speedlites have heads that can be angled in at least one direction. The most common method of bouncing flash is to angle the head upward to bounce the light from a ceiling down onto your subject.

However, the surface you bounce the light from must be neutral in color, as the flash will be tinted by the surface color if there is any present. Another potential problem is that by bouncing the flash you are increasing the distance the light has to travel to reach your subject. It's all too easy to exceed the effective distance of your flash unless your flash has a high GN or you use a large aperture or high ISO.

BLUE 
This shot required two off-camera Speedlites. One was used to illuminate the subject from above, while the other was used to light the blue background.

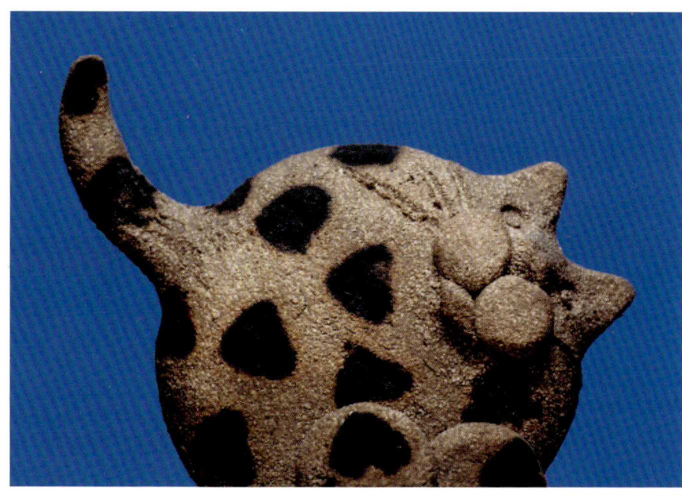

› Off-camera flash

Taking a Speedlite off-camera allows you to direct the light in a more creative way. This means you can use flash as a side light to create interesting shadows and emphasize texture, or as a backlight to create silhouettes, produce rim-lighting, or illuminate translucent subjects.

There are two main ways to trigger an off-camera Speedlite: either via an E-TTL cord or wirelessly. E-TTL cords provide a wired connection between the camera's hotshoe and the Speedlite. They come in a variety of lengths and are a relatively inexpensive—Canon produces the OC-E3 E-TTL, but there are also third-party alternatives. The problem with an E-TTL cord is that the Speedlite can only be as far from the camera as the length of the cord, and the cord can also be tripped over.

A neater solution is a wireless connection, which comes in two forms: optical and radio. Optical systems require two Speedlites. A "master" Speedlite is fitted to the camera and a second, off-camera Speedlite, is used as a remote "slave." When the master flash fires, the slave detects its flash and fires in turn. With a compatible Speedlite, optical triggering allows the use of E-TTL metering, making exposures easy to calculate. The drawback is that the various Speedlites need to

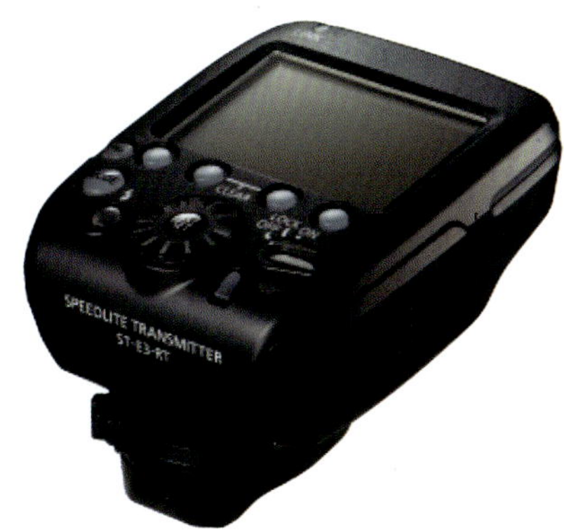

OFF-CAMERA ⌃
Canon's new Speedlite Transmitter ST-E3-RT is a radio trigger that can be used to fire 430EX III-RT and 600EX-RT Speedlites. Unlike some third-party systems it is E-TTL II compatible.
© Canon

be able to "see" each other, which can sometimes limit your positioning.

Radio triggering requires a radio trigger unit that is attached to the camera's hotshoe and fires your off-camera Speedlites when the shutter-release button is pressed. Radio triggering doesn't require "line-of-sight," but it is often not E-TTL compatible, which means the flash exposure needs to be set manually. Canon's 430EX III-RT and 600EX-RT both have built-in radio triggering.

ACCESSORIES

It's possible to shoot successfully with just your Rebel T6/EOS 1300D, a lens, and a memory card. However, it's an unusual photographer who just sticks with the equipment they initially purchased. Optional accessories can make your life easier and help increase the odds of you shooting a masterpiece.

The Rebel T6/EOS 1300D is a system camera, which means it can be fitted with a wide variety of accessories to enhance its capabilities. Canon produces a wide range of accessories, including Speedlites, battery grips, and remote releases. As with lenses and flashes, you don't have to stick solely to the Canon brand—there are many third-party alternatives that work just as well and are sometimes cheaper.

Which accessories you need will largely depend on your preferred subject area: some photographers don't want or need to be encumbered by a tripod, while others won't leave home without one. However, it pays not to rush into buying a particular accessory, but to be honest with yourself about how much use it will get— something that just sits gathering dust after being used once or twice isn't really a worthwhile investment.

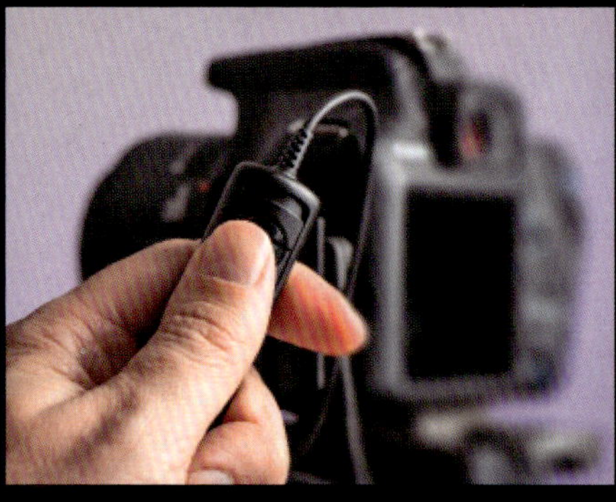

REMOTE RELEASE ⌃
Some accessories work well together: the RS-60E3 remote switch works well with a tripod for instance.

LANDSCAPE »
For genres such as landscape photography, a tripod is almost a necessity.

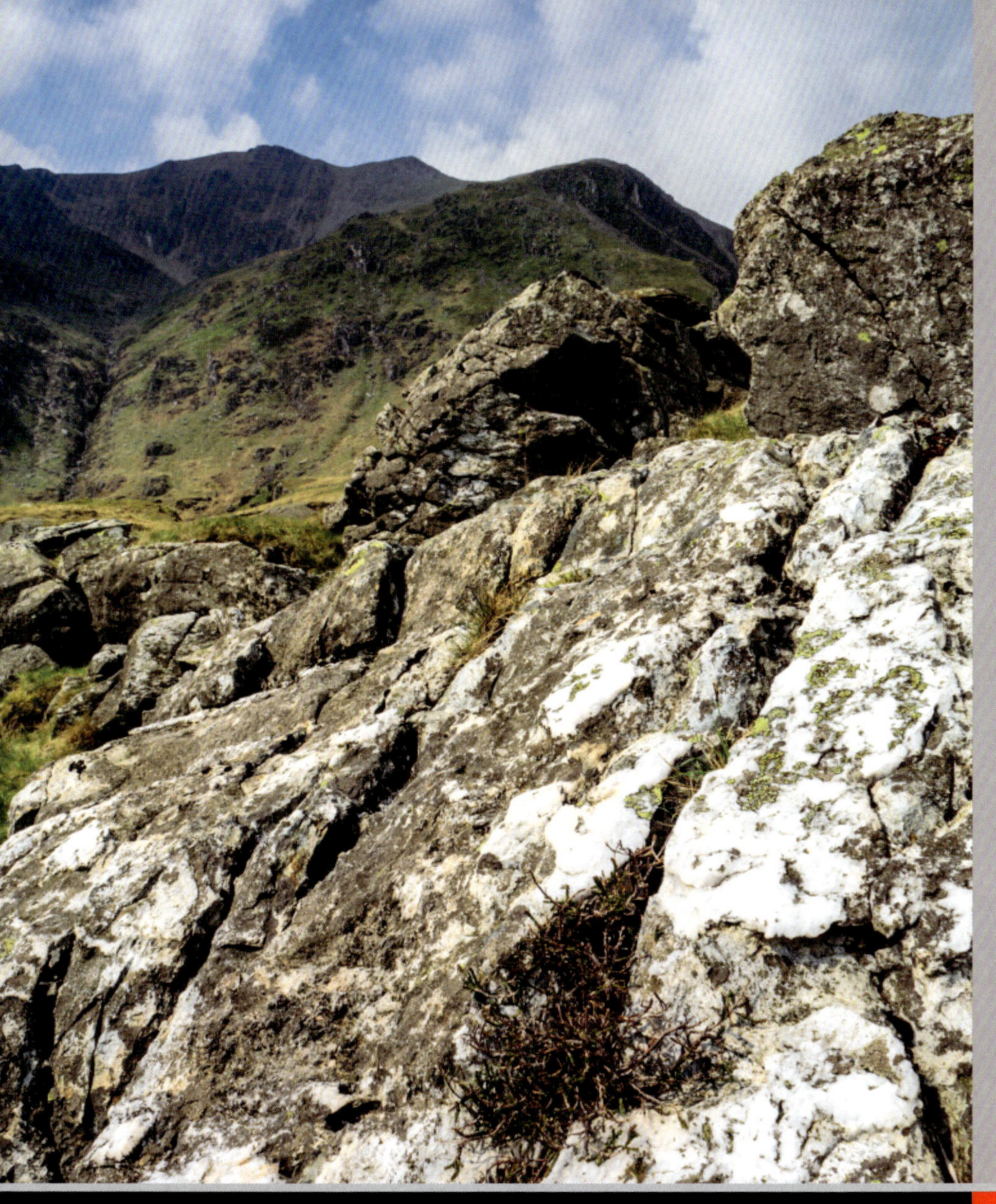

6

» CANON ACCESSORIES

› GPS receiver (GP-E2)

The GP-E2 fits to your Rebel T6/EOS 1300D's hotshoe and records the location information (longitude, latitude, elevation, and direction) of your images to the EXIF metadata. This information can be read by software such as Adobe Lightroom, so your images can be quickly sorted by location and shown on a world map. The GP-E2 will also automatically update the clock in your Rebel T6/EOS 1300D so it remains accurate.

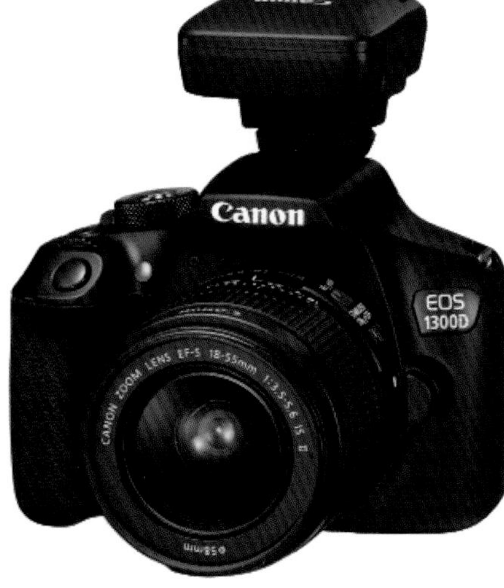

CANON GP-E2 ⋙
© Canon

› DC Coupler (DR-E10)

Canon's DR-E10 DC Coupler replaces the battery in your Rebel T6/EOS 1300D, allowing you to power the camera from a domestic wall socket (in conjunction with the Canon CA-PS700 AC Adaptor). It's most useful when you're using your camera continuously for long periods of time, such as printing directly from your camera, running a slide show, or viewing images on an HDTV. You can also use the older ACK-E10 AC Adaptor in a similar way.

› Remote switches

A remote switch allows you to fire the shutter without touching the camera. The RS-60E3 is a remote switch that connects to your Rebel T6/EOS 1300D via a short cable. You can also use remote switches with an N3-type connector designed for EOS cameras such as the 5D MkIII via an RA-E3 Remote Switch Adaptor (the Rebel T6/EOS 1300D has an E3-type socket).

» FILTERS

A filter is a piece of glass, gelatin, or optical resin that is designed to alter the light that passes through it in a specific way. Filters are sold either as round and threaded (enabling them to be screwed to the front of a lens), or square/rectangular (to be slotted into a holder attached to the lens).

Round filters are usually made of high-quality optical glass, with a metal or heavy duty plastic surround. The main drawback is that if you have two or more lenses with different filter thread sizes you either need to buy another filter of the same type in a different size, or buy a step-up or step-down adaptor ring to use the same filter on those lenses.

Filter holder systems are more easily adapted to different sizes of lens as they are attached via cheap adaptor rings.

There is a number of different filter holder systems to choose from. Cokin produce a popular range of holder systems, including the A system, which takes 67mm filters; the 84/85mm P system; the 100mm Z-Pro system; and the 120mm X-Pro system. Other filter system manufacturers include Formatt, Hitech, Lee Filters, and NiSi.

Notes

Don't use **AWB** if you use a colored filter, as **AWB** will try to correct for the color of the filter.

A step-up adaptor ring lets you fit a large filter onto a lens with a smaller filter thread; a step-down adaptor ring lets you fit a small filter onto a lens with a larger filter thread. The latter isn't recommended, though, as it can lead to vignetting.

The filter thread size is shown on the front face of all Canon lenses. It can also be found on the inside of the lens cap.

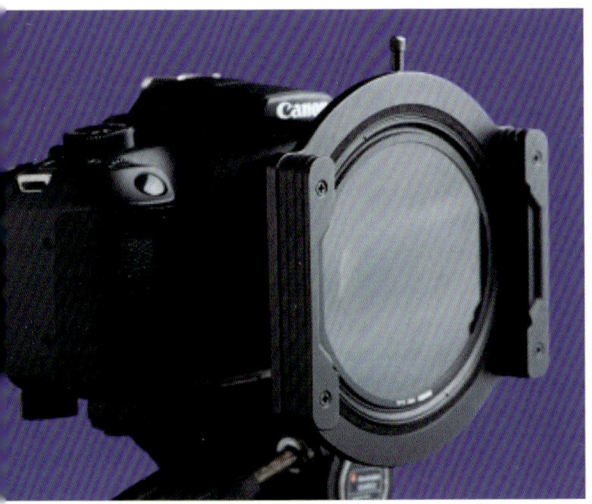

FILTER HOLDER «
NiSi 100mm filter holder.

› UV or skylight

UV and skylight filters absorb ultraviolet light, which is typically found at high altitudes and on hazy days. UV light can introduce a distinctive blue cast: skylight filters have a slightly pink tint to them, helping to compensate for this, while UV filters are more neutral. As neither filter affects exposure, they are often also used to protect the front elements of lenses from damage, although dedicated "protection" filters are now available for that purpose.

Notes
ND filters are often sold using an optical density figure. A 1-stop ND filter has an optical density of 0.3, a 2-stop filter has a density of 0.6, and so on.

Use a fixed ISO value when using ND filters. If you use ISO AUTO, the ISO will increase in an attempt to negate the effect of the filter.

› Neutral density filters

A neutral density (ND) filter is semi-opaque, so it reduces the amount of light reaching the sensor. This simulates shooting in lower light conditions, enabling you to use slower shutter speeds or larger apertures than would otherwise be possible. ND filters are available in a variety of strengths, from 1-stop (which is equivalent to halving the ISO speed) to very dense 10- or 15-stop filters that can often extend exposures that would be fractions of a second into whole seconds, sometimes even whole minutes.

As long as the ND filter isn't too dense, the Rebel T6/EOS 1300D's exposure and AF systems should be able to cope without a problem. However, the very dense 10–15-stop filters generally block too much light for the viewfinder AF system to work, although sometimes (in bright conditions) the Live View AF is just about able to manage. If this happens, focus *before* fitting the filter, then switch to MF so that focus doesn't shift when the filter is attached.

When an "extreme" ND filter is used, you won't be able to see through the viewfinder, so frame your shots before the filter is fitted.

» MONOCHROME

10-stop ND filters are typically used to extend shutter speeds and blur movement. This produces a slightly surreal effect when shooting subjects such as tidal water, which often suit a black-and-white approach, rather than color.

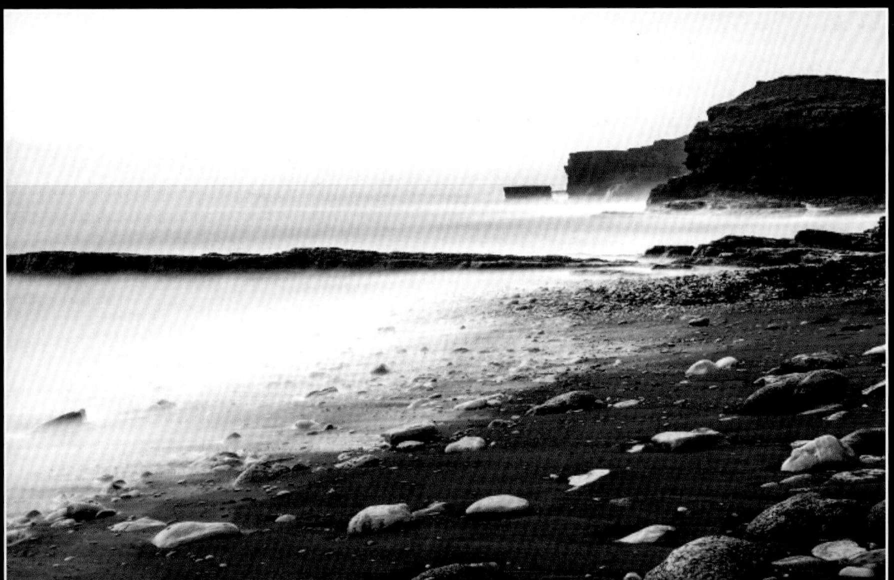

Settings
> Focal length: 35mm
> Aperture: f/11
> Shutter speed: 133 sec.
> ISO: 100

› Polarizing filters

When light is reflected from a non-metallic surface it is scattered randomly, reducing the color saturation (or transparency) of the surface—light scattered this way is said to have been "polarized." A polarizing filter (or polarizer) cuts out polarized light from every plane but one, restoring the color saturation (or transparency) of the surface.

Polarizers are made of glass, mounted in a holder that can be rotated through 360° to vary the strength of the polarizing effect. As a polarizer is slightly opaque, it will reduce the amount of light reaching the sensor. The camera's TTL exposure metering will automatically adjust when a polarizing filter is fitted, unless you're shooting in **M** mode, in which case the exposure adjustment must be set manually. The amount of compensation required will vary, but 2 stops is a good starting point.

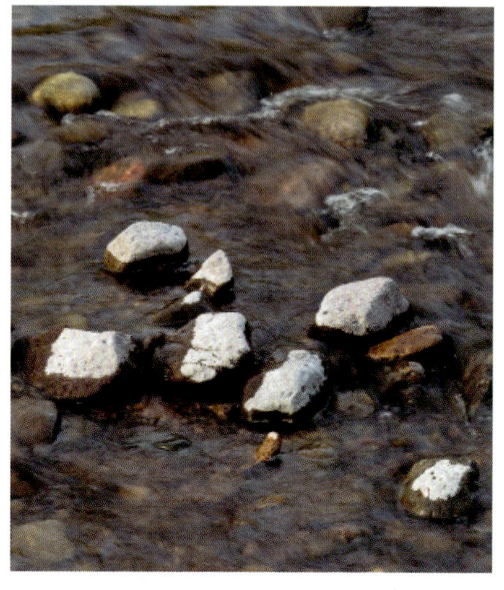

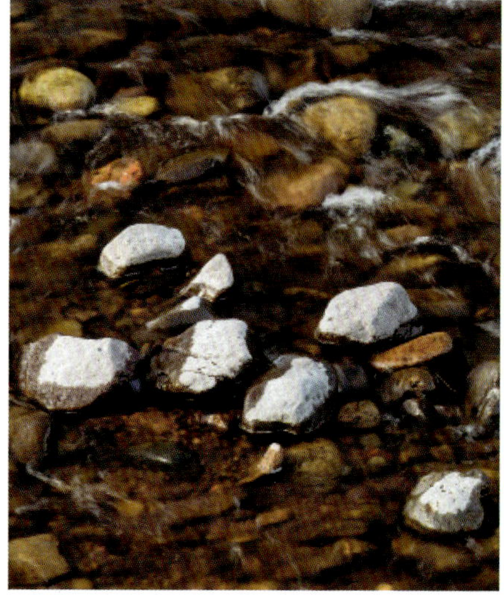

WATER »

Without a polarizer there's a milky glare to the surface of this river (top). With a polarizing filter fitted this glare is removed, making the water appear more transparent (bottom).

» CLOUD

Polarizing filters can be used to deepen the blue of a sky. The effect is strongest when the polarizer is at 90° to the sun; as you change the angle, the effect diminishes, and beyond 110° (or below 70°) a polarizer has little or no effect on the sky at all. The effect works well when there's some cloud in the sky, as the deepening of the blue sky helps the clouds to stand out more.

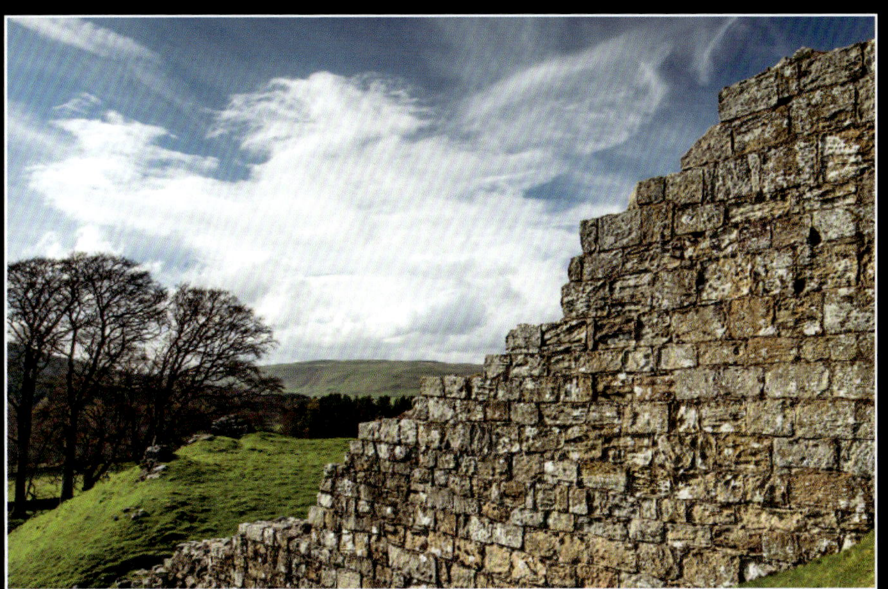

Settings

> Focal length: 24mm
> Aperture: f/14
> Shutter speed: 1/100 sec.
> ISO: 100

› Graduated ND filters

A graduated ND filter is a close relation of the ND filter, although the graduated version has a clear bottom half and a semi-opaque top half. They are used to balance the exposure across an image, when one part of a scene is far brighter than the other (exceeding the camera's dynamic range and causing overexposure in the brighter area).

Graduated ND filters are sold in a variety of strengths (most often from 1–3 stops) and the greater the brightness difference in your scene, the stronger the filter you need to use. As well as strength, graduated ND filters are also differentiated by the way that the clear area transitions to the semi-opaque area: the transition can be soft, hard, or very hard. Graduated ND filters with a hard transition are easier to position accurately, as the transition is more clearly seen, but they are more difficult to use when the difference between the light and the dark areas of a scene isn't perfectly straight.

GRACIATED ⌄
GRADUATED ⌄
Lee Filters 3-stop (0.9) graduated ND filter.

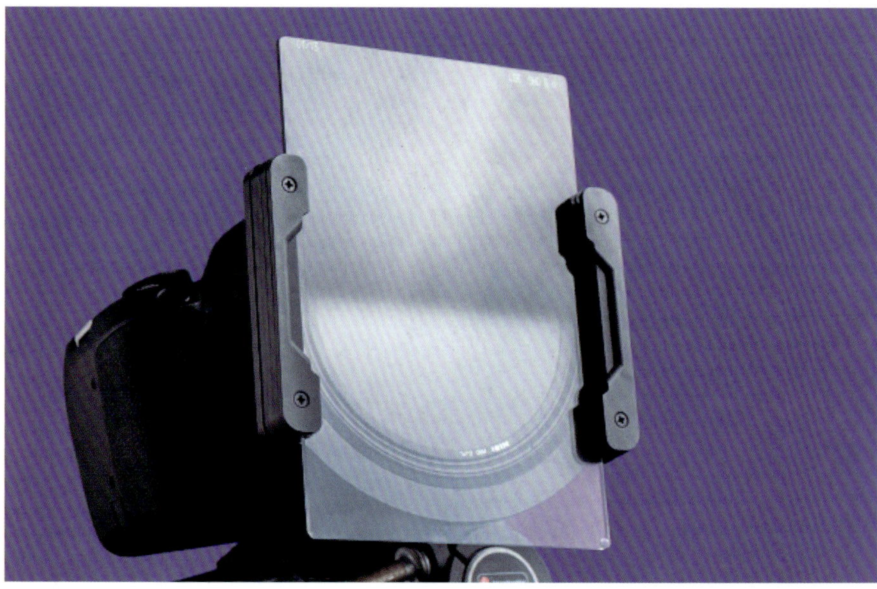

» SKY

Landscape photographers typically benefit from owning and using graduated ND filters, as the sky is often brighter than the foreground. The brightness difference between the sky and the foreground in this scene was such that I needed a 3-stop graduated ND filter to balance the exposure.

Settings
> Focal length: 24mm
> Aperture: f/14
> Shutter speed: 0.4 sec.
> ISO: 200

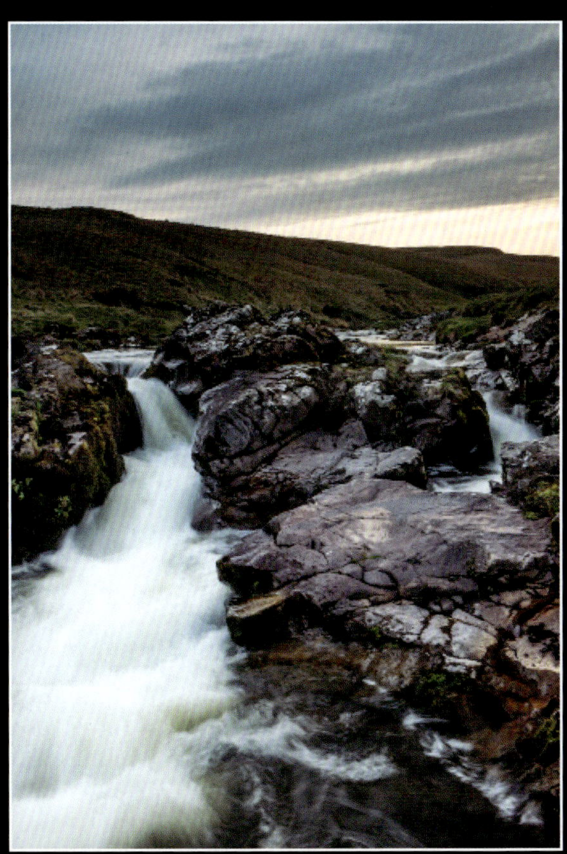

There's a lot to be said for handholding a camera—it means you can react quickly to events and recompose fluidly as the situation demands. However, if there's less need to think on your feet and you're working in less-than-ideal light, you'll benefit from giving your camera more solid support.

› Tripods

Using shutter speeds longer than 1 sec. is a creative way to blur movement, but it's impossible to handhold a camera at such long shutter speeds, making a tripod all but essential. Tripods also force you to slow down and think about your photography, allowing you to make subtle tweaks to composition and even lighting before you fire the shutter. A tripod will be useful when shooting movies as well—footage shot with a handheld camera can be jerky and can even induce nausea in whoever views the footage.

When you choose a tripod, it's important to think about factors such as weight and height. If a tripod is too heavy you'll be less inclined to carry it far, but one that is too light may not provide adequate stability in anything but a light breeze. Carbon fiber tripods offer a good compromise between weight and stability, but they are more costly than plastic or aluminum models.

Tripods are available in a variety of heights, but the ideal maximum height is one that reaches your eye level without using the center column (raising the center column raises the center of gravity of the camera/tripod combination, making it less stable). However, long-legged

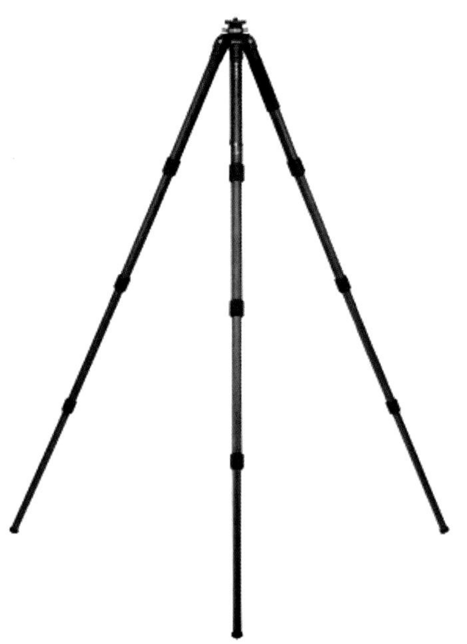

CARBON FIBER »
Benro Mach3 TMA48CXL carbon fiber tripod.
© Benro

tripods are invariably heavier and more bulky than their shorter relations; height is therefore another compromise that often has to be made.

Tripods come either with a head fitted or legs only (with a screw fitting that allows the attachment of a separate head). The latter option is a more flexible—and expensive—option that lets you choose the head that best suits your needs.

There are three basic types of tripod head: three-way, ball, and geared. Three-way heads are the simplest type and the most common, with individual locking handles that allow you to move the head in three axes.

Ball heads are light, strong, and quick to set up, as they only have a single locking mechanism. However, it can be fiddly to make minor adjustments.

Geared heads are the easiest to make fine adjustments to, as they combine three distinct axes of movement (like a three-way head) with geared micro-adjustments. The downside is their complexity makes them far heavier and more expensive than the other two types.

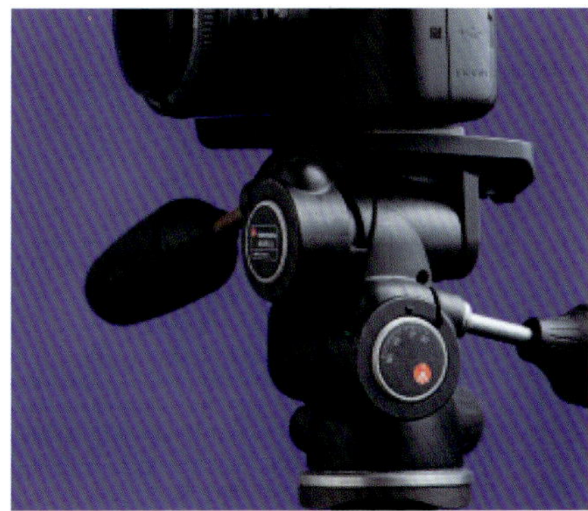

SUPPORTED ▲
Manfrotto 3-way tripod head.

Notes
If you're using a tripod and your lens has Image Stabilization, switch IS off.

Ideally, the legs of the tripod should be set so the tripod won't tip over when the camera is attached. On uneven ground you may have to set the legs at different heights to achieve this.

When shooting long exposures try not to move around your tripod too much. It's easy to either knock the tripod or, on soft ground, cause one of the legs to sink slightly.

7 MACRO

Macro is the art of shooting the very small. Most lenses won't focus closely enough for true macro photography, so you either need a macro lens or to temporarily modify your standard lenses.

A macro lens is one that is able to project an image onto a sensor that's life size or larger. This means that if you were able to physically measure the projected image of your subject on the sensor, it would be exactly the same size or larger than the subject itself in "real life." A life-size image is said to have a reproduction ratio of 1:1, twice life-size 2:1, and so on.

The reproduction ratio is one of two ways that manufacturers show the macro capabilities of a lens; the other is the magnification figure. Unfortunately, lens manufacturers tend to use one or the other, but rarely both. To convert a reproduction ratio to a magnification figure, divide the number on the left of the reproduction ratio by the number on the right (so 1:4 would give a magnification figure of 0.25x). To convert in the other direction, divide 1 by the magnification to get the figure that should be placed on the right side of the reproduction ratio.

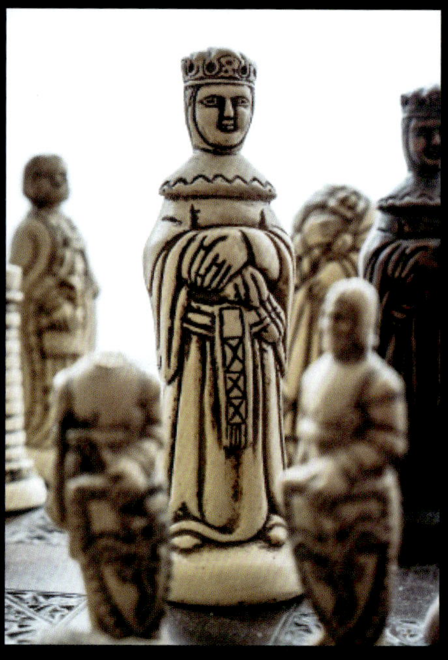

CLOSE ⌃
The kit zoom that can be bought with the Rebel T6/EOS 1300D is ideal for shots like this, which are close-ups, but not true macro images.

MACRO »
A true macro lens will let you achieve a 1:1 reproduction ratio. For this shot of a dewdrop under a blade of grass, I used a Canon 100mm macro lens.

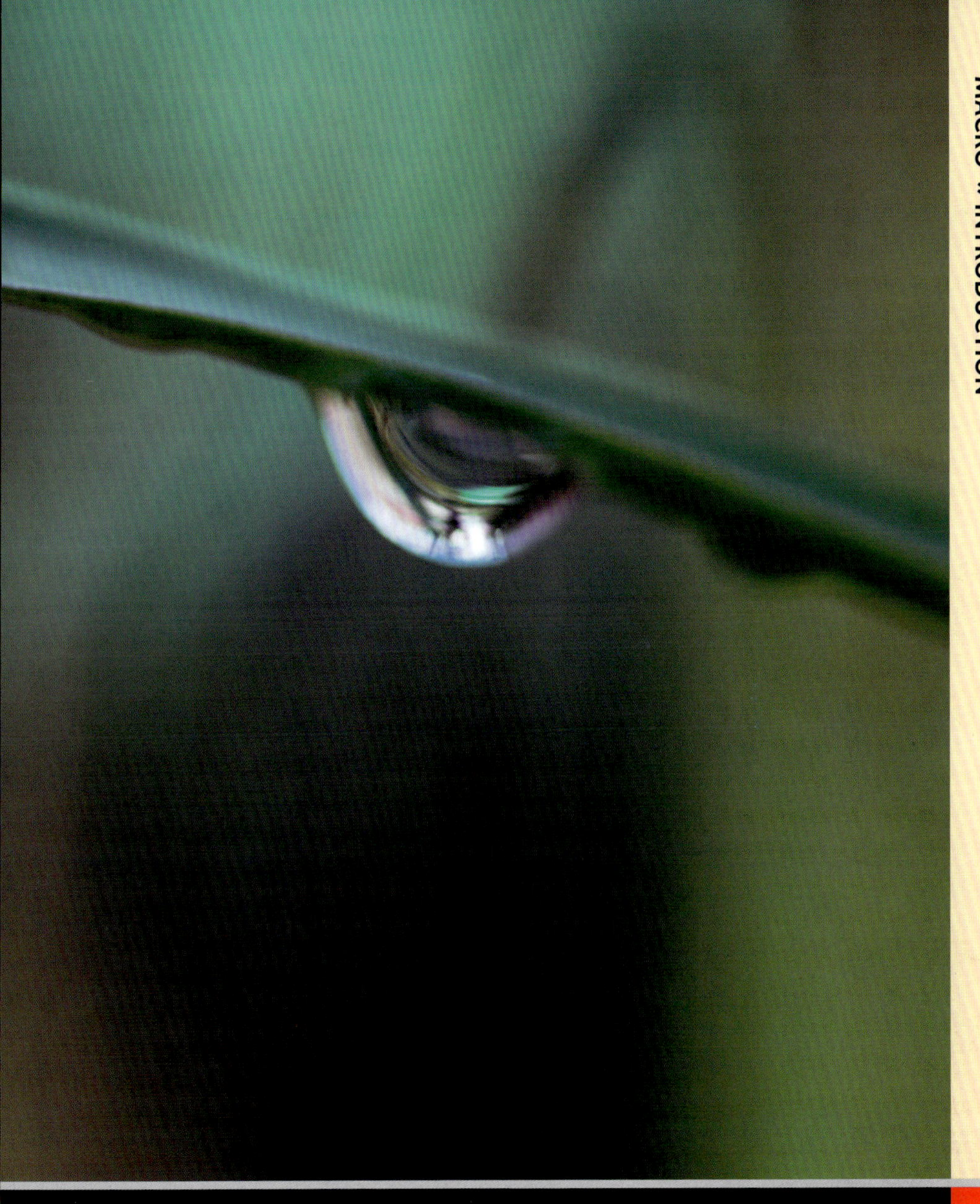

» MACRO SOLUTIONS

Remarkably, it's possible to shoot macro images without purchasing a dedicated macro lens. With the addition of the equipment described here it's possible to extend the focusing capabilities of any lens. This equipment won't give you the image quality of a true macro lens, but it is a viable way to try macro photography without spending a lot of money.

› Close-up attachment lenses

A close-up attachment lens screws directly into the filter thread on the front of a lens and reduces the minimum focusing distance. Close-up attachment lenses are appealing as a first step into macro photography because they're easy to use and don't interfere with either the autofocus or exposure system.

Close-up attachment lenses are available in a variety of strengths, which is indicated by a diopter value: the higher the diopter value, the greater the magnification. It's also possible to stack close-up attachment lenses to increase the strength of magnification, but image quality will take a noticeable drop. For optimum image quality it's better to use one close-up attachment lens with a prime lens, rather than a zoom.

Canon currently produces two close-up attachment lenses: a +2 diopter (Type 500D) to fit 52mm, 55mm, 72mm, and 77mm filter threads, and a +4 diopter (Type 250D) to fit 52mm and 55mm filter threads.

STEPPING RINGS «
Just like screw-in filters it's worth buying the largest close-up attachment lens you can, and then adapting it for your different lenses.

› Reversing ring

If you switch a lens around so that the front element faces into the camera, it instantly becomes a macro lens. A reversing ring is a metal ring that has a bayonet fitting on one side (which will fit the lens mount of your camera) and is threaded on the other (allowing you to screw a lens to the ring via its filter thread).

As reversing rings don't usually make an electronic connection between the lens and the camera, both AF and aperture control will be disabled. This means it's actually easier to use older, manual focus lenses with an aperture ring, rather than EOS lenses. Simply attach the lens and set the mode dial to **M**. Then, set the shutter speed as normal and adjust the aperture ring on the lens until the correct exposure is obtained.

MINOLTA »
You don't need to stick to Canon lenses with a reversing ring: old Minolta MD lenses are a good choice and are in plentiful supply.

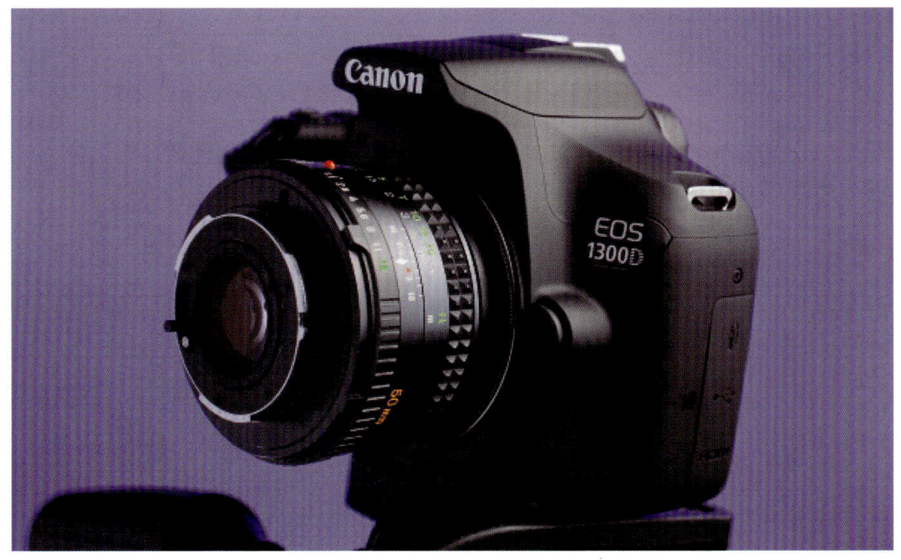

› Extension tubes

Extension tubes (also known as extension rings) are hollow tubes that fit between the camera and lens. This decreases the minimum focusing distance of the lens and increases the magnification.

Extension tubes from third-party manufacturers are often sold in sets of three rings of different lengths, which can be used separately or combined to create the maximum magnification.

As there's no glass in an extension tube there is very little loss of image quality, regardless of the make you buy, but there is an important difference between different brands of extension tube. The cheapest extension tubes lack the electronic connection between the lens and the camera, so AF and aperture control are disabled.

Canon produces two extension tubes: the EF 12II (with 12mm of extension) and the EF 25II (25mm extension). Both of these extension tubes retain AF and aperture control.

INTERNET »
Web sites such as Ebay are a good place to find pre-owned close-up equipment, such as this Russian Soviet-era set of bellows I use. They don't fit directly onto an EOS camera, but all that was required was an M42-to-EOS adaptor.

› Bellows

Bellows work on the same principle as extension tubes, but they are extended or compressed along a guide rail, which makes it easier to adjust the magnification. Once the magnification is set, the bellows are locked into position ready for shooting.

The downside to using bellows is that they're heavier and more cumbersome than extension tubes, so most bellows systems are used in studios with the set-up mounted on a tripod. Bellows are also far more expensive than extension tubes.

Canon doesn't make bellows for the EOS system, but EOS-compatible units are made by companies such as Novoflex.

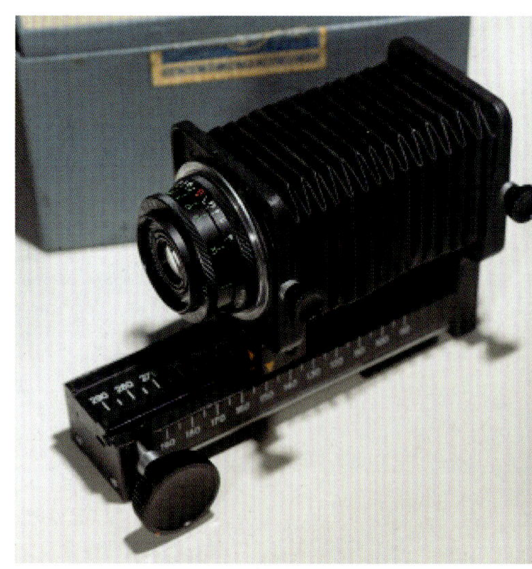

» FOCUS

It can be tricky to focus on macro subjects through the viewfinder, as the viewfinder is relatively small and the AF points don't cover the entire area of the viewfinder. Live View is a far better option, as you can position the AF point virtually anywhere in the scene (I picked the number 19 as the focal point for this shot).

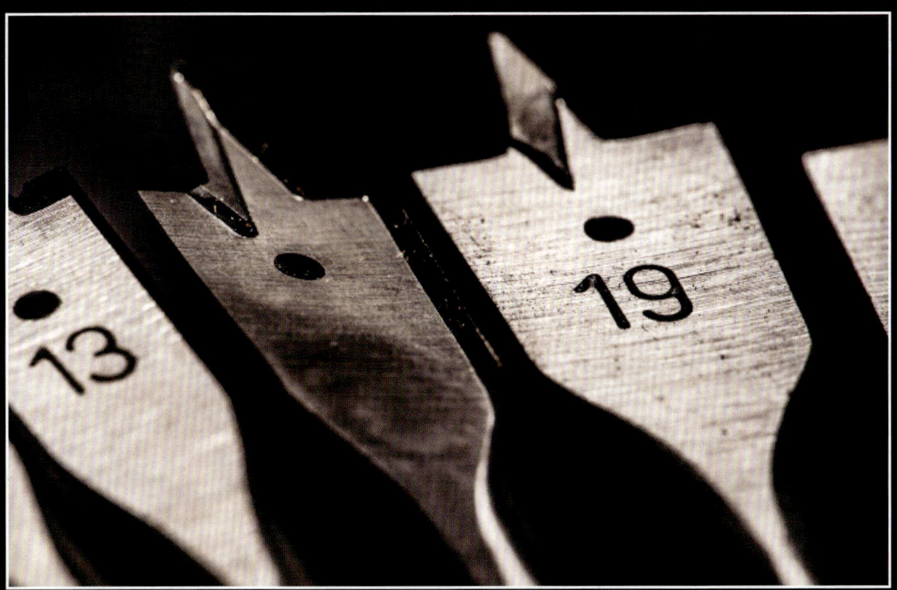

Settings

> Focal length: 100mm
> Aperture: f/16
> Shutter speed: 1/250 sec.
> ISO: 100

» TECHNIQUE

There are a variety of challenges that you'll face when shooting macro, and knowing what these are is a useful first step to solving them before you shoot.

› Working distance

The working distance of a macro lens is the distance from the lens to the subject for the required reproduction ratio. Longer focal length lenses have a greater working distance than those with a shorter focal length, and a large working distance is useful for several reasons. The main one is that it allows you to keep your distance from your subject. This means that you won't accidentally knock your subject with the lens and you'll also be less likely to scare away or distract a living subject—such as an insect—as you shoot.

The downside of using a longer focal length macro lens is that they are usually more expensive than shorter focal length lenses, and are inevitably heavier and more cumbersome to use; if you're handholding your camera then this extra weight can increase the risk of camera shake.

KEEPING YOUR DISTANCE ⌄

It's all too easy to knock a plant accidentally. Once knocked, the plant can often shake for some time, particularly when it's on a branch or a long, thin stem.

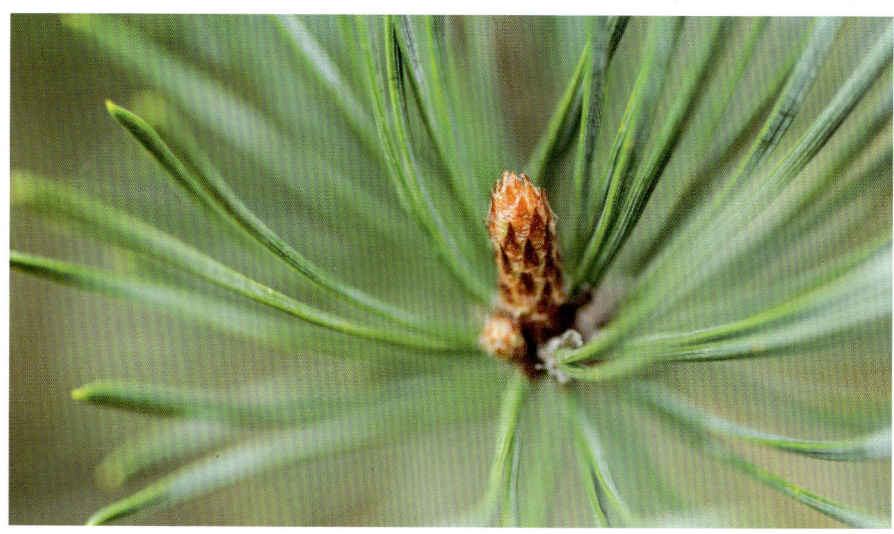

» ABSTRACT

Shooting close-up and macro is a great way to create abstract imagery. This can be done by concentrating purely on the details of a subject rather than the form or shape of the subject. This sheet of cracked glass made an excellent subject for an abstract image, creating a slight mystery as to what it actually is.

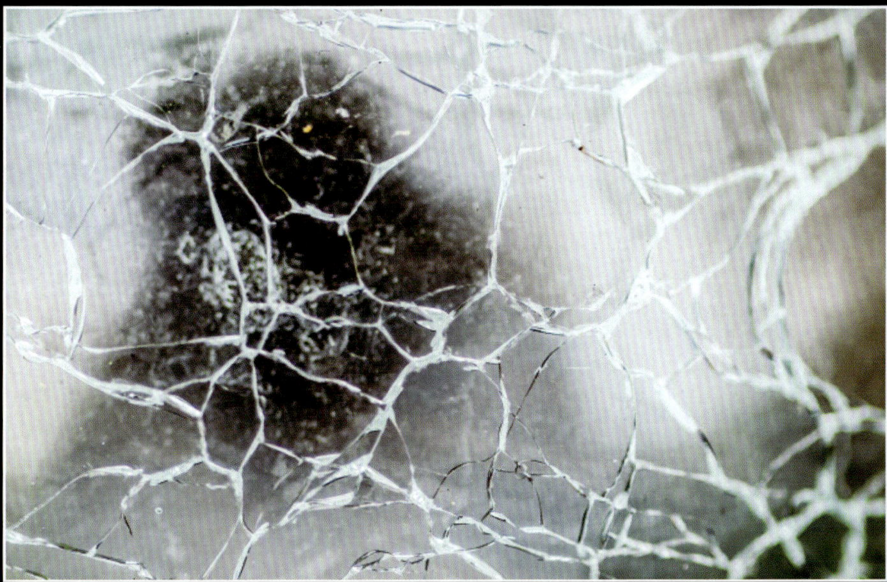

Settings
> Focal length: 100mm
> Aperture: f/5
> Shutter speed: 1/400 sec.
> ISO: 400

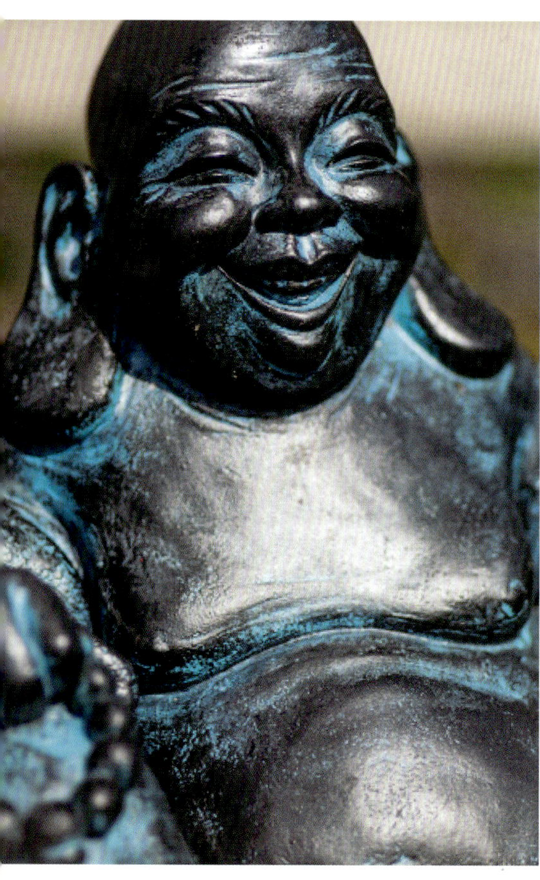

EYE ⌃
As there's so little depth of field in macro photographs, you need to think carefully about where you focus. For this shot I focused on the eyes of the statue to ensure they were sharp; it would have looked unusual if the eyes were out of focus.

Depth of field reduces with focus distance, so the closer you focus, the less depth of field you will have. When you shoot macro images this means you will have very little depth of field. As so little is sharp, selecting the most appropriate point of focus is very important, particularly if your subject is three-dimensional. Depth of field is less critical if a subject is a flat plane, but care should still be taken to ensure that it's perfectly parallel to the camera.

A subject that moves brings added problems, as it often doesn't take much movement for the subject to drift out of focus. If your subject is blowing in the wind, try to shelter it with your body. You can also select Continuous shooting and AI Servo AF (when using the viewfinder) and expose a number of frames. You can then edit the sequence later, deleting the images that don't have critical sharpness.

» SHUTTER SPEED

Despite the depth of field limitations, there is one good reason why you'd use a large aperture when shooting macro imagery—using a large aperture means that you can prioritize a faster shutter speed. This is useful when you're handholding your camera, as any movement of the lens will be magnified. Subjects that are prone to slight movement—such as flowers in a breeze—are also more likely to be unsharp for similar reasons.

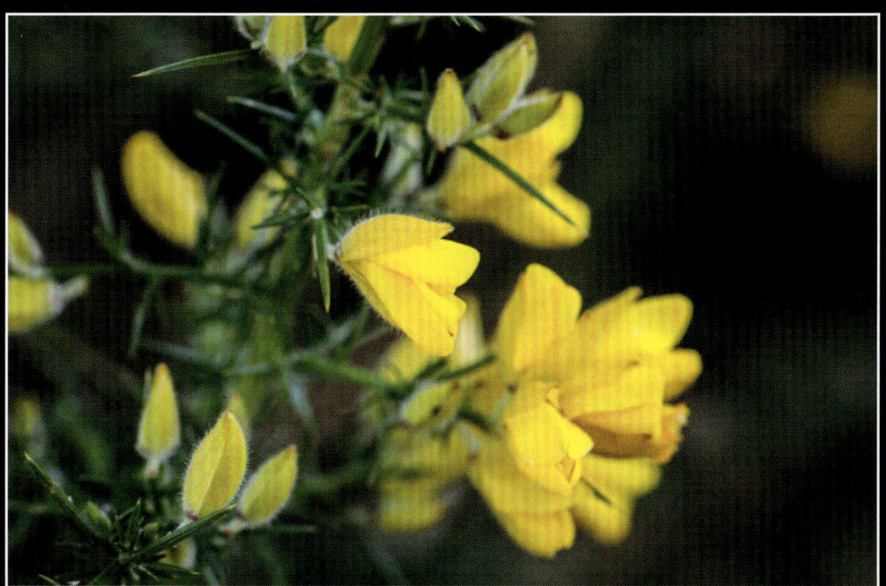

Settings
> Focal length: 100mm
> Aperture: f/8
> Shutter speed: 1/100 sec.
> ISO: 400

Using a small aperture to maximize depth of field means that you either have to use a slower shutter speed or a higher ISO. Alternatively, illuminating your subject will allow you to use faster shutter speeds without the need to increase the ISO (which is useful if your subject is moving or if you're handholding the camera). Any light source will help—even a flashlight—although the level of exposure control possible with flash makes it a more compelling solution.

Unfortunately, the Rebel T6/EOS 1300D's built-in flash is far from ideal—because of its position on the camera, the lens tends to get in the way and cast a shadow on your subject. An on-camera external flash is better, especially if the light can be softened by a diffuser (see chapter 5), but best of all is off-camera flash, which can be positioned so its light flatters your subject.

Another useful illumination source are ring lights. These lights "wrap" around the front of the lens creating a subtle and soft illumination for macro subjects. Canon currently produces two dedicated macro flashes: the Macro Twin Lite MT-24EX and Macro Ring Lite MR-14EX.

ROUND ⌄
Ring lights often create round highlights when they are used to illuminate reflective subjects and glass. The effect isn't unattractive, but it does give the game away about how the subject was lit.

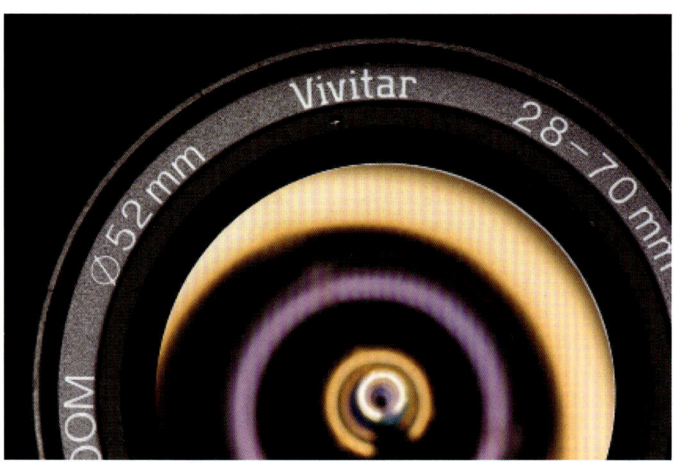

» MACRO LENSES

› Canon lenses

Canon currently produces six prime macro lenses. All but one of them offers a 1:1 (or better) reproduction ratio, and all but one can also be used as a conventional lens for non-macro photography.

The two shortest focal length lenses are the EF 50mm f/2.5 Compact Macro and EF-S 60mm f/2.8 Macro USM. These are small, lightweight lenses that can double as short telephotos suitable for subjects such as portraiture (albeit with relatively short working distances compared to Canon's other macro options). However, you could argue that the 50mm isn't a true macro as it only offers a 1:2 reproduction ratio.

The most specialized of Canon's macro lenses is the manual focus MP-E 65mm f/2.8 1–5x Macro. This lens boasts a 5:1 reproduction ratio, allowing you to capture macro images that are five times life size, although the downside is that the lens cannot be used for non-macro work.

Canon's most popular macro focal length is 100mm, and it produces two such lenses: the EF 100mm f/2.8 and the EF 100mm f/2.8L. The latter is the newer lens, with L-series status and a hybrid IS system that's effective when shooting macro images.

The largest, heaviest, and most expensive Canon macro lens is the EF 180mm f/3.5L Macro USM. With the longest working distance of all the Canon macros, this is the perfect lens when working with subjects that benefit from you keeping your distance.

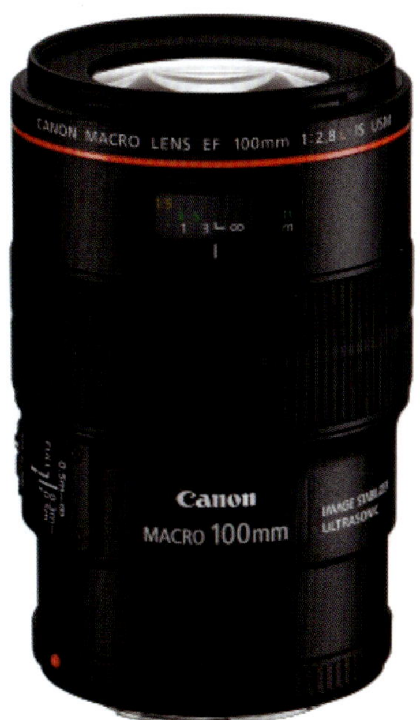

100MM »
Canon's latest 100mm macro lens has gained L-series status.
© Canon

7

› Third-party lenses

Canon isn't the only manufacturer of macro lenses—there are third-party options that often match and even exceed Canon's offerings (and include focal lengths that Canon doesn't produce).

The grid below shows the current range of lenses produced by Sigma, Tamron, and Tokina for the Canon EOS lens mount (lenses marked * are EF-S only).

Lens	Minimum focus distance (cm)	Reproduction ratio	Filter thread size (mm)	Dimensions (length x diameter in mm)	Weight (g)
Sigma					
50mm f/2.8 EX DG	19	1:1	55	66.5 x 71	320
70mm f/2.8 EX DG	25	1:1	62	95 x 76	527
105mm f/2.8 APO EX DG OS HSM	31	1:1	62	126 x 78	725
150mm f/2.8 EX DG OS HSM	38	1:1	72	150 x 80	1150
180mm f/2.8 EX DG OS HSM	47	1:1	86	204 x 95	1640
Tamron					
60mm f/2 Di II LD SP AF	23	1:1	55	80 x 73	390
90mm SP f/2.8 SP Di	29	1:1	55	97 x 71.5	405
90mm SP f/2.8 SP USD Di VC	30	1:1	62	117 x 79	609
180mm f/3.5 SP Di	47	1:1	72	166 x 85	920
Tokina					
35mm f/2.8 AT-X PRO DX*	14	1:1	52	60 x 73	340
100mm f/2.8 AT-X	30	1:1	55	95 x 73	540

» FOCUS

Live View is very useful when focusing on a macro subject, as you can zoom into the image and check critical focus across the entire frame (use the (SET) button, set to activate depth of field preview, as outlined on page 138). When shooting this image I used Live View and zoomed into the stamens of the foreground flower to ensure that the image was sharp where I intended it to be.

Settings
> Focal length: 100mm
> Aperture: f/5.6
> Shutter speed: 1/500 sec.
> ISO: 400

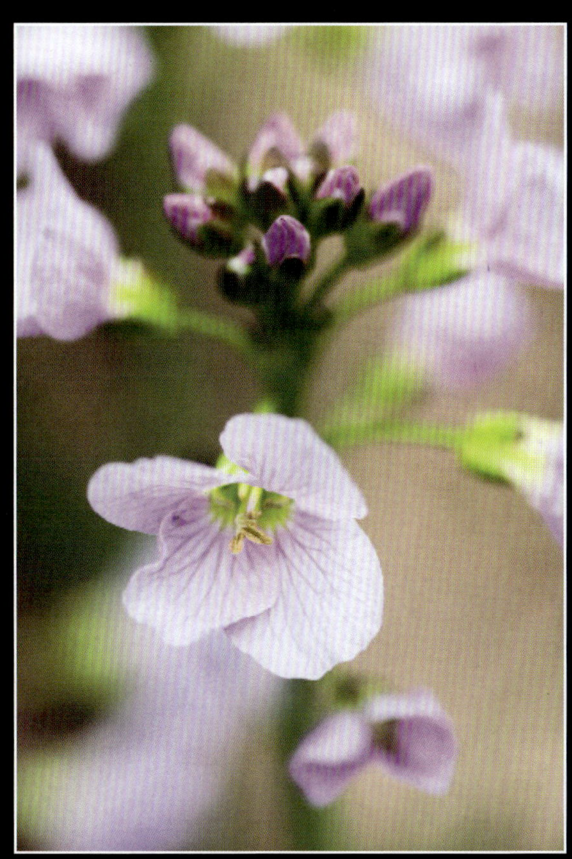

8 IN THE FIELD

The Rebel T6/EOS 1300D may be Canon's entry-level DSLR, but that doesn't mean it can't be used to produce professional-looking images. The key is understanding how you can get the best out of the camera.

Modern cameras are generally more than capable of withstanding years of use, but this doesn't mean you should mistreat your Rebel T6/EOS 1300D.

One way to do your camera harm is to get it wet, as water and electronics make for an unhappy combination. You don't need to stop shooting when it's raining or very humid though—with a few precautions, such as a rain cover, it's possible to shoot in even heavy rain.

If your Rebel T6/EOS 1300D does get wet, wipe it dry as best you can before covering it up again. Once you're back indoors, check the camera thoroughly, and dry it again if necessary. The lens will also need to be checked: remove any moisture on the lens surface with a lint-free lens cloth.

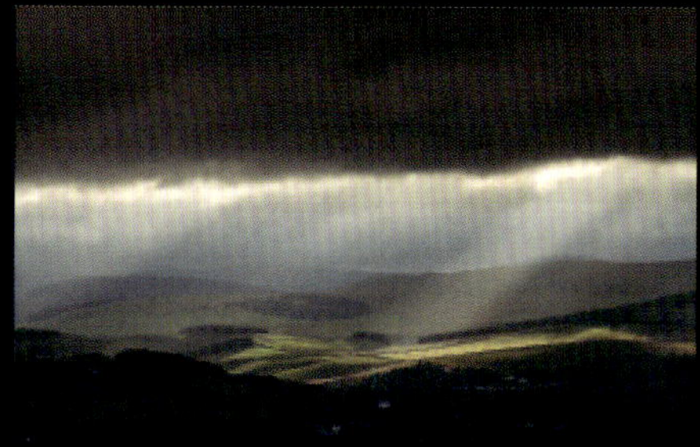

INCLEMENT »
Changeable weather—the type that brings rain—often produces the most interesting light in landscape photographs.

IMAGINATION »
Photographs don't need to be literal. This shot was created at dusk looking across a cityscape. During a long exposure the camera was deliberately moved sideways, up, and down to produce an image made up of streaks of light.

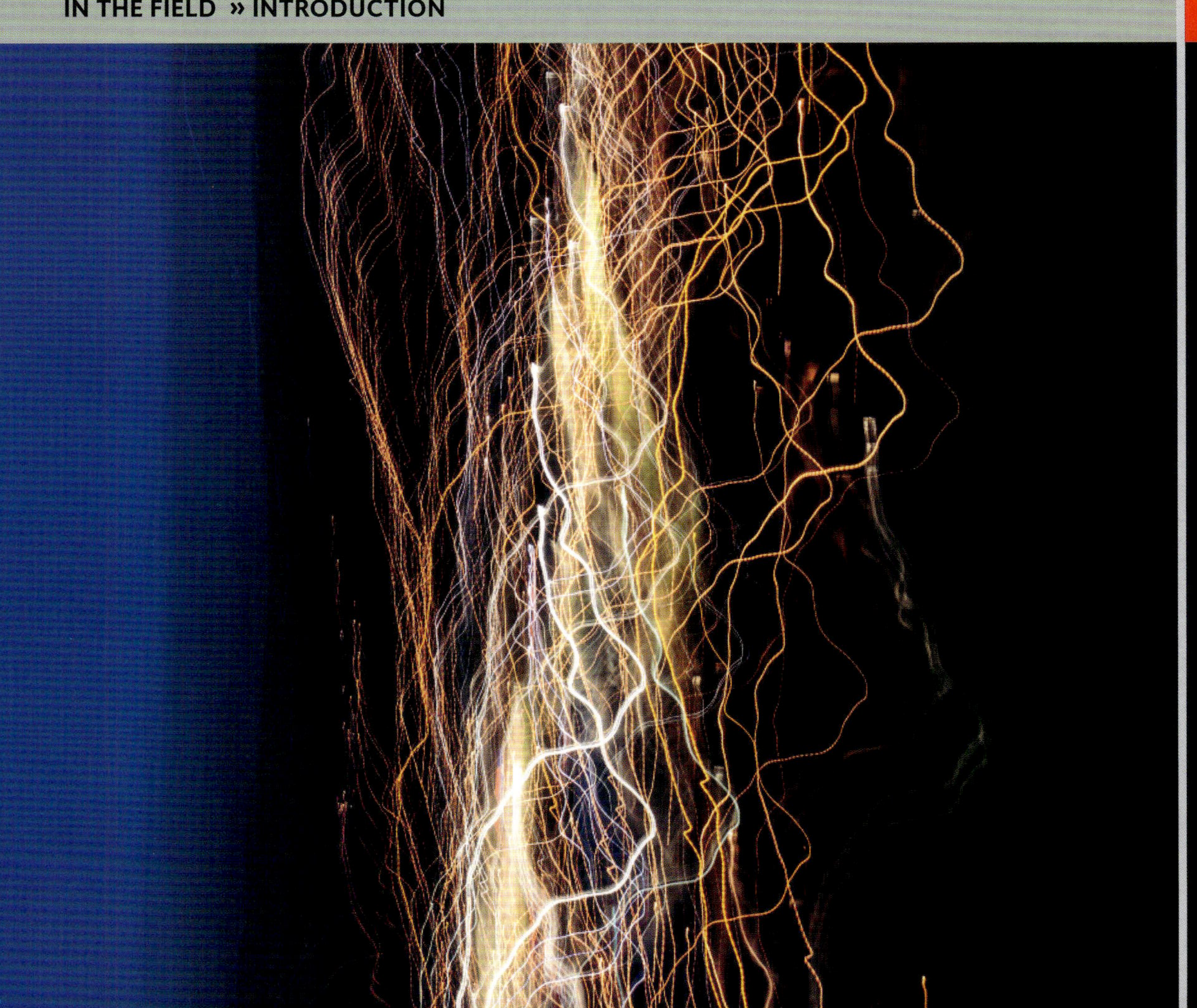

» ADVERSE CONDITIONS

› Heat

The ambient temperature at which you shoot is a potential source of problems as well. Canon recommends a maximum operating temperature of 104°F (40°C) for the Rebel T6/EOS 1300D, and you should try to avoid using your camera in temperatures hotter than this—or at least keep the camera cool in the shade when it is not in use.

Cold can affect a camera too; lubricants in the camera can freeze in extremely cold conditions and batteries become far less efficient. When you return indoors, let your camera slowly return to room temperature and check that condensation hasn't built up on the lens or LCD screen. Keeping a large packet of silica gel in your camera bag will help prevent excessive moisture building up.

› Dust

The Rebel T6/EOS 1300D doesn't have an automatic cleaning system like other cameras in the EOS range, which can lead to dust on the sensor—this is seen as fuzzy blobs in a photograph, usually in areas of light, even tone, such as the sky.

Depth of field has an influence on the visibility of dust, and using small apertures (to increase depth of field) will make dust more apparent and more sharply defined. Therefore, one way to minimize the appearance of dust is to use the largest aperture required to achieve the required depth of field and not use smaller apertures unnecessarily. Of course, cleaning the sensor is the only real removal solution.

A fine coating of dust on a lens can also impair image quality, in this case by increasing the risk of flare. If you're shooting in dusty conditions, keep your camera inside a bag when it is not in use. If you need to change lenses, try to do this as quickly as possible, using your body to shield the camera from any breeze.

» COASTAL

Shooting at the coast means being aware of two dangers to a camera: sand and salt water. If you get sand (or dust) on the front element of the lens, use a blower to avoid touching—and potentially scratching—the glass.

Salt water is corrosive to the metal in a camera's circuitry, and a fine spray can wet your camera just as effectively as dropping it in water. You should therefore dry your camera as soon as possible if it gets wet, and check it again when you get home for salt deposits.

Settings
> Focal length: 18mm
> Aperture: f/11
> Shutter speed: 1/50 sec.
> ISO: 100

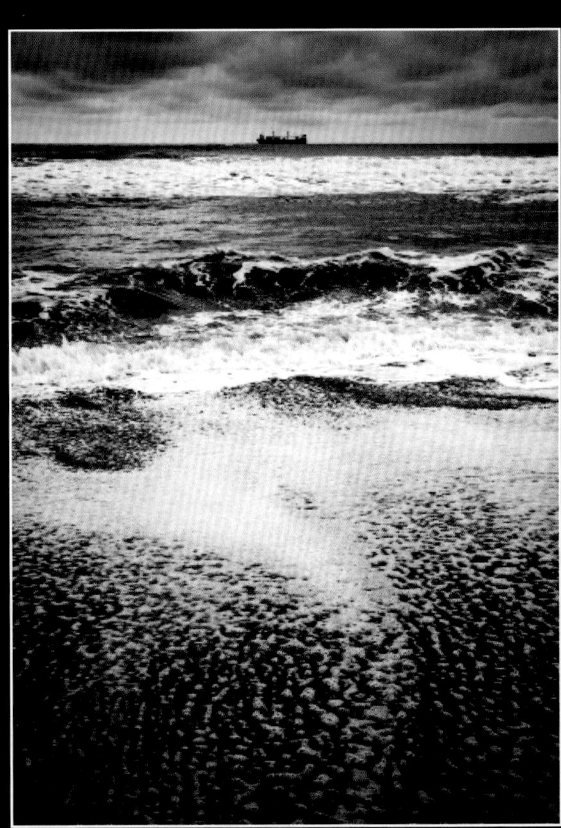

A good exposure is one in which just the right amount of light is allowed to reach the sensor to make an image. Exposure is set by three different controls: the shutter speed, aperture, and ISO. Shutter speed and aperture determine physically how much light enters the camera, while the ISO control determines the amount of light actually needed to make the exposure to start with.

› Shutter speed

Shutter speed is measured in precise fractions of a second: 1/125 sec., 1/250 sec., 1/500 sec., 1/1000 sec., and so on. The difference between each of these shutter speed values is known as a "1 stop," and represents either a halving of the light let into the camera or a doubling of the light.

For example, there's a 1-stop difference between shutter speeds of 1/125 sec. and 1/250 sec., and there's also a 1-stop difference between 1/500 sec. and 1/250 sec. Changing the shutter speed from 1/250 sec. to 1/125 sec. doubles the time the shutter is open for, which doubles the amount of light reaching the sensor. Conversely, changing the shutter speed from 1/250 sec. to 1/500 sec. halves the amount of time the shutter's open, halving the amount of light reaching the sensor.

The Rebel T6/EOS 1300D lets you adjust the shutter speed in more precise ⅓-stop increments. In the example above, 1/160 sec. and 1/200 sec. are the ⅓-stop values between 1/125 sec. and 1/250 sec., and 1/320 sec. and 1/400 sec. sit between 1/250 sec. and 1/500 sec.

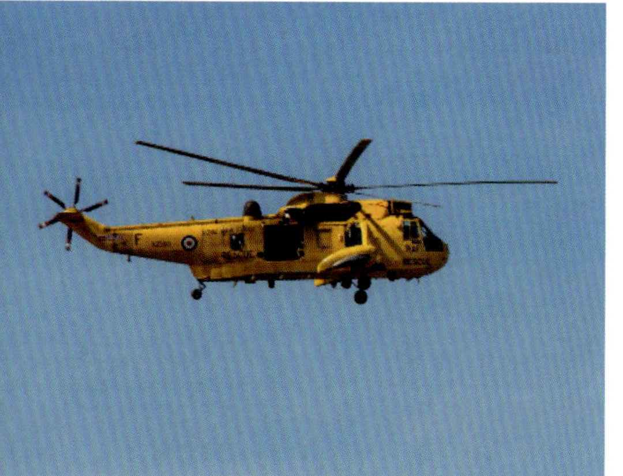

Note
ISO is also adjusted in stops: ISO 100, 200, 400, and so on are all 1-stop apart in terms of exposure.

SPEED «
This image was shot at 1/2000 sec. This shutter speed is so fast that the rotor blades of the helicopter look static.

› Aperture

The size of the aperture in the lens is measured in f-stops, which describe the diameter of the aperture as a fraction of the focal length. So, on a 50mm lens the physical diameter of the aperture at f/2 would be 25mm, at f/4 it would be 12.5mm, and so on.

The most commonly found f-stops on a lens (from widest to smallest) are f/2.8, f/4, f/5.6, f/8, f/11, f/16, and f/22, although the maximum and minimum apertures of lenses do vary. As with shutter speeds, each f-stop represents either a doubling or halving of the amount of light let through. So, f/5.6 will allow half as much light through the lens as f/4, but twice that of f/8. As with shutter speed, you can adjust the aperture on the Rebel T6/EOS 1300D in ⅓-stop increments to make very fine exposure adjustments.

› Reciprocal relationship

There's a reciprocal relationship between shutter speed, aperture, and ISO, so if one is changed, at least one of the other two controls must be altered to maintain the same amount of exposure.

As an example, let's say that the meter in the Rebel T6/EOS 1300D recommends an exposure of 1/125 sec. at f/11 using ISO 800. f/11 is a relatively small aperture, so you may prefer a larger setting to reduce

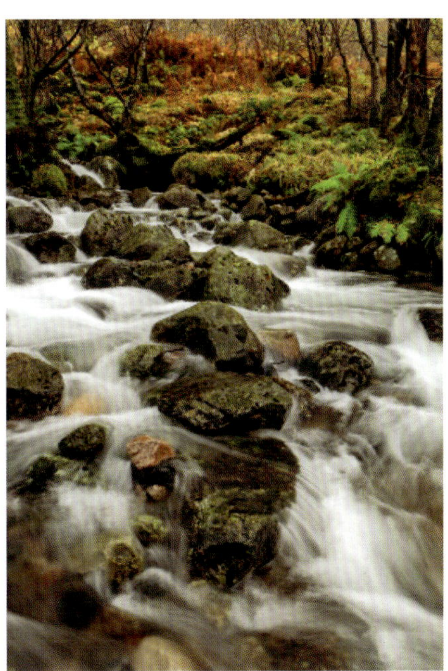

RECIPROCAL
This photograph was taken using a shutter speed of 1/15 sec. and an aperture of f/11, at ISO 200. The grid below shows that I could have chosen a number of different shutter speed and aperture combinations, which would have enabled me to achieve the exact same exposure overall.

	Shutter speed (sec.)			
	Slower		Faster	
1/4	1/8	1/15	1/30	1/60
	Aperture			
	Smaller		Wider	
f/22	f/16	f/11	f/8	f/5.6

depth of field—f/5.6 for example. This will allow more light through the lens, so you either need to use a faster shutter speed or a lower ISO in order to maintain the same level of exposure overall.

The difference between f/11 and f/5.6 is 2 stops so, after setting the aperture at f/5.6 you could either set the shutter speed at 1/500 sec.; reduce the ISO to 200; or adjust both the shutter speed and ISO by 1 stop each (to 1/250. sec and ISO 400), to split the difference. Each of these would ensure that the exposure stays the same overall.

› Metering

There are two types of exposure meter: incident and reflective. Incident exposure meters measure the amount of light falling onto a scene; this is the method that is typically used by handheld light meters. The meter built into your Rebel T6/EOS 1300D is a reflective exposure meter, which measures the amount of light reflected by the scene back toward the camera. This may seem like a small difference, but it has a very important consequence.

Reflective exposure meters work on the assumption that the scene that has been metered has an "average" reflectivity. An averagely reflective scene is one that reflects approximately 18% of the light that falls onto it (which equates to a mid-gray). Subjects that are averagely reflective include grass and the bluest part of the sky.

However, problems arise with reflective metering when the scene doesn't have average reflectivity. Some scenes, such as brightly lit snow or sand, have a higher-than-average reflectivity. Reflective exposure meters often underexpose this type of scene in order to average the tonal range of the image to the mid-gray ideal.

Conversely, a scene with a darker-than-average reflectivity (a black cat on a dark carpet for example) has the opposite effect and will most likely lead to overexposure.

In either situation, you will usually need to apply positive or negative exposure compensation to get the correct exposure.

ADJUSTED «
This scene, which was dominated by dark tones, required a -1⅓-stop exposure adjustment (set using exposure compensation).

» LIGHT

The way a subject is lit can affect the accuracy of metering. Spotlit subjects often cause overexposure as they're generally surrounded by areas of deep shadow. For this shot I switched to partial metering, metering from the sunlit stonework. This meant that the staircase (which was in shadow) had no effect on the final exposure.

Settings
> Focal length: 18mm
> Aperture: f/5
> Shutter speed: 1/4 sec.
> ISO: 100

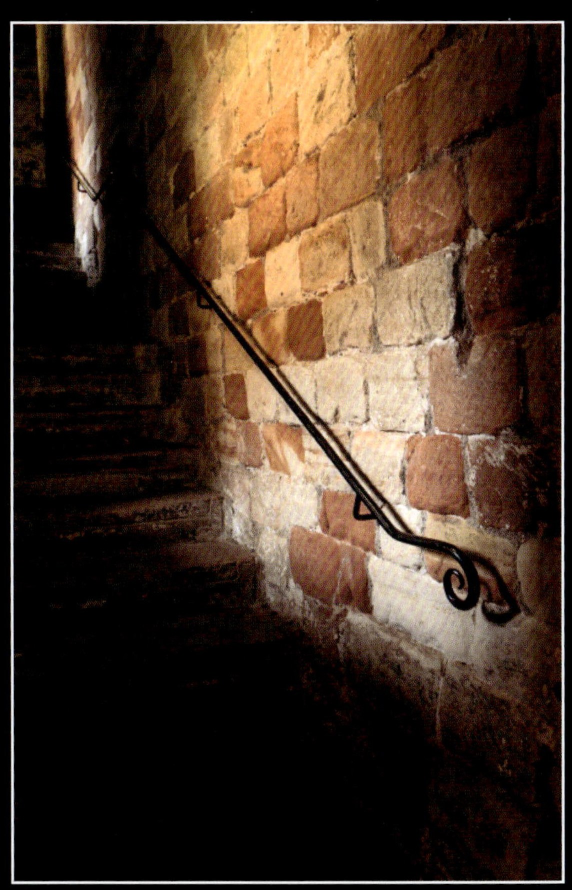

A histogram is a graph that shows the distribution of tones in a still image. You can view the histogram for a still image either before shooting (during Live View), or on the detailed playback screen after the exposure has been made. Histograms are very useful tools, which will allow you to judge the exposure of an image. By interpreting a histogram correctly you'll know whether you need to make adjustments to the exposure before you shoot (in Live View) or reshoot after viewing the histogram in playback.

The key lies in being able to "read" a histogram successfully. The left half of a histogram shows the range of tones in an image that are darker than mid-gray, with black at the extreme left edge. The right half of the histogram shows the tones in an image that are lighter than mid-gray, with white at the extreme right edge.

If a histogram is skewed to the left, this may be an indication that the image is underexposed; if skewed to the right, it may be overexposed. The vertical axis of the histogram simply shows the number of pixels in an image of a particular tone.

If a histogram is squashed against either the left or right edge it has been clipped. This means there are pure black or pure white pixels in the image respectively: those pixels have no usable image data.

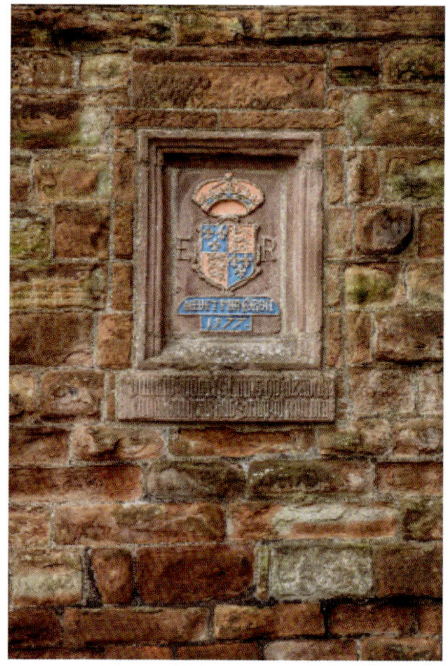

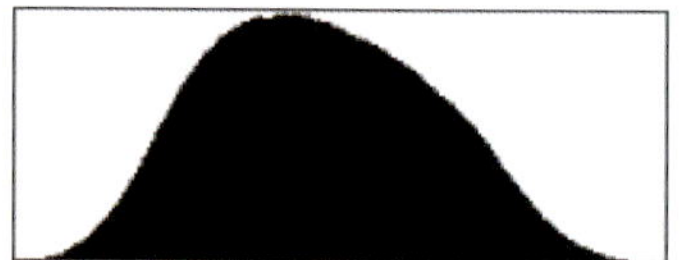

BELL CURVE »
There's no ideal shape for a histogram; the shape is dependent on the range of tones in the scene. A scene that's mainly comprised on midtones, such as this stone wall, will have a histogram shaped like a bell curve.

› White balance and histograms

The type of histogram described previously is known as a brightness (or "luminance") histogram, because it shows you the distribution of the brightness levels in the image. However, in playback, the Rebel T6/ EOS 1300D can also display red, green, and blue (RGB) histograms stacked one above the other.

The information conveyed by RGB histograms is subtler than a brightness histogram, in that each one shows the distribution of red, green, and blue that combine to make each pixel in the image. A pure red pixel only has red in it, with no green or blue components; a pure magenta pixel is an equal mix of red and blue; and a white pixel is an equal mix of red, green, and blue at their maximum values of 255 (black is the complete absence of red, green, and blue).

An RGB histogram lets you check whether one particular color is clipping and adjust your exposure accordingly. This can also happen when the white balance is incorrect; an image that is too "warm" will often be caused by clipped highlights in the red histogram, while a "cool" image is usually the result of clipping in the blue histogram. Simply using a different white balance preset or creating a custom WB can solve the problem.

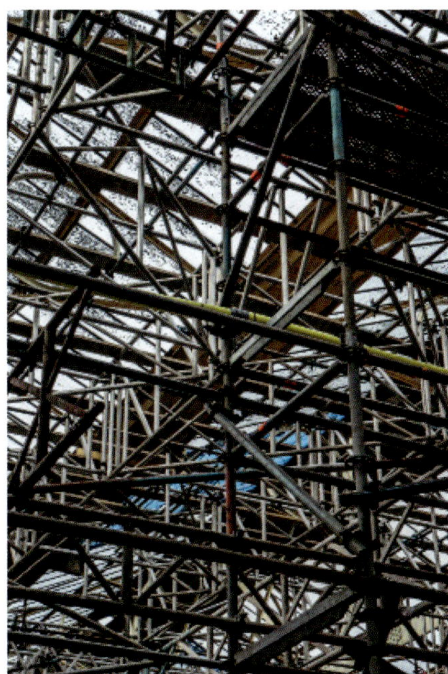

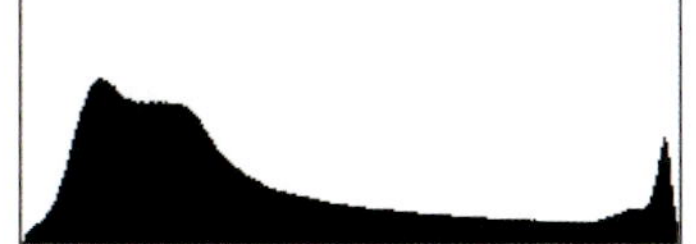

PEAKS　　　　　　　　　　　》
A scene that is high in contrast, with extreme dark and light tones, will have two distinct peaks at either end of the histogram.

8

› Dynamic range

The dynamic range of a camera is its ability to record usable detail in both the shadows and the highlights, without clipping. The greater the dynamic range of a camera, the better able it is to cope with high-contrast scenes.

The Rebel T6/EOS 1300D has a respectable dynamic range (certainly far greater than most compact or cellphone cameras), but you may well encounter situations where the contrast levels are too high. Exposure then becomes a compromise between retaining detail in the shadows or in the highlights. Typically, losing shadow detail is more esthetically acceptable than losing highlight details—dark shadows in an image look more natural than pure white highlights.

There are several techniques that can help in high-contrast situations. Using graduated ND filters (see page 194) can help balance the exposure across an image if you're shooting landscapes, for example, while fill flash is effective for filling in shadows. As well as flash, reflectors (sheets of reflective white or metallic material) can also be used to bounce light into shadows to reduce contrast.

CONTRAST ⌄

This is the type of scene that tests a camera's dynamic range: bright, near-white highlights in the form of clouds and dark shadows under the tree cover.

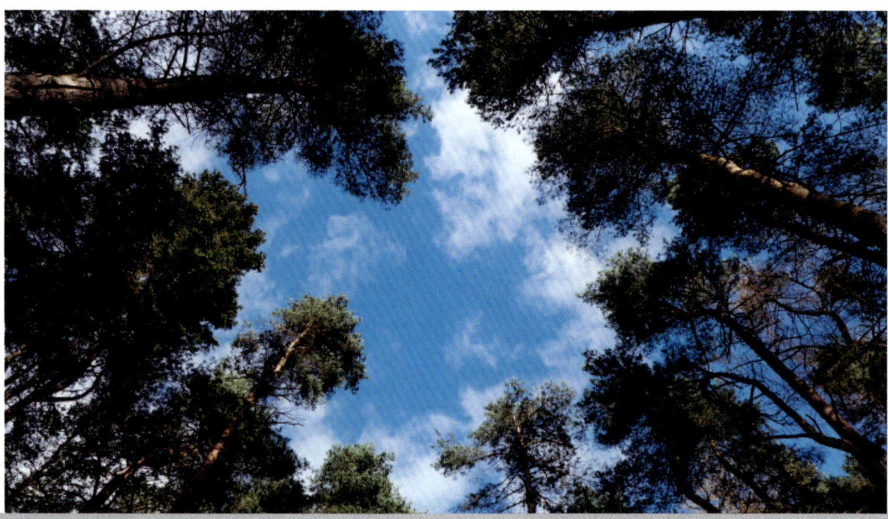

» OPPORTUNITY

Carry your camera with you whenever you can and always look out for picture opportunities. The more you look, the more you will see! Don't just look for subjects at eye-level, either. This interesting sculpture was at knee-height, so I had to squat down to view it correctly and then to shoot it.

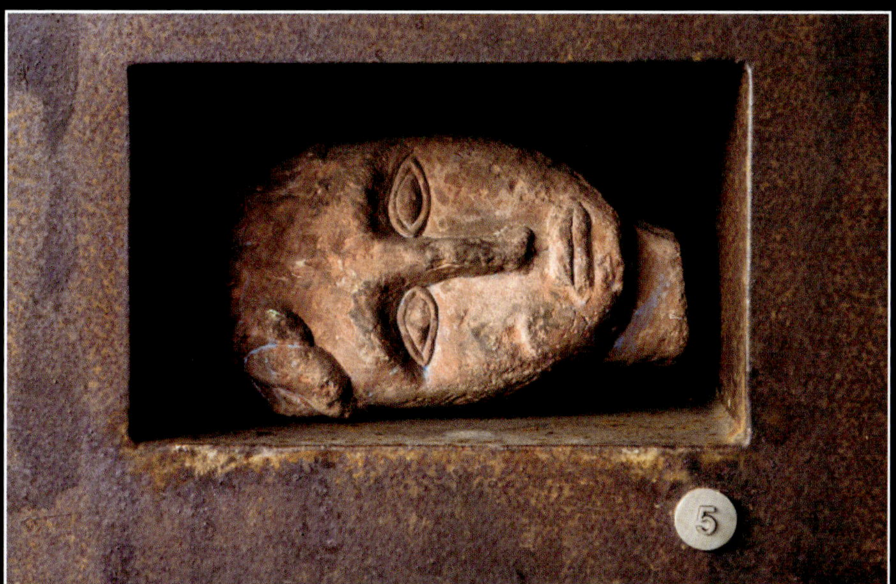

Settings
> Focal length: 50mm
> Aperture: f/3.5
> Shutter speed: 1/40 sec.
> ISO: 200

8 » BLACK AND WHITE

A black-and-white image is one that is made up of a range of grays, from black through to white. The brightness of a particular gray tone in an image is determined by the reflectivity of the subject: the more light the subject reflects, the brighter the gray tone in the final image. However, if elements in the scene reflect similar amounts of light (even if they're radically different in color) they will be very similar shades of gray when converted to monochrome. This can lead to "flat" images.

This can be overcome by the use of colored filters (or the **Filter effect** options when shooting using the ⬛M Picture Style—see page 102–103). Colored filters block out colors on the opposite side of a standard color wheel to the filter, so a red filter blocks out blue-greens, a blue filter blocks red-orange, and so on. Therefore, when using a red filter, anything that's red in the black-and-white image will be lightened, while anything that is blue will be darkened. This can help you to separate the tonal values in an image.

Landscape photographers will often use yellow, orange, or red filters to darken blue skies (with red having the greatest effect), while portrait photographers are more likely to use a green filter, which enhances skin tones. So, if you find your black-and-white images look flat, try experimenting with colored filters or the ⬛M Picture Style **Filter effect** options.

Note

Only use colored filters when you are shooting black-and-white JPEGs. Raw files retain color information even when shooting using the ⬛M Picture Style. Therefore the effects of colored filters can be emulated during postproduction when you process your Raw files.

COLOR TO MONOCHROME »
This is the same scene, shot using ⬛M with four different colored filters applied.

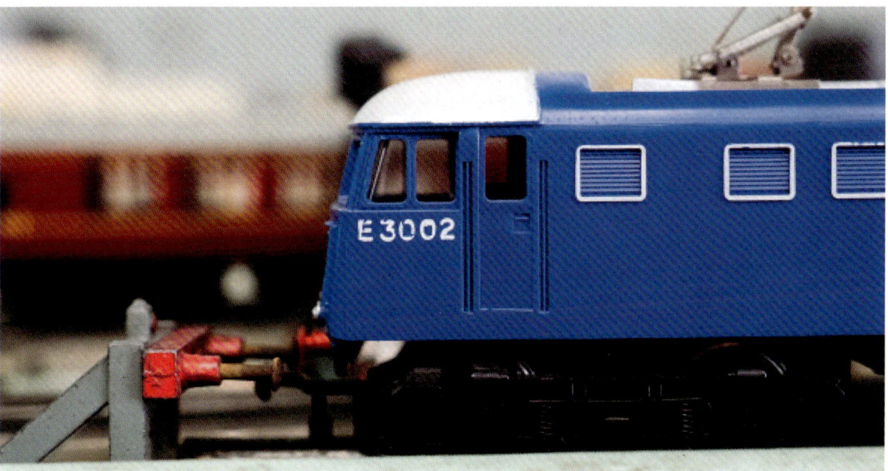

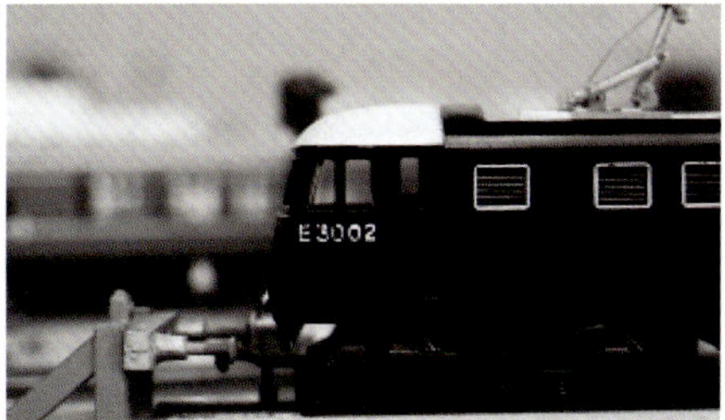

Yellow

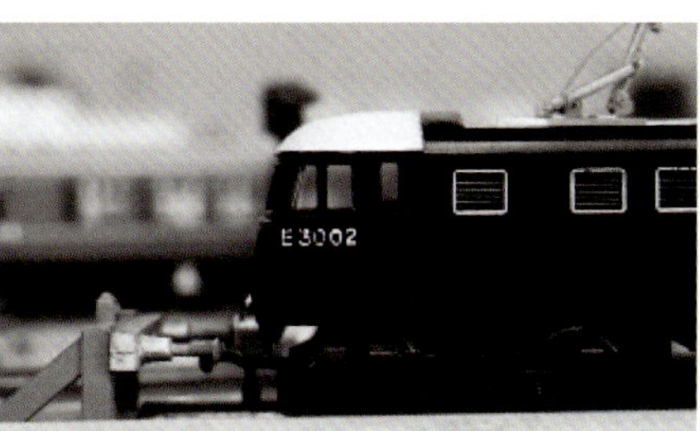

Red

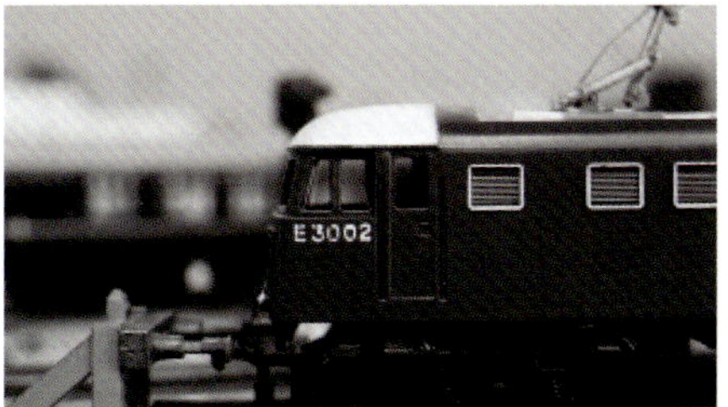

Green

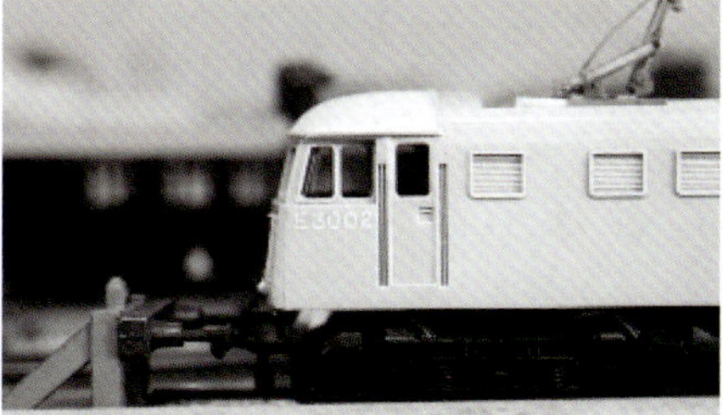

Blue

CONNECTION

Once you've shot a few images you'll need to connect your Rebel T6/EOS 1300D to another device. The most useful device is a computer, which will let you store your images permanently, but it is not the only option.

› Color calibration

A color calibrator is a hardware device that can be used to check the color accuracy of a monitor. The calibrator reads a series of color patches displayed on the monitor by the calibration software to create a profile for the monitor. Good image-editing software will then use this profile to ensure that your colors appear accurate on screen.

It's also possible to buy printer calibrators, but it's far simpler to use "canned" profiles supplied by the printer or paper manufacturer. You will need a profile for every type of paper you use to print, and will have to select the relevant profile at the printing stage. A profile specifies how the printer needs to modify its output so that a particular paper type receives the correct amount of ink in the right proportions, ensuring that the colors are reproduced correctly.

If a "canned" profile isn't available it's still not necessary to go to the expense of buying a printer calibrator. If you only want a few profiles, it's often far cheaper to use specialist companies who will create bespoke profiles for a nominal fee.

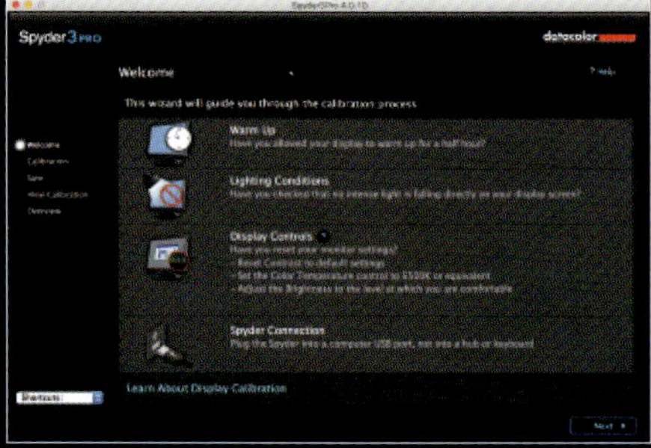

CALIBRATION ⌃
In order to calibrate your monitor successfully it's a good idea to wait for 30 minutes or so after switching it on.

COMPUTER »
Despite the rise of tablets and smartphones, nothing beats a computer when it comes to storing, viewing, and filing your images.

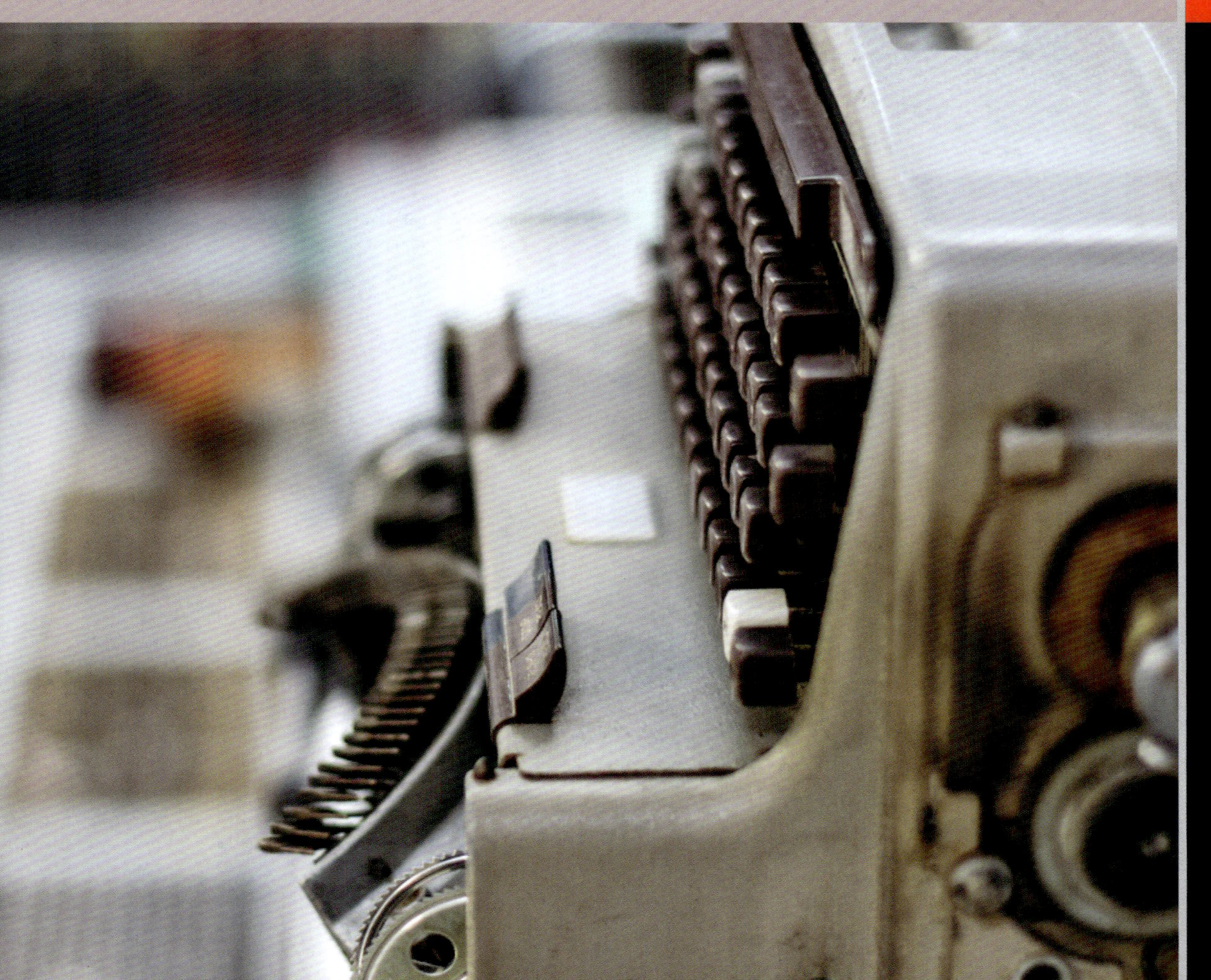

» CANON SOFTWARE

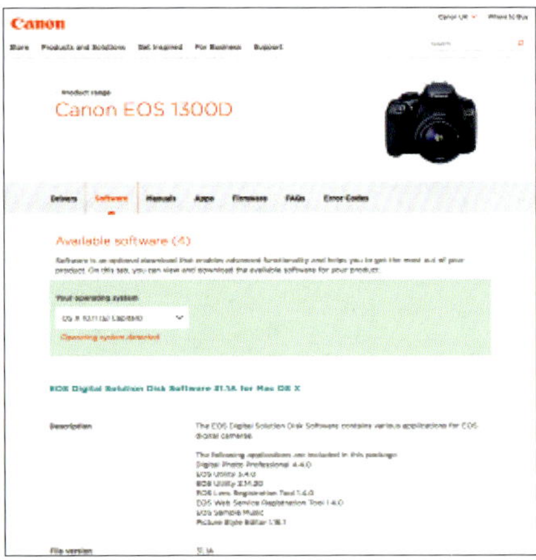

The Rebel T6/EOS 1300D isn't supplied with any imaging software, but you can download a software bundle from Canon's web site; it's not obligatory to do this, but the software is free and useful. There's not enough space in this book to give an in-depth guide to all this software, but Canon supplies comprehensive PDF instructions for each application, which can also be found on its web site.

Downloading the software (USA)

1) Go to *www.canon.com/icpd*

2) Select **North America** > **USA**

3) Enter Rebel T6 into the **Enter Model** text box (selecting the relevant camera/lens combination when prompted).

4) Click on the **Drivers & Downloads** > **Software** button.

5) Select the operating system for your computer and language.

6) Select which apps you want to download, agree to the terms and conditions by checking the box, and then click on **Download.**

7) Enter the serial number of your Rebel T6 (found on the base of the camera) when prompted.

8) Downloading should begin.

Downloading the software (UK)

1) Go to *www.canon.com/icpd*

2) Select **Europe/Middle East/Africa > United Kingdom**

3) Click on **EOS cameras** > **EOS 1300D**.

4) Click on the **Software** tab.

5) Select the correct operating system for your computer.

6) Click on **Download** in the relevant EOS Digital Solution software box.

7) Agree to the disclaimer and then enter the serial number of your Rebel T6/EOS 1300D (found on the base of the camera) when prompted.

8) Downloading should begin.

> ### *Note*
> As the owner of a Canon camera you're eligible to join the CANON iMAGE GATEWAY. This is a free service that gives you 10GB of online storage space for images and videos. These can be viewed by other members or shared via social media web sites.

Installing the software

1) On a Windows PC, double-click on the downloaded software file; on a Mac, double-click the Installer icon found on the desktop after the downloaded DMG file has been opened.

2) The Canon software installation screen should appear automatically. Click on **Easy Installation** to install all the software, or click on **Custom Installation** to select which programs are installed. Follow the instructions on screen to continue.

3) When the installation is complete, click on either **Finish** or **Restart** as required.

4) Archive or delete the downloaded file. Note that you can download the software—including updates—at any point, so it's arguably easiest to delete the file and save hard drive space on your computer.

> ### Warning!
> Uninstall any previous versions of Canon software from your computer before installing the new software.

Digital Photo Professional

Digital Photo Professional (or DPP) is most useful for processing your Rebel T6/EOS 1300D's Raw files and converting them to either JPEG or TIFF format for further adjustment or use. If you've set **Dust Delete Data** (see page 106–107) you'd use DPP to automatically clone out dust spots.

EOS Utility

This useful utility enables you to import images from your Rebel T6/EOS 1300D onto your computer, or organize the images on the memory card. It can also be used to capture images directly onto your computer when your camera is attached.

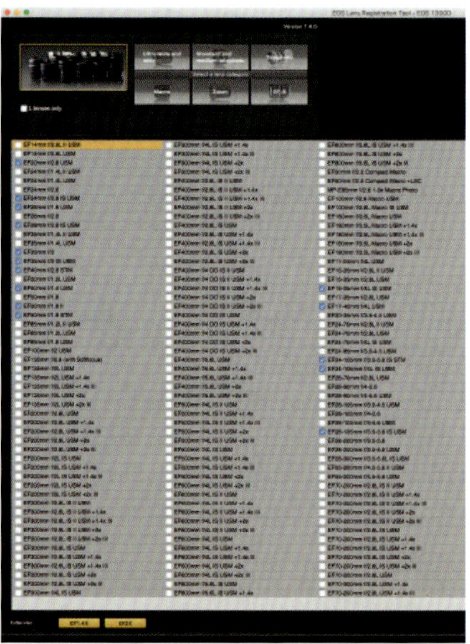

Picture Style Editor

Picture Styles Editor allows you to edit, save, and copy Picture Styles to your Rebel T6/EOS 1300D, which you can then use when shooting JPEGs.

Lens Registration Tool

The Lens Registration Tool lets you update the list of lenses to which **Lens aberration correction** can be applied automatically in-camera. Your camera must be connected to your computer to use this software.

EOS Web Service Registration Tool

This app lets you upload images to social media services, such as Facebook and Twitter, directly from your camera. To use this service you must first open a CANON iMAGE GATEWAY account.

LENS PROFILES «
Lens Registration Tool lets you change the lenses registered on your Rebel T6/EOS 1300D. This determines the options available when **Peripheral illumin. correct.** is selected.

» CONNECTING TO A COMPUTER

There are several ways you can transfer images saved to the memory card in your Rebel T6/EOS 1300D. The most battery efficient method is to remove the memory card and plug it into a card reader attached (or integral) to your computer. Alternatively, you can connect your Rebel T6/EOS 1300D directly to your computer via a USB cable, or by using Wi-Fi (as described on pages 235–237).

Using a USB cable will also enable you to shoot remotely (saving the images directly to your computer), and allow you to apply changes to your camera, such as adding custom Picture Styles created using Picture Style Editor.

Warning!

Before connecting your Rebel T6/EOS 1300D to your computer, install the Canon software, ensure that the camera is switched off, and check that the battery is fully charged.

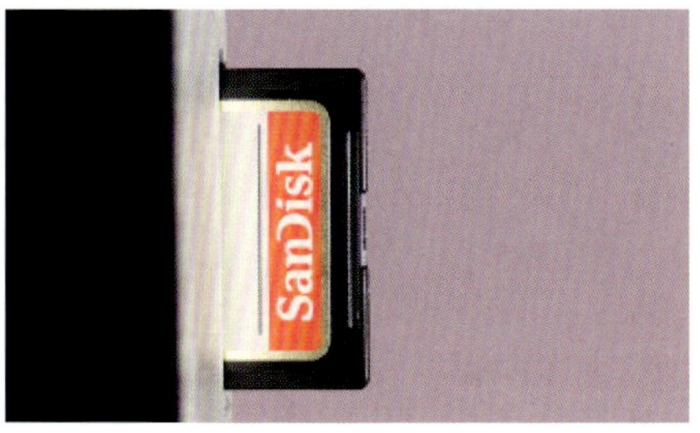

Connecting via a USB cable

1) Attach the USB cable to the Digital terminal underneath the terminal cover on your Rebel T6/EOS 1300D.

2) Insert the other end of the USB cable into a free USB 2.0 (or higher) port on your computer.

3) Turn on your Rebel T6/EOS 1300D.

4) On Windows PCs click on **Downloads Images From EOS Camera using Canon EOS utility**. Canon EOS utility should now automatically launch. Check **Always do this for this device** if you want to make this a default action when you connect your Rebel T6/EOS 1300D.

On Mac OS X, Canon EOS Utility should run automatically when the camera is attached.

5) Follow the instructions on screen for Canon EOS Utility.

6) Quit Canon EOS Utility when you're finished, turn off your Rebel T6/EOS 1300D, and unplug it from your computer.

SLOT «
Many computers have built-in SD card slots, which means you don't necessarily need to connect your camera via a USB cable to copy your images to your PC.

9

» TETHERED SHOOTING

If you connect your Rebel T6/EOS 1300D to your computer via a USB cable you can use a technique known as "tethered shooting." Tethered shooting allows you to view a Live View image on your computer monitor, make adjustments remotely to the camera, and then shoot. The resulting image is transferred directly to your computer for saving. Tethered shooting requires the installation of EOS Utility.

Enabling tethered shooting

1) Connect your Rebel T6/EOS 1300D to your computer as described previously.

2) Launch EOS Utility (if it doesn't launch automatically) and click on **Remote shooting**.

3) Click **Preferences** and select **Destination Folder** from the pop-up menu (Mac) or tab (Windows) at the top of the dialog box. Select the folder that you want your images to be saved to. Alter the other settings as desired.

4) Select **Linked Software** from the pop-up menu (Mac) or tab (Windows) at the top of the dialog box. Select the software that you want to use to edit your images.

5) Click **OK** to continue.

6) Click the **Live View shoot...** button to see the camera's output on your computer's monitor.

7) Alter settings such as **White balance** and **Focus**—found at the right and below the Live View window—as required.

8) Click on the EOS Utility shutter-release button to capture the image.

9) When you're done, disconnect your Rebel T6/EOS 1300D from your PC as described previously.

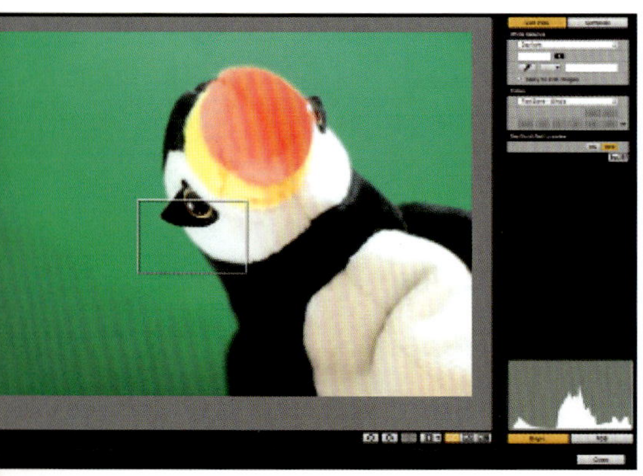

» CONNECTING TO A TV

Showing your images on an HDTV is a very sociable way to share them with friends and family. You can connect your Rebel T6/EOS 1300D to an HDTV via a Type C mini-pin HDMI cable—this isn't supplied with the camera, but is readily available online and in most electronics stores.

Notes
Wi-Fi/NFC must be set to **Disable**.

The Rebel T6/EOS 1300D cannot be connected to analog televisions.

Connecting your camera to an HDTV

1) Ensure that both your Rebel T6/EOS 1300D and TV are switched off.

2) Open the camera's terminal cover and connect the HDMI cable plug to the HDMI OUT port.

3) Plug the other end of the HDMI cable into a free slot on your TV.

4) Turn on your TV and switch to the correct channel for external HDMI devices.

5) Turn on your Rebel T6/EOS 1300D. Press ▶ on your camera to view your images on the HDTV. Press **DISP.** to change the display format if necessary.

6) When you're finished, turn off the Rebel T6/EOS 1300D and TV before disconnecting.

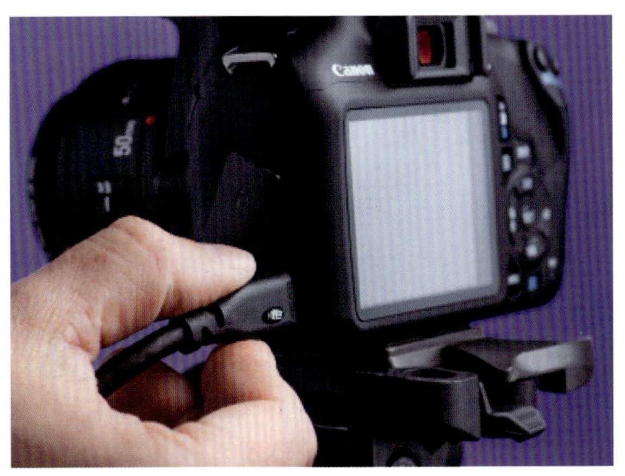

THIRD-PARTY «
As with most accessories, you don't need to stick to the Canon brand when it comes to buying an HDMI cable.

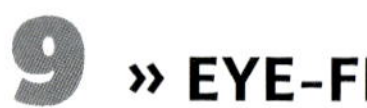 » EYE-FI

Eye-Fi is a third-party SD memory card with a built-in Wi-Fi transmitter. This allows you to transfer files wirelessly between your Rebel T6/EOS 1300D and a Wi-Fi-enabled computer or hosting service.

To set up the Eye-Fi card check the manual that came with your card before use. For more information about Eye-Fi go to *www.eye.fi*

Enabling Eye-Fi

1) Press MENU and select **Eye-Fi Settings** from the 🔧 menu.

2) Set **Eye-Fi trans.** to **Enable** (when **Disable** is selected, the Eye-Fi card won't automatically transmit your files and 📶 will be shown on the shooting settings screen).

3) Once a still image has been shot, the Eye-Fi symbol turns from a gray 📶 to one of the other icons below. When the still image has been transferred to your computer, 📷 will be displayed on the shooting information screen.

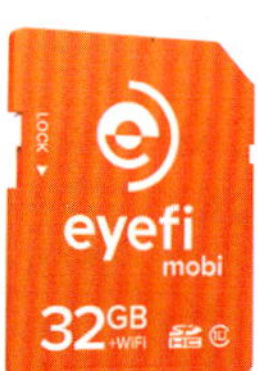

EYE-FI MEMORY CARD
© Eye-Fi, Inc

Checking an Eye-Fi Connection

1) Press MENU and select **Eye-Fi Settings** from the 🔧 menu.

2) Select **Connection info**. to display the connection information screen.

3) Press MENU to return to the main **Eye-Fi Settings** menu.

> **Notes**
> The battery in your Rebel T6/EOS 1300D may be depleted more quickly than usual when using an Eye-Fi card to transmit images.
>
> **Eye-Fi Settings** only appears on the 🔧 menu when an Eye-Fi card is installed.
>
> Eye-Fi operation is not possible when **Wi-Fi/NFC** is set to **Enable**.

Displayed symbol	Status
📶 Gray	Not Connected
📶 Blinking	Connecting
📶 Solid white	Connection to access point established
📶 (↑)	Transferring

» WI-FI

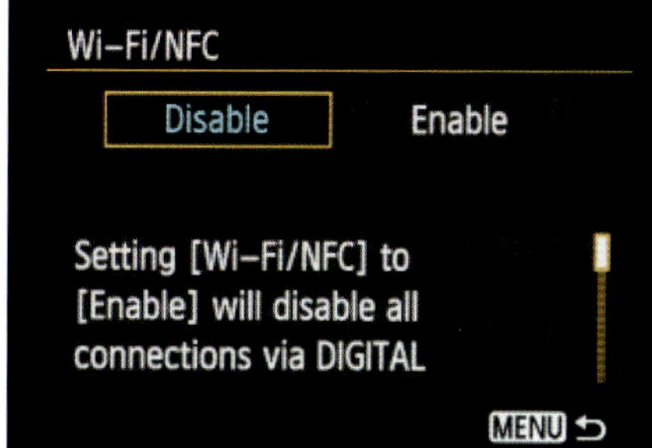

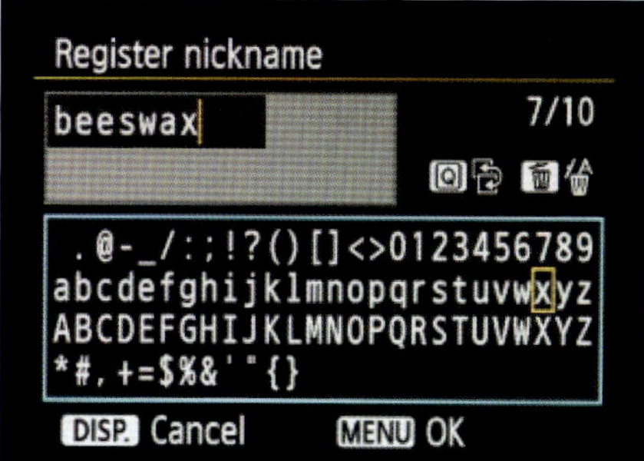

Although you can use an Eye-Fi memory card, the Rebel T6/EOS 1300D also has built-in Wi-Fi that lets you transfer files wirelessly. Images can be transferred to smartphones and tablets, web services, or to Canon's own Connect Station. If your smartphone or tablet has the Canon Connect app installed you can also control your camera remotely.

((ŗ)) lamp	Connection status
On	Wi-Fi connection made
Blinking slowly	Connection/ reconnection in progress
Blinking quickly	Sending data
Blinking reasonably quickly	Connection error

Enabling Wi-Fi

1) Select **Wi-Fi/NFC** on the menu followed by **Enable** (if you take your Rebel T6/EOS 1300D into an area where a Wi-Fi-enabled device wouldn't be welcome select **Disable**).

2) If this is the first time you've selected **Wi-Fi/NFC** you'll be prompted to enter a nickname. Create a memorable nickname using the text entry system. If you want to change the nickname at a later date select **Wi-Fi function** from the main menu. Press **DISP.** to view the **General sett.** screen and then select **Edit nickname**.

3) The ((ŗ)) lamp can be used to check the status of the Wi-Fi connection. Use the grid at the left as a guide.

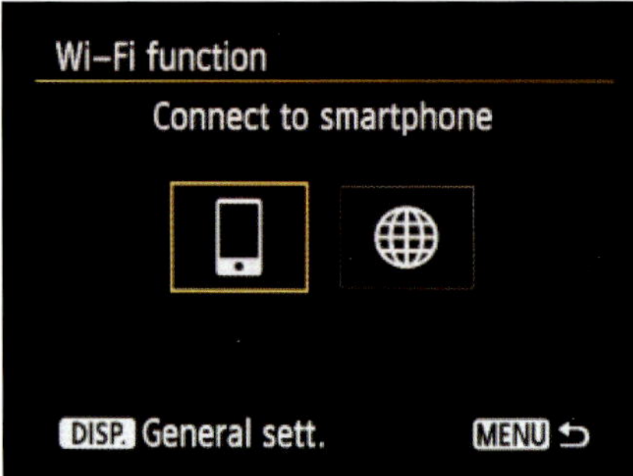

There are two connection options when **Wi-Fi function** is selected after setting up a nickname: **Connect to smartphone** and **Upload to Web service**. The procedure—such as whether a password needs to be entered—will depend on how your device or wireless network is configured.

Possibly the most useful function if you're interested in controlling your Rebel T6/EOS 1300D remotely is the **Connect to smartphone** option (see following page if your smartphone has NFC capability).

To make the most of the smartphone option you'll need to download the free Camera connect app produced by Canon, which is available for Apple iOS and Android devices. Once the app is installed and a connection has been made, you can view a Live View feed from your Rebel T6/EOS 1300D on your device, set shooting functions, and make exposures.

After you've made an exposure you can use your device to browse images on the Rebel T6/EOS 1300D's memory card and copy them to your device (the images will be automatically shrunk to suit the size of your device's screen). The limitation with Camera connect is that you can't copy movie files (although this is perhaps unsurprising as movie files are generally far larger than still images).

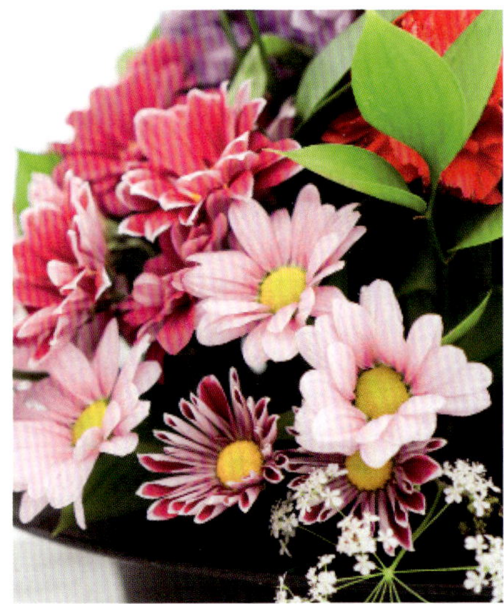

SHARING »

By copying your photos to your smartphone you can immediately share them on your favorite social media web site.

› Wi-Fi options

There is a number of hoops you have to go through to set up a wireless connection between your Rebel T6/EOS 1300D and another device. Fortunately, some devices—such as some smartphones and Canon's own Connect Station—can be connected in a very simple way using NFC (Near Field Connection).

By bringing the **N** mark on the Rebel T6/EOS 1300D close to the **N** mark on the other device, the two will establish a connection, allowing the wireless transfer of data (a gentle tap between the two devices may be necessary).

To use NFC, set **Allow NFC connections** to ✓ on the **Wi-Fi/NFC** menu screen. NFC capability also has to be enabled on your smartphone (which also needs Canon's Camera connect app installed as well). The downside to NFC is that your camera and the device need to remain in close proximity during the data transfer.

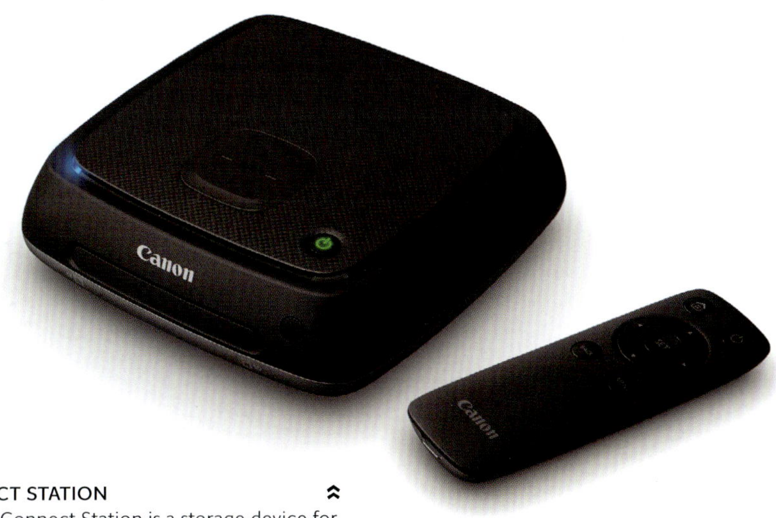

CONNECT STATION ⌃
Canon's Connect Station is a storage device for photos (up to 1TB) with connections that allow those photos to be printed wirelessly, shared on social media, or displayed on an HDTV.
© Canon

» CONNECTING TO A PRINTER

There are two ways to make prints directly from still images saved to the memory card of your Rebel T6/EOS 1300D: you can either connect the camera to a PictBridge printer via a USB cable, or you can tag DPOF printing instructions to the images and then plug the memory card into a compatible printer or take it to a printing service. DPOF instructs the printer which and how many images to print, as described on pages 240–241.

The advantage of using the USB/PictBridge method compared to DPOF is that PictBridge supports the printing of both Raw and JPEG images; DPOF only supports JPEGs.

Connecting to a PictBridge printer

1) Ensure that the camera and printer are switched off. Make sure the memory card containing the images you want to print is installed in the Rebel T6/EOS 1300D.

2) Open the Rebel T6/EOS 1300D's terminal cover and connect the supplied USB cable to the Digital Terminal.

3) Connect the cable to the printer, following the instructions in the manual supplied with the printer.

4) Turn on the printer, followed by the Rebel T6/EOS 1300D. Press ▶ on the camera and the 🖉 PictBridge icon will be displayed at the top left corner of the LCD to show that a connection has been successfully made.

5) Press ◀ / ▶ to find the image you want to print and then press (SET).

6) The print options screen will appear (see grid opposite). Set the required options and select **Print** to start printing.

7) Repeat steps 6 and 7 if you want to print additional images.

8) Turn off the Rebel T6/EOS 1300D and printer and disconnect the USB cable.

> *Notes*
> Make sure you start with a fully charged battery when you're printing directly from your camera,
>
> **Wi-Fi/NFC** must be set to **Disable.**

Printing effect	Description
⊠ On	Print will be made using the printer's standard setup
⊠ Off	No automatic correction applied
⊠ Vivid	Greens and blues are more saturated
⊠ NR	Image noise reduction is applied before printing
B/W B/W	Black-and-white image is printed with pure blacks
B/W Cool tone	Black-and-white image is printed with blueish blacks
B/W Warm tone	Black-and-white image is printed with yellowish blacks
▣ Natural	Prints an image with natural colors
▣ Natural M	Finer control over colors than Natural
Default	Printer dependant—see your printer manual
◷	Date and file number imprinting: choose between overlaying the date, file number, or both on the print
▤	Number of copies: specify the number of prints to be made
Cropping	Allows you to trim and rotate your image before printing

Paper settings	Description
▱ Paper size	Select the size of the paper loaded in the printer
▰ Paper type	Select the paper type
▤ Page layout	Select how the image will look on the printed page

Page layout	Description
Bordered	Print will be made with white borders around the edge of the paper
Borderless	Set edge-to-edge printing if your printer supports this facility
Bordered 🅸	Shooting information will be imprinted on the border on prints 9 x 13cm or larger
XX-up	Allows you to print with 2, 4, 8, 9, 16, or 20 image thumbnails on A4 paper
20-up 🅸 / 35-up ▯	20 or 35 images will be printed as thumbnails on A4 or Letter-sized paper; 20-up 🅸 adds shooting information
Default	Prints using your printer's standard settings

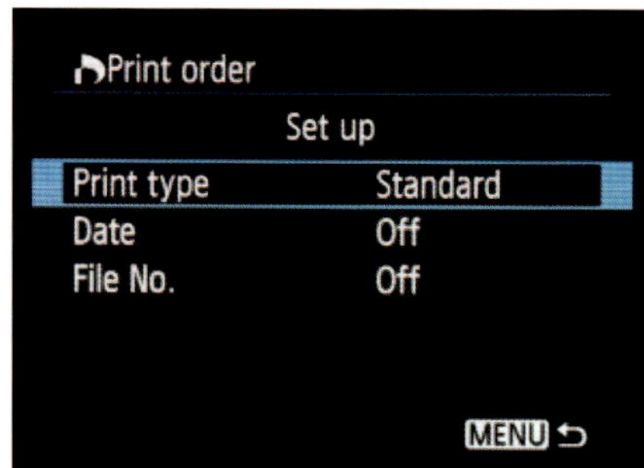

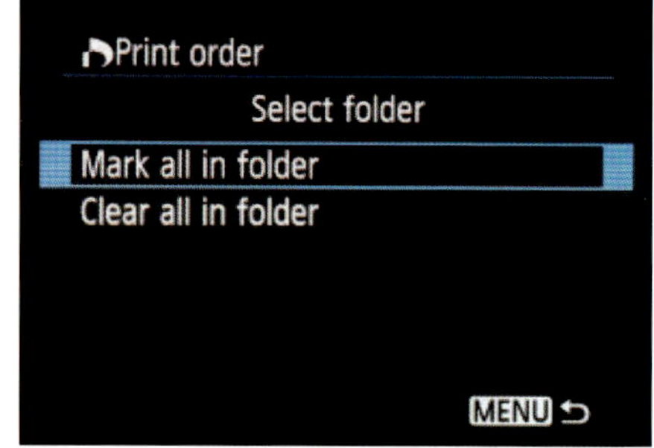

If you've shot JPEG images you can also use DPOF (Digital Print Order Format) to prepare them for printing. DPOF adds printing instructions to the Rebel T6/EOS 1300D's memory card, which include which images (and how many copies of those images) should be printed, and whether the shooting date or the file name should be overlaid on the print. Once DPOF instructions have been added to the memory card you either plug the memory card directly into a compatible printer or take it to your chosen photographic printing service.

Setting DPOF

1) Press MENU, navigate to ▶, and select **Print order**.

2) Select **Set up**.

3) Set the **Print type**: **Standard** for a normal print, **Index** for a sheet of thumbnails of the image, or **Both**.

4) Set **Date** to **On** if you want the date to be imprinted on your prints; set **Date** to **Off** if you don't want the date added.

5) Set **File no.** to **On** if you want the image file numbers added to your prints, or **Off** if not.

6) Press MENU to return to the **Print Order** menu screen.

Marking all images in a folder for printing

1) On the **Print order** screen select **By** 📁.

2) Select **Mark all in folder** followed by the desired folder. Select **OK** to continue and a print order for one copy of each compatible image in the folder will be set,

or select **Cancel** to return to the **Select folder** screen.

3) To clear the print order, select **Clear all in folder** and then select the desired folder. Select **OK** to continue, or **Cancel** to return to the **Select folder** screen.

Marking all images for printing

1) On the **Print order** screen select **All image**.

2) Select **Mark all on card**. Select **OK** to continue and a print order for one copy of each compatible image on the memory will be set (select **Cancel** to return to the **All image** screen).

3) To clear the print order select **Clear all on card**. Select **OK** to clear all the DPOF instructions from the memory, or **Cancel** to return to the **All image** screen.

Print ordering individual images

1) Choose **Sel. Image** from the **Print order** screen.

2) Press ◄ / ► to skip between the images on the memory card, or jump through the images by turning ⚙. To view three images at once press ▨/⊖; to restore single-image view press ⊕.

3) If **Standard** was selected when setting **Print type**, press ▲ / ▼ to set the number of prints to be made from the currently displayed image. The number of times the selected image will be printed is shown next to the 🖪 icon at the top left corner of the LCD (with the current total number of prints at the right of this figure).

4) If **Index** was selected, press ▲ to add the currently displayed image to the DPOF instructions to be printed as thumbnails. An ✓ in the box next to the 🖪 icon indicates that the image has been selected. Press ▼ to deselect it again if required.

5) Repeat as required from step 2 and then press MENU to return to the main **Print order** menu screen.

Direct printing

If your Rebel T6/EOS 1300D is connected to a PictBridge printer, select **Print** from the **Print order** menu screen. Follow the instructions on screen and the printer will print according to the DPOF instructions you've set.

» GLOSSARY

Aberration An imperfection in a photograph, usually caused by the optics of a lens.

AEL (automatic exposure lock) A camera control that locks in the exposure value, allowing a scene to be recomposed.

Angle of view The area of a scene that a lens takes in, measured in degrees.

Aperture The opening in a camera lens through which light passes to expose the sensor. The relative size of the aperture is denoted by f-stops.

Autofocus (AF) A reliable through-the-lens focusing system allowing accurate focus without the photographer manually turning the lens.

Bracketing Taking a series of identical pictures, changing only the exposure, usually in ⅓-, ½-, or 1-stop increments.

Buffer The in-camera memory of a digital camera.

Center-weighted metering A metering pattern that determines the exposure by placing importance on the light meter reading at the center of the frame.

Chromatic aberration The inability of a lens to bring spectrum colors into focus at a single point.

Codec A piece of software that is able to interpret and decode a digital file such as Raw.

Color temperature The color of a light source expressed in degrees Kelvin (K).

Compression The process by which digital files are reduced in size. Compression can retain all the information in the file, or "lose" data usually in the form of fine detail for greater levels of file-size reduction.

Contrast The range between the highlight and shadow areas of a photo, or a marked difference in illumination between colors or adjacent areas.

Depth of field (DOF) This is controlled primarily by the aperture: the smaller the aperture, the greater the depth of field.

Diopter Unit expressing the power of a lens.

dpi (dots per inch) Measure of the resolution of a printer or scanner. The more dots per inch, the higher the resolution.

DPOF Digital Print Order Format.

Dynamic range The ability of the camera's sensor to capture a full range of shadows and highlights.

Evaluative metering A metering system where light reflected from several subject areas is calculated based on algorithms.

Exposure The amount of light allowed to hit the digital sensor, controlled by aperture, shutter speed, and ISO. Also, the act of taking a photograph, as in "making an exposure."

Exposure compensation A control that allows intentional over- or underexposure.

Fill-in flash Flash combined with daylight in an exposure. Used with naturally backlit or harshly side-lit or top-lit subjects to prevent silhouettes forming, or to add extra light to the shadow areas of a well-lit scene.

Filter A piece of colored or coated glass, or plastic, placed in front of the lens.

Focal length The distance, usually in millimeters, from the optical center point of a lens to its focal point.

fps (frames per second) A measure of the time needed for a digital camera to process one photograph and be ready to shoot the next.

f-stop Number assigned to a particular lens aperture. Wide apertures are denoted by small numbers (such as f/1.8 and f/2.8), while small apertures are denoted by large numbers (such as f/16 and f/22).

HDMI High Definition Multimedia Interface.

HDR (High Dynamic Range) A technique that increases the dynamic range of a photograph by merging several shots taken with different exposure settings.

Histogram A graph representing the distribution of tones in a photograph.

Hotshoe An accessory shoe with electrical contacts that allows synchronization between a camera and a flash.

Hotspot A light area with a loss of detail in the highlights. This is a common problem in flash photography.

Incident light reading Meter reading based on the amount of light falling onto the subject.

Interpolation A method of increasing the file size of a digital photograph by adding pixels, thereby increasing its resolution.

ISO The sensitivity of the digital sensor measured in terms equivalent to the ISO rating of a film.

JPEG (Joint Photographic Experts Group) JPEG compression can reduce file sizes to about 5% of their original size, but uses a lossy compression system that degrades image quality.

LCD (Liquid crystal display) The flat screen on a digital camera that allows the user to preview digital photographs.

Macro A term used to describe close focusing and the close-focusing ability of a lens.

Megapixel One million pixels is equal to one megapixel.

Memory card A removable storage device for digital cameras.

Noise Interference visible in a digital image caused by stray electrical signals during exposure.

PictBridge The industry standard for sending information directly from a camera to a printer, without the need for a computer.

Pixel Short for "picture element"—the smallest bit of information in a digital photograph.

Predictive autofocus An AF system that can continuously track a moving subject.

Raw The file format in which the raw data from the sensor is stored without permanent alteration being made.

Red-eye reduction A system that causes the pupils of a subject's eyes to shrink, by shining a light prior to taking the main flash picture.

Remote switch A device used to trigger the shutter of the camera from a distance, to help minimize camera shake. Also known as a "cable release" or "remote release."

Resolution The number of pixels used to capture or display a photo.

RGB (red, green, blue) Computers and other digital devices understand color information as combinations of red, green, and blue.

Rule of thirds A rule of composition that places the key elements of a picture at points along imagined lines that divide the frame into thirds, both vertically and horizontally.

Shutter The mechanism that controls the amount of light reaching the sensor, by opening and closing.

Soft proofing Using software to mimic on screen how an image will look once output to another imaging device. Typically this will be a printer.

Spot metering A metering pattern that places importance on the intensity of light reflected by a very small portion of the scene, either at the center of the frame or linked to a focus point.

Teleconverter A supplementary lens that is fitted between the camera body and lens, increasing its effective focal length.

Telephoto A lens with a large focal length and a narrow angle of view.

TIFF (Tagged Image File Format) A universal file format supported by virtually all relevant software applications. TIFFs are uncompressed digital files.

TTL (through the lens) metering A metering system built into the camera that measures light passing through the lens at the time of shooting.

USB (universal serial bus) A data transfer standard used by the Canon Rebel T6/ EOS 1300D—and most other cameras— when connecting to a computer.

Viewfinder An optical system used for composing and sometimes for focusing the subject.

White balance A function that allows the correct color balance to be recorded for any given lighting situation.

Wide-angle lens A lens with a short focal length and, consequently, a wide angle of view.

» USEFUL WEB SITES

CANON

Canon Worldwide
www.canon.com

Canon US
www.usa.canon.com

Canon UK
www.canon.co.uk

Canon Europe
www.canon-europe.com

Canon Middle East
www.canon-me.com

Canon Oceania
www.canon.com.au

GENERAL

David Taylor
Landscape and travel photography
www.davidtaylorphotography.co.uk

Digital Photography Review
Camera and lens review site
www.dpreview.com

Photonet
Photography discussion forum
www.photo.net

EQUIPMENT

Adobe
Image-editing software such as Photoshop
and Lightroom
www.adobe.com

Apple
Hardware and software manufacturer
www.apple.com

Phase One
Photographic editing and cataloging
software
www.phaseone.com

Sigma
Third-party lens manufacturer
www.sigma-photo.com

Tamron
Third-party lens manufacturer
www.tamron.com

Tokina
Third-party lens manufacturer
www.tokinalens.com

PHOTOGRAPHY PUBLICATIONS

**Photography books &
Expanded Camera Guides**
www.ammonitepress.com

Black & White Photography magazine
Outdoor Photography magazine
www.thegmcgroup.com

CANON REBEL T6/EOS 1300D